THE COMPLETE GUIDE TO
HOME
AUTOMATION

DAVID ALAN WACKER

BETTERWAY BOOKS
CINCINNATI, OHIO

Also by David Alan Wacker:

The Complete Guide to Home Security

Cover photos top and bottom left by Pamela Monfort. Cover kitchen by Kitchen Concepts, Inc., Cincinnati, OH.

Cover photo bottom right by Unity Systems, Inc., Redwood City, CA.

Page layout by Studio 500, Charlottesville, VA.

Typography by Blackhawk Typesetting, Charlottesville, VA.

97 96 95 94 93 5 4 3 2 1

Library of Congress Cataloging-in-Publication Data

Wacker, David Alan.
    The complete guide to home automation / David Alan Wacker.
        p. cm.
    Includes index.
    ISBN 1-55870-301-2
1. Dwellings — Automation. 2. Dwellings — Electric equipment. I. Title.
TH4812.W33 1993
696—dc20
                                                                93-24794
                                                                CIP

Dedicated to
Lora, Anna, and especially Julia, our newest addition,
for all their love, support, and understanding.

Acknowledgments

A special thanks to:

Gary Skinner, Sentient Homes Inc., Westminster, CO
H. Brooke Stauffer, SMART HOUSE L.P.
Jay McLellan, Home Automation Inc.
Mike Stein, User Interface Technologies
Jeff Stein, JDS Technologies

The following companies graciously provided photographs and illustrations:

AMX Corporation
Andersen Windows
Aqua/Trends
Aritech-Moose Security Products
Custom Command Systems
Enerzone Systems Corporation
Group Three Technologies

Home Automation Inc.
JDS Technologies
Leviton
Mastervoice, Inc.
Mitsubishi Electronics America
Multiplex Technology, Inc.
Roll-A-Way Insulating Security Shutters
SMART HOUSE L.P.
SolarTronics
Sony
Sound Track
Square D Company
Ultrak, Inc.
Unity Systems, Inc.
Universal Electronics, Inc.
X-10 USA, Inc.

Preface

Home automation conjures up images of sci-fi movies and Saturday morning cartoons. We grew up watching Rosie, the Jetsons' robot housekeeper, remote control in hand (so to speak), wielding complete control over every aspect of their daily lives. George didn't even need to shower, shave, or dress himself, it was all done for him — automatically. Automatic everything — a pushbutton world.

Today, while we still have to dress ourselves (for now), many of our home's functions, such as lighting, heating and air conditioning, entertainment, security, water management, etc., can be controlled (automated). Automating your home puts you in control; enjoy the convenience of automatic lighting, heating, cooling, entertainment, security, and much more, all at the touch of a button. Home automation is real, the products exist, and you can buy them now, not in the future.

Once the exclusive domain of the wealthy, with many systems costing $50,000 or more, the average homeowner can now put together a good, reliable system for less than $1,000. Even most professionally installed whole-house integrated systems go for less than $10,000. And prices should continue to drop as more systems are sold and as home automation becomes more commonplace.

Contents

Introduction

WHAT IS HOME AUTOMATION?

Webster's Dictionary defines automation as: (1) The technique of making an apparatus, a process, or a system operate automatically. (2) The state of being operated automatically. (3) Automatically controlled operation of an apparatus, process, or system by mechanical or electronic devices that take the place of human organs of observation, effort, and decision, reducing human intervention to a minimum. The term *home automation*, as used in this book, is defined as the control of lighting, audio/video, heating, air conditioning, appliances, draperies, sprinklers, and more, by one or more of the following: remote control, timer, sensor, telephone, voice command, or situation.

Home automation means different things to different people. To some, it may be as simple as a few lights on a timer. To others, it may mean an environment in which all the systems in the house that provide comfort, security, entertainment, and communications are highly sophisticated and can react and adapt automatically to changes in the environment.

Home automation systems not only make "running" your household more convenient, they save you money, perhaps as much as a third of your utility bills. These systems turn off your lights, appliances, and heating, cooling, and sprinkler systems when they are not needed. You can customize your system to suit your lifestyle and easily change its programming as the need arises. Automation is very flexible and can usually be done without special wiring. It is easily retrofit into an existing home.

Home automation systems are designed as "behind the scenes" systems; they operate the home for normal day-to-day activities without homeowner intervention, while allowing quick and simple homeowner override for manual operation. Home automation systems provide personal and property security, manage climate control, and control lighting and appliances with reliable, afford-able, and easy-to-use technology. They provide enhanced personal and property security, unparalleled comfort and efficiency, and complete control of electrical circuits, based on personal schedules and/or events occurring in and around the home.

A new generation of homes is now emerging with features that seem as outlandish today as the microwave oven did 25 years ago. These homes will feature intelligent products that will be able to communicate, or "talk," with other intelligent products in the home. These homes, known as *intelligent homes, smart homes*, or *automated homes*, will have the capacity for total home control, voice messaging, and much more.

WHAT CAN BE AUTOMATED?

Almost anything electrical that is normally controlled by pushing a button or flipping a switch can be automated. Controllable items include (but are not limited to):

- All types of lighting (incandescent and fluorescent), both indoor and outdoor
- Heating, ventilating, and air conditioning (HVAC) systems
- Home entertainment systems such as TVs, VCRs, stereos, and CD players
- Plant watering systems (indoor and outdoor)
- Fans and other ventilation systems
- Remote-controlled circuit breakers
- Door openers and electronic locks
- Motorized windows and skylights
- Window coverings such as draperies, blinds, awnings, and shutters

Automating a home can be very simple or extremely complex. Certain home automation systems are all-in-one packages from a single manufacturer. More often, however, home automation systems integrate off-the-shelf equipment from various manufacturers. Automated items can be controlled by computer controllers, touchscreens, sensors, pushbutton wall switches, hand-held remote controllers, voice command, telephone control (from any touchtone phone in the world), and timers.

A typical home automation system consists of a central computer, which controls two or more household functions or subsystems (temperature, security, lights, appliances, multi-room monitoring, and entertainment audio/video), by using any combination of communication links (wired or wireless).

Sensors are the eyes and ears of a home automation system. They sense current conditions and send a message to the central controller (brain), which in turn makes a decision and initiates a sequence of events. This can be as simple as turning on the porch light at dusk or as complicated as opening and closing windows and blinds based on the difference between indoor and outdoor temperature and humidity.

The main types of sensors used in home automation are:
- occupancy
- photocell
- temperature
- humidity
- rain/moisture
- water leak

Occupancy sensors (primarily motion and sound) can be used to activate household systems (e.g., HVAC, lighting, entertainment) when you enter a room and turn them off after you leave. Temperature sensors can turn on/off a vent or open/close a window in response to temperature or humidity changes. Photocells can be used to turn lights on or off and to open and close draperies, blinds, rolling shutters, etc. Rain/moisture sensors automatically close/open windows or skylights and turn off your yard sprinkling system if it is raining. Sensors buried in your driveway can announce the arrival of incoming guests and turn on porch and walkway lighting.

HOW CAN AUTOMATION BENEFIT YOU?

One of the benefits of programmable home automation is the ability to create multiple acts, or instructions, that can be initiated by pressing a single button. Simple one-button commands such as AT HOME, WAKE UP, AT WORK, AWAY, AWAY-EVERYBODY, GOOD NIGHT, VACATION can activate a whole series of preprogrammed events. Here are several examples of simple commands and their possible results:

WAKE UP — Wake up to music or TV. Illuminate hallway, bathroom, and bedroom. Open window coverings. Turn on electric water heater.

AT WORK — Shut off all appliances left on, set back the thermostat, monitor the house for such emergencies as fire, break-in, water leak, etc.

AT HOME — Turn exterior lights on at dusk and off in late evening.

AWAY (one or more family members out) — Turn exterior lights and hall lights on at dusk, leave porch light, driveway light, and entry light on until AT HOME is received. If AT HOME is not received, turn lights off at dawn.

AWAY-EVERYBODY (all family members out) — Same as AWAY, but turn various interior lights on and off periodically to give the house a "lived-in" look.

VACATION — Maintain normal AT HOME exterior lighting schedule, turn interior lights on and off periodically to simulate occupancy.

AT NIGHT — Lower central heating or air conditioning while occupants sleep. Automatically shut off music or TV and lights after occupants fall asleep.

Automation allows you to increase the convenience of your home's lighting by automatically turning lights on when you enter a room and off again after you leave. Path lighting is also possible — no more fumbling for light switches during that late night rendezvous with the refrigerator. Control your lights (on, off, dim) from many different places without adding expensive new wiring.

Automation deters burglars by making your house always look lived-in, whether you are there or not. You need never come home to a dark house again. Feel safe and secure in your house as outside lights come on when someone walks up. Light predetermined areas at predetermined times or turn lights on and off at random. If you hear a suspicious noise, automation allows you to flood the house with light at the touch of a button. Upon detecting a fire, the automation system will sound an alarm, call the monitoring station, close the ventilation dampers (reducing the spread of the fire), and automatically light your fire escape routes. Talk to and see whoever is at the front door without opening it, even if you are not home.

Home automation can save up to 40% on utility bills by automatically turning off unused lights and appliances. It can intelligently heat and cool rooms only as needed, turning the heat down at night, and back up before you wake up. Automation allows you to have different preset heating and cooling schedules for weekdays, weekends, when you have guests, or when you are on vacation. This is not only convenient, it's energy efficient and saves money.

Wake to TV or music and freshly brewed coffee. Open and close draperies and curtains at desired times of the day or by remote control. Control ceiling fans, humidifiers, and dehumidifiers. Have your whirlpool or spa heated before you arrive home. Run pool pumps and filters automatically. Automatically turn the sprinkler system off when it is raining. One command can turn on the TV, start the VCR, and set the room lighting for comfortable viewing by turning off or dimming designated lights and closing the draperies. Automatically turn down the stereo when the phone or doorbell rings. The possibilities are endless.

Sometimes an "automated" solution to a problem can introduce needless complexity and expense. However, it is necessary to point out the advantages of a systems approach. For example, if you want one lamp to turn on and off at the same times daily, a five dollar mechanical timer may be a better solution than, say, an X-10 module and timer controller. If, however, you have three table lamps, two ceiling fixtures, a coffee pot, and an air conditioner to control, and prefer weekdays to have different schedules than weekends, using individual mechanical timers would clearly be impractical.

THE BIG FOUR: X-10, SMART HOUSE, CEBUS, AND LONWORKS

SMART HOUSE, CEBus, and LONWORKS have been simulated at trade shows and in demonstration houses, and they are slowly but surely moving into the marketplace. Well-known manufacturers are supporting efforts both financially and developmentally. Manufacturing all the necessary devices and actually implementing them in typical consumer homes are the factors holding up SMART HOUSE, CEBus, and LONWORKS from becoming reality.

Of the big four, X-10 is the recognized leader in home automation technology, with more than two million homes using X-10 products. With X-10, inexpensive pushbutton consoles can turn appliances on and off and can dim or brighten any incandescent light in the house. The X-10 power line technology sends signals along the existing power lines in your home — no special wiring is required. This makes the X-10 system very affordable and easily expandable.

Several factors account for the universal popularity of X-10 technology. First, the fact that the product works and has been available for years has made it a popular choice for both individuals and installers who want the benefits of home automation now, not in the future. Second, X-10 has kept the pricing of its components low, making it far more economical for other firms to adopt the X-10 product than to try to invent their own. Finally, X-10 products have always been designed for installation in existing homes without any wiring changes; most are readily installed by do-it-yourselfers.

Future X-10 products are expected to incorporate two-way communications and other sophisticated features, but no change in the basic communication scheme is anticipated. This means that X-10 technology will continue to be a viable medium for home automation well into the foreseeable future.

SMART HOUSE
SMART HOUSE is an integrated wiring and gas plumbing system with built-in electronic intelligence. It was created through the endeavors of the National Association of Home Builders (NAHB) and its National Research Center. The system provides a pathway for the electronic signals that can manage all operations in the house. Homeowners will be able to operate appliances anywhere in the house with wall switches, handheld remote controllers, sensors, a video touchscreen, or any touchtone telephone at home or away.

The SMART HOUSE system means increased convenience for the homeowner. Plug your VCR into a SMART outlet and watch movies on a TV in another room; speakers in one end of the house can play music from a stereo at the other end; standard telephones can be used as intercoms; computers and printers can be located in separate rooms. SMART HOUSE can be linked to utility companies, facilitating remote metering and energy-saving load management techniques. The homeowner will have a greater ability to control the time of use and the operation of household appliances to take advantage of the utility's rate structure. All this and more can be done without any additional wiring..

In SMART HOUSE, the integrated "hybrid branch cable" wiring system distributes power, audio, video, security, telephone, and control communications wherever the homeowner chooses. Three SMART HOUSE hybrid cables replace the myriad of wires used in houses today. The Branch Cable delivers 120 volt AC (VAC) and control communications to each wall receptacle. Conventional wiring will still be used for large appliances with high current demands. The Applications Cable handles low-voltage signaling for switches and sensors. The Communications Cable contains wiring for up to four telephone lines and two coaxial cables to send and receive video, audio, and data information.

Along with innovative hybrid cabling, SMART HOUSE uses distributed-control technology to provide reliable, efficient, and cost-effective home automation. SMART HOUSE uses a system controller and SMART outlets to coordinate a network of computer-like operations and manage the flow of information among appliances. This minimizes the possibility of a complete system failure as the result of a single problem.

One option available to homeowners desiring future SMART HOUSE compatibility is to prewire new construction using SMART-REDI. SMART-REDI will provide your family with exciting new features plus all the benefits of a traditional home. Enhanced lighting controls in a SMART-REDI house enable homeowners to dim their lights from multiple locations. In addition to meeting the National Electrical Code requirements for ground fault protection, SMART-REDI provides additional safety to homeowners by adding surge suppression protection to all outlets on the main power cable, protecting the system electronics and all household electrical appliances, entertainment equipment, and other products from surges in electrical current.

Whole-house audio/video distribution is provided throughout a SMART-REDI home — signals generated from both inside and outside. For example, one cable hookup can distribute programs to all TVs in the home; a videotape in a VCR can be viewed on any TV in the home; and a closed circuit camera at the front door can be programmed so that a specific TV channel will al-

ways display a view from that camera. The SMART-REDI telephone gateway supports up to four telephone lines with as many as thirty-two telephone outlets throughout the house and makes it possible to page family members throughout the house by way of an ordinary touchtone phone.

A SMART-REDI home can be upgraded at a later time to FULL-SMART with the addition of controllers and SMART outlets. SMART-REDI wiring for a 2,500 square-foot home currently costs $9,000 to $12,000. Upgrading to FULL-SMART will add $3,000 to $5,000 to the cost.

One point that has always caused confusion is just how SMART HOUSE relates to CEBus, the Electronic Industry Association's home automation standard. Although both are potential home automation standards, they are not exactly direct competitors. SMART HOUSE plans to be a closed standard, meaning all products using the technology would be licensed and pay a fee to SMART HOUSE L.P.; while CEBus will be an open standard, with the technology developed made available to any interested manufacturer. Also, although a retrofit product is planned, SMART HOUSE is aimed at the high-end new home construction market. The CEBus standard will be based more on existing wiring and allow a much broader retrofit market.

CEBus

The Consumer Electronic Bus, or CEBus, is a home automation standard (IS-60) of the Electronic Industries Association (EIA), which defines the communications protocol, language, and media interface specification that allows any device in the home to communicate with any other. The CEBus standard can be divided into three major areas: the physical media and the topology (power line, coax, twisted pair, etc., and how they are connected); the communication protocol (used for network access and constructing messages); and the communication language (allowing all devices to communicate a common set of actions to be performed). While the communication protocol and language are common to all CEBus devices, the media and topology may vary considerably from home to home, depending on the homeowner's needs and the types of devices desired in the home.

CEBus consists of several sub-standards grouped together under the CEBus banner. They are:

- IRBus — Infrared Bus
- TPBus — Twisted Pair Bus
- PLBus — Power Line Bus
- CXBus — Coax Bus
- RFBus — Radio Frequency Bus
- Node O — Standard for physical central distribution point
- Node Protocol — Software used by appliances to send messages
- Router Protocol — Software to interconnect TP, PL, and CX
- Brouter Protocol — Software to interconnect IR and RF Buses with the others
- CAL — Software used by appliances to issue commands

A home using CEBus may utilize one or all of the media supported by CEBus and available for product communications, including:

- The existing 110/220V power line wiring of the home (called PLBus in CEBus.) In CEBus, it is usable by devices normally plugged into an electrical outlet. Intellon Corporation's AC power line proprietary Spread Spectrum Carrier technology has been selected as the CEBus power line standard.

- Eight conductor twisted pair wiring. This can be used by CEBus devices that normally use "low voltage" wiring such as thermostats, security sensors, telephones, and intercoms. The four pairs (called TPBus in CEBus) can be used in place of the normal telephone wiring or to supplement existing wiring. The pairs in the cable are named TP0, TP1, TP2, and TP3. CEBus distributes DC power (18 volts) on TP0 to power devices that attach to twisted pair wiring, such as thermostats or sensors.

- A pair of coaxial cables. These can be used by CEBus devices that normally connect to "video" cable. The coax pair (called CXBus in CEBus) is used to supply CEBus messages, cable programming, and in-home generated video (cameras and VCR) to any video device in the home. One cable in the coax supplies the CATV programming, the other distributes the internal signals and external antenna signals. An amplifier/block converter provides proper signal distribution to all branches of the cable in the home.

- CEBus devices can also utilize radio frequency (RF) communications in the 900 MHz range and infrared signals (IR) similar to existing handheld remotes.

Each physical medium used in the home, and the products that connect to it, comprise a CEBus "local medium network." A home may contain several networks connected by devices called routers. A router is a two-way CEBus device that simply takes the information present on one medium and places it on another. Routers are required between any two media used in the home to ensure that any two devices can communicate without being connected to the same medium.

Because of the wide choice of media, existing homes can use the CEBus standard as easily as new homes. An existing home can immediately utilize its power line for CEBus devices, and CEBus radio frequency and infrared devices require no wire installation. Twisted pair, coaxial, and fiber optics (although better suited for new construction) can be retrofitted later if so desired.

Because CEBus can operate via standard power lines, infrared signals, and radio frequencies, wiring costs are comparable to those of standard wiring. Additional special twisted pairs and coaxial wiring and network support device installation would cost approximately $700 for a 2,400 square-foot home. Products carrying a CEBus-compatible chip will initially add $20 to $50 to the retail price of non-CEBus appliances.

LONWORKS

The newest player in the home automation field is Echelon's LONWORKS. Despite its late start, LONWORKS' development is keeping pace with SMART HOUSE and CEBus. What makes LONWORKS different from SMART HOUSE and CEBus is its ability to operate by a standard Neuron Chip IC. This Neuron Chip contains everything necessary to handle communications and interface directly with application hardware, so there is no need for additional parts or devices. LONWORKS products containing the Neuron Chip communicate with one another through the power line, twisted pair, coaxial cable, radio frequency, and fiber optics so, like CEBus, there is no need to rewire.

LONWORKS is neither a new way of wiring as SMART HOUSE is, nor is it a new way of building a product as CEBus is; rather, it is a standardized networking process adapted from network systems currently used in factories. The fact that similar networks are already being used makes LONWORKS the least expensive technology of the three to develop and implement. For a device to communicate on the LONWORKS network, it must have an integrated chip. Development of the Neuron Chip is underway at Motorola and Toshiba.

The LON concept is based on embedding a single multifunction chip in appliances, switches, lights, etc., to allow them to communicate with other similarly equipped devices and controllers. The chip, dubbed the Neuron, incorporates communications, control, scheduling, and input/output support. One of the key differences between the LON and other networks is that each Neuron Chip communicates with other chips on what is known as a "peer-to-peer" basis, and can operate independently and even send commands to other Neurons.

Compared to SMART HOUSE and CEBus, LONWORKS is a very inexpensive home automation network. The cost of the network is paid in added product cost for Neuron Chip installation and media interface, currently $8 to $10 per appliance. Echelon expects the cost to drop to $5 in 1993, and to $2 by 1995. A complete Intelligent Node now costing $20 will sell for $10 by 1995. LONWORKS can also be used in both new construction and retrofit. Regardless of what kind of home one has, LONWORKS can be integrated quite easily.

To learn more about home automation before spending large sums of money, I recommend that you subscribe to *Electronic House* magazine ($14.95 per year). *Electronic House* is one of the best sources available on home automation products, technical information, new product information, and home, theater, and audio/video products. Their annual Buyers Guide issue and monthly New Products section are invaluable in keeping abreast of the ever-changing home automation industry. (See Appendix 1 for the address and phone number for *Electronic House* and other helpful periodicals.)

1.
Prewiring for Home Automation

Prewiring is of great interest to people building homes because it is far less expensive to run wiring while a home is under construction than after it is built. Once a home is completed, wiring can be added only by "fishing" wires through walls, a time-consuming and expensive procedure, or by surface wiring, which is not aesthetically pleasing. Thus, there is strong motivation to prewire for home automation during construction. Prewiring takes some planning, effort, and expense up front, but it will save much more time and money in the long run if it is done right.

The way you prewire a house depends on what you expect home automation to look like a few years down the road. In the U.S., the major approaches to home automation fall into several categories: SMART HOUSE, CEBus, LONWORKS, X-10, and proprietary bus/hard wiring. All of the above approaches except SMART HOUSE are designed to work in conjunction with "standard" house wiring. SMART HOUSE represents a major departure from traditional residential wiring. A concept called "closed loop power" is employed, which keeps outlets turned off until a device properly identifies itself. All outlets and wiring are completely different from those currently in residential use.

CEBus, the standard being developed by the Electronic Industries Association, seems destined to become the major home automation standard for existing homes in the United States. The standard is intended to be an all-encompassing communications system for the home covering multiple media — infrared, power line, coaxial cable, twisted pair, and radio frequency. It is specifically designed to work in existing homes with few wiring changes. Unless you plan to do a SMART HOUSE prewire (SMART-REDI) through your builder, a wiring plan that follows CEBus guidelines is recommended. Whether or not CEBus becomes a dominant standard, you will be prepared for most communications now and in the future.

ELECTRICAL POWER WIRING

CEBus signals that travel over the power wiring, infrared signals, and radio frequency signals are completely compatible with all existing house wiring. Some of the more sophisticated CEBus features, however, utilize coaxial cable and twisted pair wiring; not all homes have adequate coaxial cable or twisted pair installed to fully utilize CEBus.

Generally, AC power wiring does not need much special attention other than to ensure that there are enough outlets in all rooms, with special attention to the master bedroom and media room. Individual 110VAC outlets can be "homerun" (connected directly to the control panel) back to the power distribution panel. While it is not practical to homerun all power wiring, it might be worth putting major appliances and a few key outlets on their own circuits. This would allow future control of those circuits at the power source. Square D now offers a remote-controlled circuit breaker that fits into a standard circuit breaker slot. With homerun power wiring, these breakers can be used for controller safety purposes.

Much of power wiring is determined by code requirements and standard wiring practices. Nevertheless, since power wiring will carry many of the automation signals as well as driving most devices you will connect, be sure you have enough outlets specified, particularly where you will have concentrations of equipment, such as your entertainment center and nightstand areas.

Outside wiring should not be forgotten when planning your prewiring. The homeowner should give some consideration to whether any outdoor controls will be needed in the future. Some of the possibilities to consider are pool or spa controls, outdoor audio speakers, security cameras or sensors, lighting controls, and sprinkler controls. The type of wiring needed will be similar to that used inside the house, although the homeowner should be sure that wire to be buried or exposed to weather conditions is designed for that purpose.

COAXIAL CABLE

In prewiring for home automation, the best practice is to run dedicated wires of each type, "homerun" style, from each room to a central distribution box, "Node O," located in a utility room or basement. CEBus uses a series of RG-6 coax cable pair branches that originate at Node O. Each branch goes to a different area of the house and terminates in a four-way splitter. Each of the splitter outputs goes to a pair of jacks within the area serviced by the branch. Total cable length between Node O and any final tap may not exceed 150 feet. The wiring may be looped from point to point within the room, or multiple termination points may be selected within a room.

A typical whole house installation might start with running a pair of coaxial cables to each room, wired back to a Node O. An extra run of cable could also be sent to the attic area for TV or FM antenna connection or terminated outside the home for cable TV connection. While most whole house cable systems use a single cable to each room, full access to CEBus features requires two. The two coax lines permit both "inbound" and "outbound" video signals and make the home ready for CEBus coaxial requirements. Large rooms may require more than one outlet to allow for changing furniture and entertainment equipment locations.

Coaxial cables should be terminated at wall plates, and should be homerun, e.g., run from the wall plate to a panel in the basement or utility room. For the best television picture possible, use a #10 braided double-shielded RG-6 cable. It's also a good idea to ask what your local cable company requires before purchasing. In some areas, the FCC requires using quad-shielded cable.

For now, if you are just distributing antenna or cable signals, one or two multi-line splitters will be adequate for your distribution system. Splitters, commonly used when running cable TV wiring, are generally discouraged because you lose signal strength each time the cable is split. An inexpensive amplifier can boost signals if you have long runs or many splits.

For example, running two coaxial cables to each video outlet is an excellent idea. But you must remember to label them to avoid confusion later. A good way to do this is to use two different brands of cable, which will be easy to identify anywhere along the cable. When installing gray PVC jacketed cable in multiple runs, one can be striped with a colored permanent marker for identification as it comes off the reel.

TWISTED PAIR

This low voltage wiring can be used for just about any low voltage application including telephone, security sensors, LAN (Local Area Network) data, audio distribution, intercom, and infrared signal repeaters. All pending home automation standards (CEBus, SMART HOUSE, and LONWORKS) include twisted pair (TP) wiring schemes to send control data between components.

Twisted pair is categorized into five levels according to their electrical performance. The levels are specified by voice or data application requirements, and generally relate to cable constructions of 2-8 pairs. The five levels are:

- Level 1 — For analog and digital telephone and low speed data applications.
- Level 2 — For low speed data (< 4 Mbits/sec) and any Level 1 application.
- Level 3 — For medium speed data and LAN (< 16 Mbits/sec) and any Level 1 or 2 application.
- Level 4 — For extended distance LAN (< 20 Mbits/sec) and any Level 1, 2, or 3 application.
- Level 5 — For high speed LAN (< 100 Mbits/sec) applications.

Once you determine the performance level, you should choose the cable features that meet the requirements of the National Electrical Code (NEC). The NEC is a set of

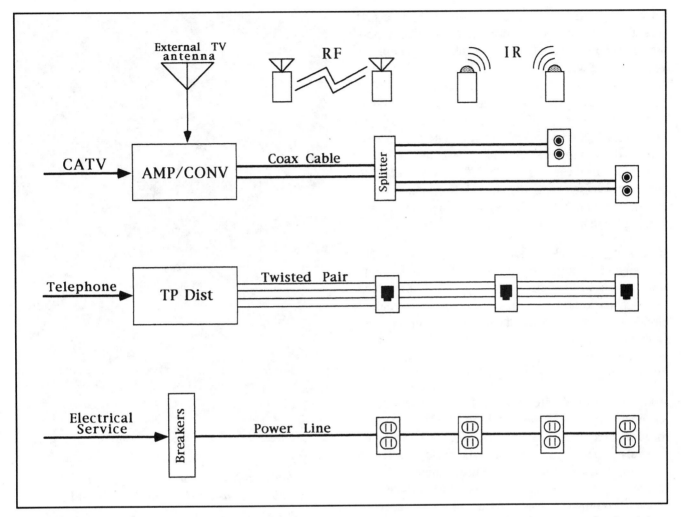

CEBus can use any combination of a large number of media for communications: power line, twisted pair wiring, coaxial cable, radio frequency, and infrared.

guidelines that describe procedures designed to minimize the hazards of electrical shock, fires, and explosions caused by electrical installations. Class 1 cables are limited to 30 volts and no more than 1000 watts. Class 2 cable limitations depend on voltage. Class 3 allows the full range of 150 volts at 100 watts. Class 2 is all that's normally required for residential low voltage applications.

Twisted pair comes in a variety of sizes and qualities. The larger the wire, the more voltage it can carry. For high-powered speakers, 12 or 14 gauge is the best. Telephones, intercoms, security systems, sensors, and thermostats use less voltage, so smaller, 16, 18, or 24 gauge can be used. Experts recommend running an extra set of wires per outlet to enable a second device to be added later and to serve as a backup should the primary wire develop problems.

Wall box locations depend on the use of the wiring. Speakers may be ceiling mounted, an intercom may be located near the door, a telephone connection could be by a nightstand or desk. You don't need to have multiple gang boxes for each run. A number of manufacturers now have modular single gang wall plates that allow you to mix and match data, telephone, and coax connections. Leviton has a series that allow up to four jacks per single gang plate.

Twisted pair cable should also be run to each room. Run at least four pair to each room. Run a four twisted pair to each thermostat and two four-pair twisted pairs to telephone locations. Dedicate one of the cables to telephone and save the other cable for future expansion. You may also want to wire for a sprinkler control, spa and pool controls, door phone, weather stations, and a garage door opener.

Low voltage wiring used for security presents a few special considerations. The location of sensors is important, and planning should allow for this. For example, if you are using window and door sensors, wiring should be run that terminates close to the door or window frames. If you are using motion detectors, their installation will be easier if wiring is run close to their logical locations. At security keypad locations run a four twisted pair in addition to the standard keypad cable for future expansion. To these "security only" locations, a single pair of wires (shielded, 18 gauge) is adequate in most cases. This wire, fortunately, is inexpensive. Run lots of wire, again in homerun fashion.

If possible, it should be arranged that all audio/video equipment that might be interconnected is on the same phase or leg of the 220 volt service. This will reduce electrical noise currents between equipment on separate circuits in different parts of the house. In addition to the coaxial wiring for TVs, run four twisted pair to the same box. This wire can support infrared repeaters as well as future standards-based products.

Audio lines can be wired back to the designated media room, and the other wires should run back to a central location. Shielded 18 gauge pairs are a good choice for general use. The number of pairs to be run to a particular location depends on the planned use. If both high and low level audio lines are to be run between rooms, be sure to keep them at least three to six inches apart to avoid interactions that can cause oscillations in audio amplifiers. These oscillations cannot be heard but can burn out the speaker's tweeters.

All low level audio lines, from sources such as preamps, tape decks, and VCR audio connections, must be shielded cable. Speakers should be run with twisted pair of at least 16 gauge, with 14 or even 12 gauge being used for long runs with high-powered speakers.

When running video or phone lines in rooms where furniture layout may change, it is a good idea to run the wiring all the way around the room, about a foot above floor level. Leave a loop of line every third or fourth stud, and make the holes in the studs slightly oversized. This layout makes it possible to cut a hole anywhere on the wall and pull out enough line to install a "cut-in" box exactly where needed. Be sure when doing this that the line is secured within six inches of all existing boxes prior to closing the wall, and that all lines have one end run to an accessible junction box.

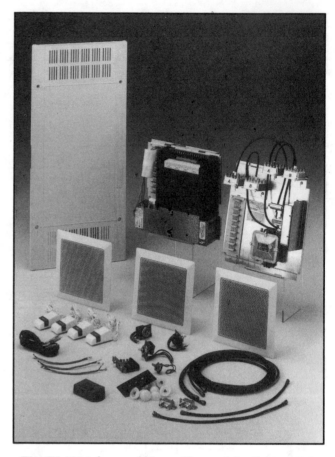

The ELAN Advanced Home Network by Square D is installed during construction to bring a new level of convenience to homes by consolidating and coordinating all audio, video, and phone services. Courtesy of Square D Company.

Before the insulation is put in the walls but after all wiring and plumbing are installed, get out a camera or camcorder and make a detailed photo/video record of every wall. It is also a good idea to make a sketch showing the distance to the first wall stud from every corner. The other studs can be found by adding multiples of 16 inches or 24 inches. The photos and sketches will make it easy to find wire, pipe, and stud locations, and see which walls are load bearing, throughout the life of the house.

Many do-it-yourself homeowners opt to run the coaxial cable and low-voltage wiring themselves. A good rule of thumb for eventual enhancement of home automation capabilities is putting in at least twice as much wire as you think you need. It doesn't take any more time to put in twin coax instead of single coax, so labor costs remain about the same. Although material costs may increase, you'll be set for the future. Labor is the major component when contractors wire a home, and doing it yourself can simultaneously save money and permit a much more extensive prewire. Nevertheless, many homeowners will prefer to have the work done for them. For the best performance for years to come, leave installation to a professional. (In some states, professional installation is required by law.)

For the best performance, buy the best wire. It's better to spend an extra few cents per foot than to suffer through problems later. Always buy shielded wire. This includes both coaxial cable, which brings cable and antenna signals into the home and distributes them to connected TVs, VCRs, laser disc players, and audio/video receivers; and twisted pair, which distributes sound throughout your home.

While it is important to plan for immediate needs, future requirements should also be considered. Planning for these future demands includes taking steps to accommodate technological advances now on the horizon. Installers and electricians will tell you that it is impossible to overwire a house; you need the extra wire to support future technologies like CEBus and LONWORKS.

SYSTEM DESIGN

Realistic system design begins with setting definite priorities and boundaries. It takes a combined effort by both the homeowner and the automation dealer/installer to make the installation a success. Homeowners must be involved in the design process — it is essential in creating a system that meets their expectations.

First, imagine your home at its most extravagant, with a home theater, whole house audio/video, HVAC control, "scene" lighting control, and a security camera at the front door or in the nursery. Second, study your home's floor plan. It will help you decide what controls you need and where to put them.

Look at each room and make a list of the control functions you want: What lights will be controlled? Temperature control? Music selection and volume control? Make sure to take into consideration furniture layout and the location of built-in cabinets and components. Next, set priorities for what is a "must have now" and what can be prewired and added later. Finally, don't over-automate. Not every light or home function needs to be automated when a standard light switch will do.

Determining the subsystems you want and what you want them to do is the best place to start your automation plans. The major automation systems and related subsystems are as follows:

- Lighting — Your home's lighting can be controlled (on, off, dim) via power line control (X-10) or proprietary circuit control (LiteTouch). Lights can be controlled based on time-of-day, remote control, or occupancy sensors. You can control a few selected lights or the whole house. "Scene" lighting can be used to create various visual "moods." Elements of lighting include: indoor lights, scene control, outdoor lights, skylights, window coverings, security lighting.

- Security and Safety — The important elements are intrusion protection, fire detection, access control, gates, cameras, and safety sensors such as magnetic, motion, glass break, smoke, gas leak, water leak, heat, vehicle/driveway.

- Energy Management — Heating and cooling are the primary areas of concern, but don't forget to consider energy-efficient appliances — water heaters, dishwashers, dryers, etc. Energy subsystems include such items as heating and cooling, hot water, zoned air flow, temperature, electronic meters, humidity, outside air.

- Entertainment — Where and what audio/video will be distributed throughout the home? Will there be a media/home theater? Location of speakers? Subsystems include: audio, video, home theater, multiroom, multi-source, remote control, outdoor.

- Water Management — The most common water management components are: lawn sprinklers, pool/spa controls, indoor plant watering systems, and bathrooms.

While you're still in the planning stage, make sure to take into consideration the placement of controls. This helps avoid "wall acne," the proliferation of control switches, buttons, boxes, etc., clustered at one or more locations, which can occur without proper planning. To help eliminate "wall acne," use multiple function wall switches such as Leviton's Wall Mounted Controllers and two-way controllers such as Enerlogic's ES-1400e.

You can purchase a "whole-house" system that consists of either proprietary products or pre-integrated subsystems that are installed by professional dealer/installers. Or you can purchase stand-alone products and integrate them yourself. This is actually easier than it sounds, as most products are designed to meet one of the existing automation standards, X-10 being the most popular. For example, all X-10-compatible products, regardless of manufacturer, can either control or be controlled by any other X-10-compatible product.

Once you've determined what you want, call for several mail order catalogs (listed in Appendix 2) and price shop. By watching for sales, you can reduce the cost of your home automation system without eliminating desired functions. If you want your system professionally installed, call several home automation companies in your area for a bid. (See the Dealer/Installer Directory in Appendix 3 for a dealer near you, or look in the Yellow Pages under Home Automation or Burglar Alarms.)

2.
The X-10 System

The X-10 Powerhouse System, which has set the standard in real-world automation for more than ten years, controls lights and appliances throughout your home from any convenient location. You plug lamps into Lamp Modules, plug appliances into Appliance Modules, and replace wall light switches with Wall Switch Modules. Controllers send command signals over your existing house wiring to the Module or Modules of your choice, allowing you to control virtually everything electrical in your home. You can also dim and brighten incandescent lamps.

All X-10 devices are transmitters, receivers, or a combination (called transceivers). X-10 transmitters send out the control signals that receivers respond to. Transmitters generally only have a house code dial and have separate buttons for each unit code. To turn unit A2 on, set the house code to "A," then press the "2" button, then "ON."

Plug-in consoles such as the Mini and Maxi are inexpensive and can be placed anywhere for convenient control of lights and appliances. The X-10 Timer Console and Telephone Responder are transmitters that incorporate automatic timed control and the ability to control X-10 devices over the phone. X-10 wireless remotes such as the Keychain Remote, Wireless Console, or Xtender Wall Switches transmit radio signals (up to 100 feet, extending another 150 feet with a Smart RF Repeater) to a transceiver. The transceiver re-transmits the X-10 signals on your power lines to lamp or appliance receivers.

Receivers include plug-in modules to control lamps and appliances, as well as wall switches to control ceiling lights and fans. Each receiver is coded to a house code (A-P) and a unit code (1-16) for a total of 256 different possible codes. You set the code with two small dials, one for the house code and one for the unit code. You can set multiple receivers to the same code, and they'll operate as a group. Receivers that control appliances respond only to ON and OFF commands; receivers that control incandescent lights respond to ON, OFF, BRIGHT, and DIM.

The downside to X-10 is that it currently employs "broadcast only" technology. This means that controllers can only "send" signals to modules, they cannot receive a "confirmation" signal that the module received the signal. Controllers and modules also need 110V AC power to function — loss of power renders the system inoperable. For this reason, *never* use non-battery backed-up X-10 modules to operate any part of your vital security or life-safety system.

The X-10 Powerhouse System (commonly referred to as X-10) is marketed by X-10 (USA) Inc., which also manufactures and supplies modules and controllers for the systems sold by Radio Shack, Stanley, Heath/Zenith, and many others. This means that a Radio Shack controller can control a Stanley module, and vice versa. In addition, many high-end whole-house automation systems such as Mastervoice's Butler-in-a-Box, Group Three Technologies' SAMANTHA, and Unity's Home Manager utilize X-10-compatible controllers and modules.

CONTROLLERS

Controllers send signals to modules or transceivers, commanding the module either to turn lights or appliances on or off, and in the case of lights, to dim or brighten. There are several different types of controllers including: Maxi, Mini, Mini Timer, Sundowner, Telephone Responder, and Wireless Remote Control. Following is a listing of the different types of X-10 controllers available and what they can do. All model numbers shown are for X-10 Powerhouse brand components.

The Maxi Controller (Model SC503) performs six functions: ON, OFF, BRIGHT, DIM, ALL LIGHTS ON, and ALL UNITS OFF for control of up to 16 groups of X-10 modules. The Maxi Controller has "two key action." This means that to turn a module on, you first press and release the number button corresponding to the Unit Code set on the module you want to turn on. You then press and release the ON button. This two key action provides an added feature. It allows "group control" and group dimming/brightening. For example, press 1, 2, 3 then ON, to turn on modules set to 1, 2, and 3 simultaneously.

The Mini Controller (Model MC460) performs the same six functions as the Maxi but only controls up to eight modules. It has four rocker keys that control modules set to Unit Codes 1-4 or 5-8 by sliding the 1-4/5-8 selector switch to the desired position.

The X-10 Mini Timer (Model MT522) is a mini controller, timer, and alarm clock all in one. The Mini Timer can turn on and off up to four X-10 modules twice a day. (Stanley has a timer controller with a built-in AM/FM clock radio that controls up to eight modules.) Each module can be set to turn on or off once only, every day at the same time, or in the Security mode, which varies the on and off time you set to be different each day.

The Sundowner (Model SD533) has a built-in photocell, which turns on up to four lights when the sun goes down and turns them off again at dawn, with no programming. There are four slide switches on the underside of the Sundowner which enable you to select the modules you want it to control in the dusk-to-dawn mode. A sensitivity adjustment allows you to set the light level at which the Sundowner detects dawn. The Sundowner also has all the features and functions of a Mini Controller.

The Infrared Mini Controller (Model IR543) allows you to turn on up to eight lights and appliances anywhere in your home using the same Universal Remote Control that you use for your TV, VCR, and cable converter. You program the Universal remote to transmit signals that can be recognized by the Infrared Mini Controller. In addition, the Infrared Mini Controller has the same features as found in a Mini Controller.

The Telephone Responder (Model TR551) is an eight-module controller that plugs into a standard 120V outlet and a standard modular telephone jack. When you call home from any touchtone phone in the world, the Responder answers the phone, just like an answering machine.

The Responder can work with an answering machine and has a "security code" feature to prevent unauthorized callers from gaining access to your system. The Responder can also be set to flash selected lights around the house when the phone rings. This feature is very useful for the hearing impaired. The Responder also functions as a manual controller with ON, OFF, DIM, BRIGHTEN, and ALL LIGHTS ON/ALL UNITS OFF commands.

The Wireless Remote Control (Model RC5000) consists of an eight unit, four function remote control, which transmits radio frequency (RF) signals to turn on or off a light or an appliance plugged into the Transceiver/Appliance Module from anywhere inside or outside your home. The Wireless Remote Control and the Transceiver/Appliance Module have a "bank switch," allowing you to have two systems in use in the same house.

Imagine being able to turn on the lights in your house as you enter your driveway. With the Key Chain Remote Control (Model KC674) and its corresponding Transceiver Module (Model TM751), you'll never have to come home to a dark house again. The Key Chain Remote transmits RF signals (from up to 100 feet away) to the Transceiver, which retransmits the signal to your other X-10 modules.

The Deluxe Wall Programmer from Leviton carries out full seven-day scheduling for up to 63 program sequences. Each program sequence can switch from one to 16 individual address codes. This unit also permits manual switching for all 256 available addresses without affecting programmed schedules entered in the unit's memory.

Leviton's Wall Mounted Controllers are available in several different versions, each operating by means of a rocker or group of rockers. All Controllers come with a matching Decora wallplate, have two 6-inch wire leads, one white (neutral) and one black (phase), and easily wire into standard single-gang wallboxes. Up to four Wall Controllers can be ganged together.

Do you wish you could put a wall switch anywhere, and use it to control any light or appliance in your home? The

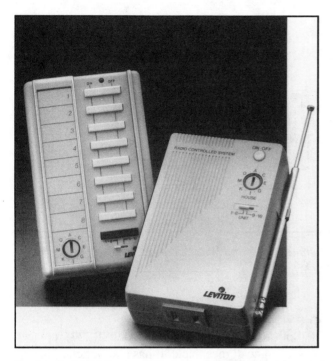

Leviton's DEC Remote Command System puts control of lights and appliances in the palm of the user's hand. The handheld transmitter sends coded signals via radio transmission through walls and ceilings to the plug-in transceiver, which conveys the signals over AC wiring to DEC receivers that switch loads on and off. Courtesy of Leviton Mfg. Co.

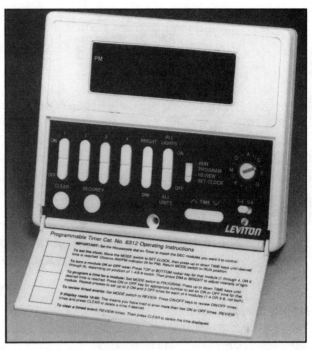

Leviton's DEC Wall Mounted Programmer (#6312) is easy to install and use, yet powerful enough to add automation security, convenience, and energy savings. Courtesy of Leviton Mfg. Co.

X-10 Xtender Wall Switch allows you to do just that. Attach the battery-powered wall switch to any wall (with the supplied Velcro) and plug in the receiver within 50 feet. When you press a button on the Xtender Wall Switch it transmits a wireless radio signal to any X-10 Wireless Receiver, Appliance Transceiver, or Security Console. The transceiver then retransmits the signal to all X-10-compatible modules on the same house/unit code, allowing you to operate lights and appliances from one location. There are three different Xtenders available. All can be set to any house code but are restricted to certain unit codes. All three models are powered by three AAA batteries.

MODULES

Modules receive the signal transmitted from a controller or retransmitted from a transceiver. They then act upon the signal by either turning the light or appliance on or off, and in the case of lights, dimming or brightening. There are plug-in and wired-in modules. Plug-in modules include: Lamp, Appliance, and Heavy-Duty Appliance Modules. Wired-in modules include Wall Switch Modules and Split Receptacle Modules. There are also several different specialty modules including: Chime Module, Universal Module, and Burglar Interface Module. Following is a listing of the different types of X-10 modules available and what they can do.

Lamp Module

The Lamp Module (LM465) is rated for incandescent lamps up to 300 watts. It can be turned on and off, and dimmed and brightened remotely from any X-10 Controller or Timer. The Lamp Module responds to ALL LIGHTS ON/ALL UNITS OFF commands from any Controller set to its Housecode. This allows you to turn on or off all lamps connected to Lamp Modules, regardless of what Unit Code the Lamp Module is set to.

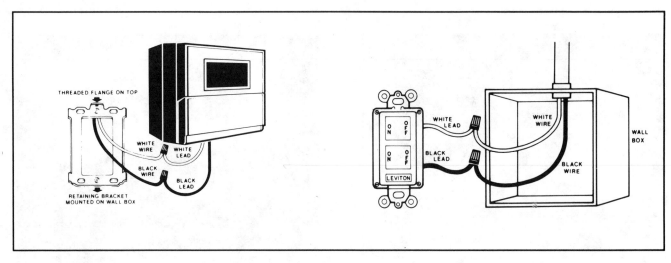

Wiring diagram for Leviton's Deluxe Wall Mounted Programmer (left) and Wall Mounted Controller (right). Courtesy of Leviton Mfg. Co.

Appliance Module

The Appliance Module is used to control appliances and fluorescent lights. It does not respond to the ALL LIGHTS ON code but does respond to the ALL UNITS OFF code. The Appliance Module has a "local control" feature, which operates in the same manner as a Lamp Module.

Appliance Modules are rated for three types of loads. The 15A resistive load is the equivalent of about 1800 watts, so it will control resistive-type loads such as coffee pots, toaster ovens, portable heaters, etc. (Extreme caution should be taken when using the Appliance Module to control portable heaters, as a fire could result if the heater were turned on by remote control while near flammable substances.) The $1/3$ HP for motor loads is sufficient to handle the motor load in appliances such as portable fans and window air conditioners.

The 220V Heavy Duty Appliance Module (Model HD243 — 15A, and Model HD245 — 20A) is designed to work on single split phase 110/220V or 120/240V systems, which is the type of wiring found in most houses. Heavy Duty Appliance Modules will not work on three-phase systems, which are sometimes found in apartments.

The HD243 plugs into a regular 220V 15A or 20A outlet and will control any 220V appliance rated at 15A or less. The HD245 will control any 220V appliance rated at 20A or less. For safety, the Heavy Duty Appliance Module does not have local control and does not respond to the ALL LIGHTS ON code but does respond to the ALL UNITS OFF code.

Split Receptacle Module

The Split Receptacle Module (Model SR227) replaces the existing wall receptacle. It has two outlets. The top outlet is controlled and works just like an Appliance Module. The bottom outlet is on all the time and works just like a regular outlet. Both outlets are rated at 15A (1800 watts) so that the Split Receptacle will control anything that you would normally plug into a regular 15A wall receptacle.

The Split Receptacle Module can be used for any kind of lamp including fluorescent lamps, but it cannot dim lamps. The module does not respond to the ALL LIGHTS ON code but does respond to the ALL UNITS OFF code. The module has a "local control" feature, but it does not work with "instant on" and remote-controlled TVs.

Wall Switch Module

The Wall Switch Module (Model WS467) is rated for incandescent lights only, up to 500 watts max. It can be turned on and off, dimmed and brightened remotely from any X-10-compatible controller. The Wall Switch Module responds to ALL LIGHTS ON/ALL UNITS OFF commands from any controller set to its Housecode.

There is also a pushbutton for manual control, which allows you to turn the light connected to it on and off manually. The slide switch located under the local control push button is a UL requirement and is used to turn the power off when changing a light bulb. The Wall Switch Module has a minimum rating of 60 watts.

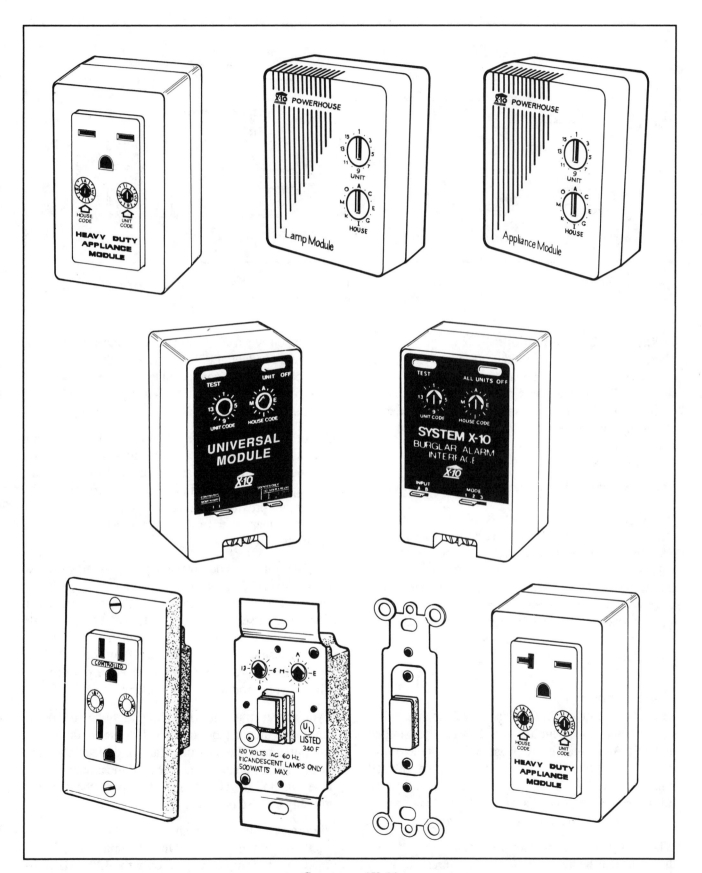

Courtesy of X-10.

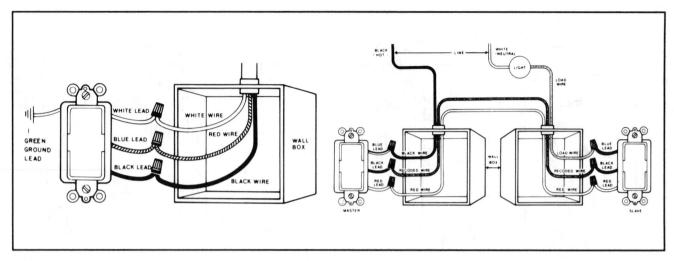

Wiring diagram for Leviton's Wall Switch Module (left) and three-way Incandescent Switch Module (right).
Courtesy of Leviton Mfg. Co.

3-Way Wall Switch Module

The 3-Way Wall Switch Module (Model WS4777) is used to control a light that is currently controlled by two switches. The set includes a master switch and a companion switch, which are used to replace the existing three-way switches. The WS4777 operates exactly the same as the Wall Switch Module.

TROUBLESHOOTING X-10 SYSTEMS

Most of the reported problems in X-10 installations stem from one or more modules not receiving signals from one or more control consoles, or with modules that work only part of the time. Most likely, these problems are caused by: (1) lack of phase coupling, (2) interference and noise, (3) power line impedance. Whether the problems are caused by lack of phase coupling, power line noise, or X-10 overpopulation, there are several ways to solve them.

Phase Problems

Your home receives 220/240V service from three wires — two hot and one neutral. An X-10 signal transmitted on phase A can only get to phase B through the power transformer located by your street power pole. Like all transmitted signals, X-10 signals weaken as they travel. It is possible, therefore, that an X-10 signal may not be strong enough to activate a receiver reliably.

Whenever you dial a neighbor's telephone number, even though he may be right across the street, the call is routed through a switch box several miles away. The same thing can happen when X-10 transmitters and receivers are used on a residential 220V service. If the transmitters (controllers) are not connected to the same 110V leg as the receivers (modules), the X-10 signal may have to travel $1/4$ mile or more before it's received.

If all of your modules work sometimes and some of your modules work all the time, but not all work all the time, you could still have a phase problem. Turning on any 220V appliance such as a range, a clothes dryer, or an air conditioner provides a temporary signal path for X-10 signals to leap over to the other phase, resulting in intermittent performance.

If X-10 signals sent out over one phase are measured as weak in the other phase, you know this is the problem. You can use Leviton's Signal Strength Indicator (model 6386), which sells for about $115, to test your X-10 system. The signal must be greater than 100 millivolts (mv) to ensure correct operation. If you don't have a Signal Strength Indicator, you might simply notice that some of your modules aren't working.

If you suspect that phase coupling might be your problem, move one or more of the offending modules to a wall outlet near the controller (all the outlets in a room are most likely on the same phase). If the modules work there but do not when placed far apart, then there's probably a phase problem.

To correct a phase problem, "couple" the two phases together using an Isolated Phase Coupler, a specially tuned circuit designed to pass only the 120 KHz X-10 signals. Install a nonpolarized 630V 0.1 mfd coupling

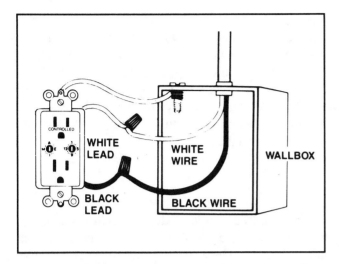

Wiring diagram for Leviton's Split Duplex Wall Receptacle Module. Courtesy of Leviton Mfg. Co.

capacitor to a neutral bus bar and then to both phases of the incoming AC power line.

With this cap in place, instead of traveling halfway down the road, the X-10 signal will jump across the fuse box and never leave the house. I recommend that anyone building an X-10 system install a phase coupler. NOTE: All such electrical work should be installed by a qualified electrician. The 630V 0.1 mfd cap can be mail ordered from Digi-Key at (800) 346-5144.

Interference and Noise

If you've installed a phase coupler and are still having intermittent problems in some areas of the house, chances are something's causing an excessive amount of electrical noise somewhere in the house, interfering with the X-10 signals somewhere along their path. You can try to make the X-10 signals stronger by using expensive repeaters and amplifiers; however, a better solution is to find the noise source and eliminate it.

Start by turning off and unplugging appliances until the troubled modules work reliably. The most likely offenders: personal computers, televisions, wireless baby monitors, fluorescent lights, and large electrical motors. Sometimes these devices only interfere when they are on. To correct this problem, simply plug the offending device into an interference filter such as the Model 15-1111 from Radio Shack.

If problems persist, start turning off circuits at the breaker panel. If a single plug-in appliance is the problem, you can use a plug-in noise filter to eliminate the

noise. If a bank of fluorescent light is causing the trouble, you may want to consider replacing the ballasts since some brands of ballasts generate excessive amounts of noise.

Certain brands of TV can generate noise and superimpose it on the power line. In most cases, this kind of noise will not cause a problem. However, if it is determined that the TV is causing a problem (which can be determined by unplugging the TV to see if the problem goes away), try plugging the TV into a filter to isolate it from the AC line. This filter may also help to isolate the load (or internal capacitance) of the TV from the AC line if it is found that the TV is attenuating the signals from your controllers.

Wireless intercom systems or baby monitors that use the house wiring to transmit can "block out" X-10 transmissions while the intercom is left in the permanent transmit (talk) mode. Unfortunately, there is no simple solution to this problem, but if the Controller and all the Modules are on one phase the first thing to try would be to change them all to the other phase. It has been found that the 6276 filter can in some cases attenuate signals from a neighbor's intercom sufficiently to allow the Controller's signals to be received by the X-10 Modules. It is not possible to have a wireless intercom and a Controller operating in the same house.

If you are plugging several items into the same outlet as an X-10 device, using cube taps, multi-outlet adapters, etc., it helps to plug all other devices into an external outlet strip, and plug the strip and the X-10 device directly into the double outlet. X-10 signals are usually filtered out by surge suppressors, so X-10 controllers and modules should be connected directly to the AC line.

What if you isolate the trouble to a particular circuit, but there's no appliance plugged in on that circuit? While it's not likely, there could be a problem with that circuit's wiring, or the circuit may be running near something else on another circuit that's inducing the noise in it. And what if you've turned off practically the whole house, and the problem persists? Then it's possible you have "dirty" (electrically noisy) power coming into your house. Dirty power comes from a neighbor's computer, fluorescent lights, or television. If this is the case, the power company should be willing to fix it.

Power Line Impedance

Each receiver and each keypad transmitter you add to a circuit in your home slightly decreases the circuit's impedance (resistance) to X-10 signals. Large numbers of X-10 devices (more than 15-20 on a particular circuit breaker) can, in some cases, load down the circuit so much that X-10 signals can't make it to their intended destinations. To avoid low power line impedance, you can move some of the X-10 devices to other circuits to spread out the load, or you can install an X-10 Signal Repeater. This fairly expensive device mounts near the circuit breaker panel and re-transmits X-10 signals whenever it hears them.

If modules turn on unnecessarily, it is also possible that the modules may have been triggered by a 120V AC power "dip" or "brownout." Lamp Modules and Appliance Modules have a feature called "local control"; this feature lets you turn the module on by turning the power switch on the light or appliance off and then on again. A circuit in the module detects this change in load and interprets it as a request to turn on. This "local control" circuit is by design very sensitive and can therefore sometimes see a momentary dip in AC power as a change in the load and therefore "think" it has been told to turn on. If this problem is suspected, it is recommended that the local control feature be disabled.

To prevent appliances with built-in thermostats (such as air conditioners, electric blankets, portable heaters, etc.) from switching themselves on when they're supposed to be off, appliance modules are designed to ignore the first locally sent override signal. The trick is to turn the "original light switch" OFF, ON, OFF, ON in rapid succession.

The first ON will be ignored, the second ON should turn on the lights. You'll still have to switch the lights off from a Mini Controller. One way around that is to replace the original switch with a Leviton wall-mounted controller or use an X-10 (RC5000) wireless control. By using the X-10 transmitter, you'll be able to switch everything on and off from anywhere in your home.

It is possible to disable the local control feature of the Appliance Module by plugging a "cube tap" into the module so that two items can be plugged into the same module. The operating range of an appliance module is seven to 500 watts at 120VAC. When the output load is less than seven watts, an appliance module can't see it. That's why you need to plug in an additional nightlight — to load the module.

Plug a 7½ watt nightlight into one of the receptacles of the cube tap and the appliance you want to control into the other. When the module is on, the appliance and the night light will be on. When the module is off, the appliance and the night light will be off. Now, even if you operate the power switch on the appliance, the night light is always "in circuit" so the Appliance Module's local control circuit is disabled. You can also modify the Appliance Module internally to disable the local control feature. To do this you need to cut the small wire link next to pin 7 on the Integrated Circuit in the Appliance Module.

Other Problems

Intermittent trouble with X-10 wall switches is sometimes caused by mold flash on the button knob, but most often it's due to a bent switch plunger. Check for mold flash by removing the cover plate, grabbing the button knob and pulling straight back. The button should pop off easily.

Examine the knob for small protrusions (mold flash) that might be rubbing against the button cavity. Remove whatever you find with a razor knife. Next, check for a bent switch plunger. Try pushing the plastic shaft with your finger. If it tends to buckle, instead of plunging, you've definitely found the problem. A little WD-40 may help, otherwise, there's not much you can do besides replacing the switch.

Plastic plungers are designed to be pushed straight in, from the exact center of the button. If you push at an angle or from the edge of the button, the increased torque will eventually fatigue the plunger shaft, rendering the switch assembly useless.

X-10 Lamp Modules can be damaged when the incandescent lamps they control burn out. This is because incandescent lamps draw an extremely large amount of current for a brief time when the filament fails. Incandescent lamps also experience a high inrush of current when the lamp is turned on. The surge in current can cause the Triac inside the X-10 lamp module to burn out. You either have to replace the module or, if you are electrically inclined, replace the bad Triac with a higher current Triac (available from Radio Shack).

X-10 modules are controlled by digitally encoded signals imposed on the power line. These signals are similar to a combination lock and, in theory, almost impossible to trigger by power line transients or electrical noise. However, thunderstorms and malfunctioning water-solenoids — found in washing machines and sprinkler systems — are two known exceptions.

Lightning can cause your entire system or individual components to stop functioning temporarily. Often this can be remedied by simply disconnecting and reconnecting the modules and control units.

Solenoid problems are very hard to track down because the malfunctioning equipment could be in your neighbor's home. The entire power line system is also temperature sensitive. As the weather gets colder and drier, you may have less interference.

You may experience trouble with X-10 wall-outlet modules responding to random ON signals (lights turning on when not commanded to do so). To answer the question, you need to determine whether the affected wall-outlet module is really malfunctioning or simply responding to random ON signals.

Start by setting a module to the same house and unit codes as the affected module, then plug it into a nearby outlet, one that's on the same electrical circuit. Plug a lamp into it, then send an ON signal to the new module to make sure it works. If so, both lamps should light. Now send an OFF signal. Both lamps should go off. If the second lamp lights when the first turns itself on, you know that random ON signals are being sent.

If the second lamp does not turn itself on when the first one does, then you have a loose bulb, a loose cord, a defective lamp socket, or a defective module. If that's the case, the fix is easy. All you have to do is tighten the bulb or loose plug.

Random ON signals (suggested when both lamps turn on) are somewhat harder to track down. Someone may have turned on security mode using a CP290 or a Remote Timer Controller. If that's the case, both modules should eventually turn themselves off. To fix it, just turn off security mode. If you find that security mode is already off in your house, check with the neighbors. Someone may be on the same house code as you, and security mode may have been inadvertently turned on over there.

Relay chatter is a problem in which modules bounce, or chatter, when commanded to turn on, which causes the module to come on sometimes and go off sometimes. Replacement is the only known remedy for relay chatter. Another problem has to do with modules that always turn on but intermittently refuse to turn off. The fix is to turn off the affected module from the same controller that was originally used to turn it on. As soon as you do that, you can usually turn the affected module on and off from anywhere.

Given sufficient static discharge, the CMOS microprocessors found in X-10 mini/maxi controllers become temporarily paralyzed. This condition is known as "latch up." When the chips are latched, the circuit doesn't respond to normal pushbutton commands, which makes the whole unit seem dead. To reduce the potential for zapping your equipment, increase the humidity level in your home, especially during the winter. You can also buy anti-static sprays to treat your carpet.

More often than not this is only a temporary situation. To correct the problem, simply unplug the unit and leave it alone for 24 hours. With an RT504 wireless controller, you have to disconnect the battery momentarily, then reinstall it. With a Leviton wall-mounted controller, you have to switch off its circuit breaker at the main electrical panel. If you fail to switch off the breaker, the zapped controller may continuously send out a signal that interferes with subsequent X-10 transmissions.

For more information on troubleshooting your X-10 system, there are several knowledgeable sources available, including: the Mr. Module column in *Electronic House* magazine, Home Automation Laboratories' *Lab Notes*, Silicon Valley Video Group's X-10 *Technical Information* compilation, and reprints of David Butler's "At Home With Technology" weekly newspaper column. (See Appendix 2 for address information.)

3.
Lighting Control

Lighting control and home automation have been closely linked since X-10 released the first control modules more than ten years ago, as lighting control is one of the basic services an X-10 system can provide. Today, X-10 modules are still a popular choice for both simple and complex lighting control systems. X-10 provides a relatively high level of control, especially considering that it requires no real installation beyond plugging controllers and modules into electrical outlets.

Proprietary lighting systems, which establish special wiring networks dedicated to lighting control, offer a greater degree of control. Most proprietary lighting networks are designed for installation during construction because their wiring replaces the traditional wiring normally found in new homes. Leaders in this area include LiteTouch, Lightolier, Lutron, and Vantage.

Lighting also plays an important role in many of the areas automation seeks to improve: entertainment, security, and convenience. Lights discourage intruders and offer comfort when returning to an empty home. Automatically turn on all inside and outside lights if you hear a suspicious noise at night. Light your escape path when the fire alarm is activated. Dim lights automatically when you start a movie. Turn off all lights and appliances from your bed with a touch of a button. Automated lighting can do all this and much more.

Most people add automated devices, such as motion detectors and timers, to their lighting systems for convenience and security reasons. A very pleasant side effect is that they are usually big energy savers as well. These devices' task is to provide the proper amount of light only when needed. In doing this, motion detectors and timers eliminate lights left on in empty rooms, and dimmers eliminate lights that are much brighter than they need to be.

Advanced lighting systems can be controlled by remote control, passive infrared control, and scene controls. These are available in both lighting-dedicated systems or as part of a whole-house control system. Either way, they can add a great deal of both convenience and safety to the modern home.

SCENE LIGHTING

Scene control refers to the ability to create different lighting looks in a room by pressing a single button. The name is borrowed from theatrical lighting, where each scene in a production has its own mix of brightness, color, and location of light. Scene lighting enhances your home's ambiance while providing greater flexibility and convenience.

Studies have proven that lighting affects moods. In most modern homes, each room is used for a variety of different activities that require different levels of brightness and lighting scenes. In a residence, for example, a living room might have several scenes available. A "reading" scene might combine wall washer indirect lights at 50% brightness, table lamps in the reading area at 100%, and track lighting to accent wall-hung artwork at 70%. A "party" scene might have higher levels on the indirect and track lighting, plus several floor lamps at 80% brightness. A "security" scene might only use a table lamp or floor lamp to make the house look occupied.

"Lightscaping" is to the backyard as "scene" lighting is to the interior of your home. Using lightscaping techniques allows a homeowner to extend entertainment hours, personalize his yard, and improve safety and security. Automation provides the necessary control functions to allow you to truly enjoy your backyard, hassle free.

Use uplighting, shining floodlights up into trees and bushes, to create moods and establish emphasis. Define paths and driveways by downlighting with floodlights. Try moonlighting, or shining a light down from high in a tree, to create emphasis and diffuse light over a large area. Use stylish, cylindrical post lights around a gazebo or deck for aesthetics and access. Use temple-shaped access lights along walkways or sidewalks for safety. Consider mushroom-shaped garden lights along the edge of plantings for definition.

INTERIOR LIGHTING

Power line carrier technology (X-10) can be used to provide any home with remote control for lights and appliances. After installation, a homeowner can completely control the use of electrical power in the home from one or more convenient locations. Incandescent lighting can be dimmed or brightened, and lights and appliances can be turned on or off, by simply pressing buttons on a manual control unit. For more convenient control, lights and appliances can be preprogrammed to turn on or off automatically at preset times.

X-10 Controls

X-10 paved the way for a low end lighting with do-it-yourself modular products. The inexpensive X-10 controls are appropriate for any home regardless of the home's size or price range. X-10 devices, such as Lamp Modules, Mini Controllers, and Timers, typically retail for $5 to $50. At that price, an X-10 lighting installation for an average home can run from $50 to $500 depending on the needs and budget of the homeowner.

To set up a basic lighting control system for your home, all you need is an X-10 Maxi or Mini Controller and Lamp Modules. Simply plug in the Lamp Modules and plug in the lamps you want controlled. Then plug in the Controller anywhere it's convenient and voilá! You have control of all the lights attached to modules. To expand your system, simply add more modules and controllers.

Leviton Wall Mounted Controller

It is possible to control and dim the room lights from a wall switch location, but it's not possible to do it using a wall-mounted module. Modules can only receive signals. They can be switched on and off locally, and they can be switched on and off or dimmed remotely, but they can't send on/off/dim signals to other modules and they can't dim themselves. To control and dim room lights from a wall location, you'll use a Leviton Wall Mounted Controller. The Leviton controller requires a neutral wire in the box. (Neutral wires are not always present at the wall switch location.) Plus you'll have to rewire the light fixture with a Leviton Fixture Receiver.

Controlling Fluorescent Lighting

To control a fluorescent bulb from a wall switch location, you can use a wall-switch relay from Domestech (available from Home Automation Laboratories). A wall-switch relay is an appliance module with an ON/OFF switch designed to fit into a standard electrical box and requiring a neutral wire in the box. Another option is to use Leviton's Decora wall switch module (model 6291) for controlling fluorescent lighting. The 6291 module was expressly designed for use with fluorescent lighting and requires a neutral wire in the electrical box. The 6291 can also be used for switch-controlled appliances and/or incandescent lighting where dimming is not required. If the fluorescent fixture happens to plug into an electrical outlet, any appliance module can be used.

Fluorescent lighting can also be controlled with Fixture Switching Modules (Leviton part number 6725 and 6726) or Box Mounted Modules (Leviton part number 6236 and 6237). Fixture Switching Modules resemble appliance modules except that they're equipped with pigtails and adhesive strips for hard wiring right inside the fixture. Box Mounted Modules are provided in boxes with 1/2-inch connectors for installation at panels and junction boxes equipped with standard 1/2-inch knockouts.

OCCUPANCY SENSORS

A simple way to save lighting energy is to turn off the lights in an unoccupied space. Occupancy sensors can perform this function automatically. Originally developed for the security industry, occupancy sensors detect the presence of occupants in a space and turn the electric lights on and off.

The major advantage of occupancy sensors is that they are a positive "off" device. Unless an occupant is detected, they do not signal a light to turn on. These are especially good for rooms that are used for short periods and then left empty for long intervals, such as bathrooms, hallways, basements, stairways, and garages. I installed a wall switch passive infrared sensor in my garage because the light switch was inconveniently located behind the door, which meant that I had to close the door in a dark garage and fumble for the switch. But no more. Now, when I open the door the light automatically turns on, it also comes on when I drive my car into the garage.

Three types of signals are used for occupancy sensors: infrared, ultrasonic, and microwave. Infrared sensors are passive and respond to changes in object surface temperature and movement. Ultrasonic and microwave sensors are active: they generate a signal and then respond to changes in the signal as it returns to a receiver at the source.

Passive Infrared (PIR) sensors use a dual-element sensing device so that when one element senses infrared energy (heat) before the other, the sensor assumes occupancy and turns to the "on" state. Ultrasonic sensors (US) use a quartz crystal oscillator to generate an inaudible signal. The ultrasonic signal is broadcast into a space, bounces off surfaces, and returns to the sensor's receiver. Changes in the signals return time indicate occupancy. Microwave sensors are similar to the ultrasonic in that a signal is generated and moving objects will cause a shift in the frequency of the returned signal.

A combination-type device is available that uses both infrared and ultrasonic sensors to turn lights on and only one signal to maintain them in the "on" position. This device helps prevent lights being turned on by false signals.

Occupancy sensors may be combined with a photo control device so that lights will go on only when a space is occupied and the available daylight is below a preset minimum level.

In new construction and renovation work, an occupancy sensor will normally be installed on the ceiling, which allows the sensor to "see" an entire space and prevents interference from obstructions. In retrofit work, there are also sensor units that can replace existing wall switches. Selection of the correct switch location and signal type is critical to proper operation.

Area coverage and beam patterns are important factors in determining which occupancy sensor should be used.

The area the unit is rated to cover — from 300 square feet to 2,000 square feet — must be considered.

Though several sensors may cover the same area, they can have different beam patterns: ellipse, circle, fan shape, square, or rectangle. The ability of a device to sense occupancy is reduced as the distance from the receiver increases. Once the appropriate sensor has been selected, it is important to install it in the proper location for effective coverage.

False triggering signals are another factor to consider. A PIR may consider a mirror image or daylighting as a signal that a space is occupied. An ultrasonic device may be triggered by vibrations or by direct air motion on the unit. A microwave sensor signal may penetrate a wall or floor and sense occupancy in a different space.

Use the following checklist to evaluate an occupancy sensor project:

- Amount of time lights operate unnecessarily
- Type of sensor (PIR, ultrasonic, microwave)
- Size and shape of the space and presence of barriers
- Sensor placement for complete coverage
- Voids in detector signal
- Adjustability of sensitivity and time delay
- Retrofit switch replacement
- Possibility of false signals (air movement, etc.)
- Desired accessories (combination, two-step, photocontrol, etc.)

Honeywell and BRK offer wall-mounted light controls that feature PIR sensors. When left in their "auto" mode, they will turn on lights as soon as a presence is detected, then turn them off a short time after the room is left empty. They have dials to adjust PIR sensitivity and the length of time the light stays on. There are models that screw into a light socket to control a single light. Wall switch models, which replace standard wall switches, can control all lights wired to that switch.

For automatic control of interior and exterior lighting, you should look at the Stanley Radio Controlled Motion Detector. The portable and wireless PIR sensor mounts easily anywhere inside or outside the home. The PIR detects movement up to 40 feet away in a 110° arc and has a sensitivity adjustment. The unit has a built-in photocell to prevent lights from turning on during the day, and a variable timed shut-off (from 10 seconds to 15 minutes).

Upon detecting motion, the detector sends an RF signal to the plug-in Mobile Base unit, which in turn sends an ON signal to all units on the same Housecode. You could use one of these units to turn on the porch light and foyer light and activate a Chime Module to warn of an approaching visitor. The unit could likewise be used to turn on and off interior lights such as hallway lights, bathroom lights, basement lighting, etc. Best of all, your PC-based controller (Enerlogic, Dynasty, etc.) can use the detector to activate more complex actions.

Sound-Activated Light Switches

In addition to infrared, you can use sound-activated light switches for automatic control of lights. Sound-activated switches replace standard wall switches and are installed the same as light dimmers. On the switch are two dials that you adjust with a screwdriver. One controls the sensitivity of the switch; that is, how loud the sound must be to turn on the light. At the highly sensitive end, a footstep is enough to turn on the lights. The other dial controls how long the light stays on before shutting off automatically. It is adjustable from a few seconds to about ten minutes. Both of the dials are covered by the switchplate so they cannot be tampered with once they're set. Sound-activated modules also come in screw-in and plug-in models.

EXTERIOR LIGHTING

Manual control of exterior lighting can be particularly troublesome to a homeowner, since you have to remember to turn it on and off. Many people will often forget, resulting in either a dark house in the evening or lights burning on through the night and even into the next day. Some of these problems can be solved by photocell control. The main problem with straight photocell control is that the controlled lamp is on whenever it is dark. This could mean well over twelve hours of operation during long winter nights. Timers can also be used for lighting control but offer little flexibility and, in most cases, do not self-adjust to changing sunset times.

The best answer for do-it-yourself programmed home control is to install a programmable X-10 control such as Enerlogic's ES-1400e. Programmable systems can respond to user or sensor input and take varied actions based on the input and preprogrammed options. These types of systems are more expensive than timed controllers but are more flexible and have many features found in very expensive whole-house control systems.

Motion Detector Lights

To control exterior lighting, you can simply replace existing floodlights with X-10 Motion Detector Floodlights, or replace standard wall switches, which control exterior lights, with X-10 Wall Switch Modules. Motion Detector Floodlights can be set to automatically turn on at dusk, then off again at dawn, or be activated only when motion is detected. The advantage of the motion detection setting is that you save energy because the lights are on only when needed. A note of caution. Do not use quartz halogen lamps in light fixtures that are X-10 controlled. The reason is that the resistance of a quartz halogen lamp can be as high as 75 ohms (compared to about 14 ohms for a regular light bulb). This attenuates the X-10 signal substantially and in some instances may not allow the signal to pass through the lamp.

Low-Voltage Yard Lights

To control low-voltage yard lights (or variable-speed ceiling fans) from a wall switch location, use Domestech's FANtastic switch module. Unlike older X-10 switch modules, which chop the AC signal and effectively output square waves (DC), these FANtastic switch modules output filtered sine waves (AC). They were specifically designed to work with induction motors and low-voltage transformers. They allow you to safely control (ON/OFF/DIM) low-voltage yard lights without overheating the transformer.

PROPRIETARY LIGHTING SYSTEMS

Proprietary lighting systems are most commonly installed during construction, as is the case with LiteTouch, which completely replaces the standard wiring with a unique wiring system of its own. These systems offer sophisticated control over your home's lighting and may offer optional interfaces with your existing security system, pool/spa controls, and HVAC control systems, such as Unity.

Although these systems concentrate on only one aspect of automation — lighting — and are not considered true "whole-house" automation systems, they have been evolving in that direction. Many currently offer security interfaces that allow you to interface your existing security system with their lighting system for a more integrated "whole-house" approach. The main drawbacks to these systems is their price, $2.50 per square foot for a complete LiteTouch system, and the fact that they are mainly designed for new construction.

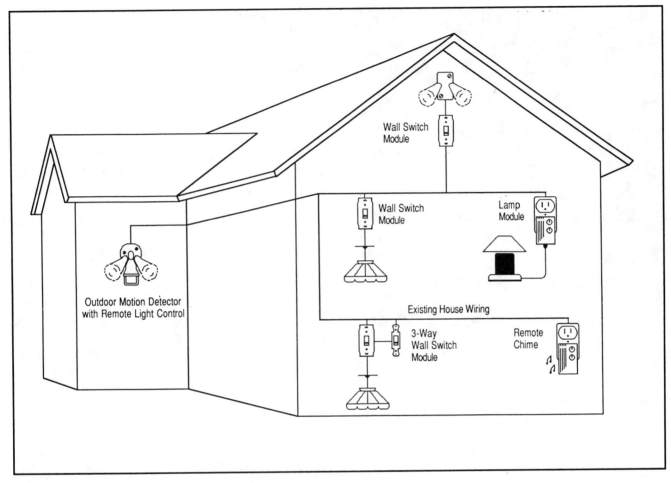

Wall Switch Module

Wall Switch Module

Lamp Module

Outdoor Motion Detector with Remote Light Control

Existing House Wiring

3-Way Wall Switch Module

Remote Chime

Courtesy of X-10.

LiteTouch 2000

LiteTouch 2000 is an innovative, microprocessor-based control system capable of switching and dimming incandescent, fluorescent, neon, cold cathode, and low-voltage loads as well as switching outlet and motor loads. The LiteTouch 2000 control system has been designed to provide convenience and flexibility impossible to achieve with conventional wiring systems. It allows multiple point switching, dimming, scene presetting, and group mastering. Designed for installation during construction, the LiteTouch 2000 system adds an average of $2.50 per square foot to the price of the home.

The heart of the LiteTouch 2000 system is the microprocessor-based central control unit (CCU), which receives all switch information, processes the commands, and transmits control data to the control modules.

The CCU has a built-in real time clock/calendar where events may be programmed to occur daily, weekly, or on a specific date. Programming entries to the system can be made using the keypad on the front of the CCU. The liquid crystal display prompts the operator through the steps necessary to initiate programming changes. The scene pre-set feature allows memory·dimmed levels to be changed not only at the CCU but from the Control Station as well.

Control Stations range from one to nine switches in a single gang with all nine switches capable of dimming. The CCU may include the Telephone Interface option, which is capable of accessing up to 900 different loads being controlled by the LiteTouch system. This feature literally turns any touchtone phone in the world into your master control station. Your personal computer can easily interface with the LiteTouch 2000 by simply plugging into the RS232 port provided on the back of the CCU.

LiteTouch 2000 is also capable of interfacing with security systems, fire alarms, photocells, wireless remotes, auxiliary relays, etc. In the unlikely event of a

Leviton's expanded Decora Electronic Controls provide sophisticated programmable and manual remote switching control for residential use. Power line carrier technology transmits switching commands on existing 120V AC wires. Modules are easily installed in standard electrical wallboxes. Courtesy of Leviton Mfg. Co.

switch or system failure, LiteTouch 2000 provides the capability to override the central controller and manually turn on your lights.

Every system needs at least one power supply. The power supplies are located in modules that mount in the system enclosures. Relay Modules, Interlock Relay Modules, Analog Output Modules, Control Stations, and the CCU require connection to a power supply. The Relay Module is specifically intended for switching fans, outlets, motors, low voltage incandescent, fluorescents, and other undimmed loads.

The Interlock Relay Module is designed for two-way motion control applications such as curtains, skylights, projection screens, and other applications where it is vital that open and close signals not be active simultaneously. The Data Input Module allows external signals such as security systems, RF Remote Control Decoder, and fire alarms to control LiteTouch loads.

LiteTouch 2000 supports two types of remotes — IR and RF. The Infrared Remote Handheld transmits to an infrared equipped Control Station, allowing wireless operation from anywhere in the room. An IR Remote can control eight switches on a Control Station, performing any function for which the switch is set. The RF Remote Handheld Transmitter and RF Remote Control Transmitter allow wireless control of any load within 150 feet of the receiver. The fixed location console version is available to control 18, 24, 30, 36, 42, or 48 loads. The portable handheld is offered in three versions for control of 6, 12, or 18 loads.

For retrofit application, LiteTouch offers the Scenario. The Scenario is a self-contained microprocessor wall-mounted single-room lighting control system, offering much of the same functions as the LiteTouch 2000. The Scenario can control four individual series of lights and can combine them to create four preset scenes. Each Scenario can be connected to other Scenarios in different locations (up to 16). LiteTouch also offers a universal remote control that can operate your television, VCR, and stereo as well as the Scenario system.

LiteCom

Honeywell's LiteCom lighting control system gives you control for up to 256 individual on/off lighting points plus 16 dimming. This means that any switch can be made to turn on or off any light in the house. You can also group any lights together at any single switch and control any single light or group of lights from any number of locations. LiteCom can control pool pumps, fans, electric blinds, and other motorized devices individually or in groups from any location. With LiteCom you can create any number of lighting "scenes" using any pattern of lights you desire.

The Master Control Panel can be placed anywhere convenient, such as the kitchen. The Master Control shows you the status of every light in the house and provides individual control of each one. Create and change lighting scenes anytime you like — programming is easy. The system also has a handheld remote control for convenient switching between scenes.

LuMaster Central Lighting Control System

The LuMaster Central Lighting Control System from Lutron adds security and convenience to your home by allowing you to take central control of lighting through-

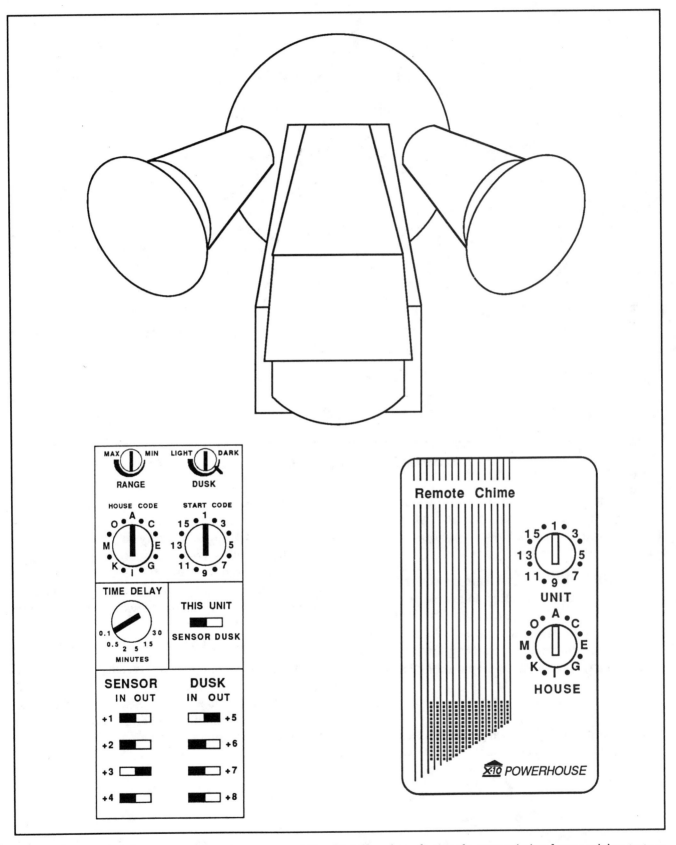

The PR511 motion detector turns on its connected floodlights and sends signals over existing house wiring to turn on additional lights and sound remote chime modules. Courtesy of X-10.

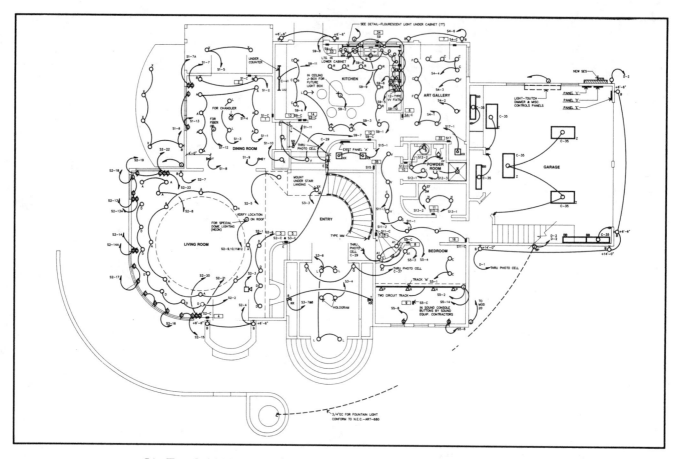

LiteTouch 2000 custom lighting diagram. Courtesy of LiteTouch Inc.

out the home. Master controls enable you to monitor and switch up to twenty Lumea dimmers and switches from a single location. The LuMaster system is easily installed.

Lutron's GRAFIK Eye preset dimming control system provides convenient four-scene, four-zone preset dimming control. GRAFIK Eye controls up to 2000 watts (800 watts per zone) and is operated by Lutron's wireless remote control, which makes it easy to transform the lighting of any space with the simple touch of a button.

Smart Start

While the common light switch performs its job well, a whole new breed of automated "smart" switches is offering consumers a high level of flexibility and convenience. One of the problems facing light switch designers is that the wiring is probably already in place. This limits the flexibility available to designers. Capri Lighting has attempted to meet the challenge with a smart switch called Smart Start. It appears to be a normal light switch, but it actually controls a two-circuit track lighting system with standard single-circuit wiring. Smart Start uses a memory chip to control its operation.

Using the positioning flexibility inherent in a track lighting system, the Smart Start can provide three distinct "scenes" to choose from. Different settings could be used for wall washing, accenting artwork, or lighting a work area. The Smart Start adds great flexibility to a lighting system, but it still requires manual operation.

Main Components:

Control Stations.

One to nine points of control in a single gang. Multiple gangs available.

Central Control Unit.

The heart of the LiteTouch System. Only one required per installation.

Enclosure.

37" h. × 20" w. × 4" d. Will hold any combination of up to four LiteTouch *Control Modules.

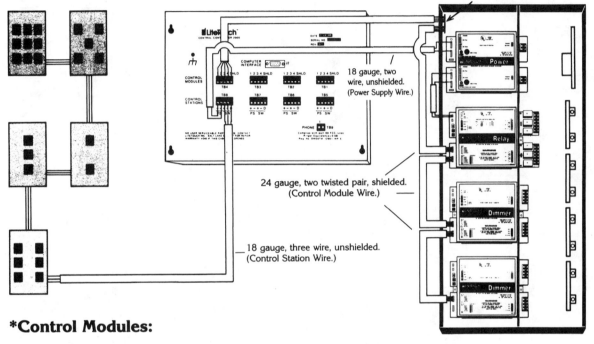

Transorb Board

18 gauge, two wire, unshielded. (Power Supply Wire.)

24 gauge, two twisted pair, shielded. (Control Module Wire.)

18 gauge, three wire, unshielded. (Control Station Wire.)

*Control Modules:

08-2140-01
Electronic Transformer Dimmer -
Provides dimming for six independent low-voltage, solid state electronic transformer loads with a total capacity of 1800 watts.

08-2100-01
Dimmer Module -
Provides dimming for six independent loads with a total capacity of 1800 watts.

08-2120-01
Dual 20 Amp Dimmer Module -
Provides two independent 20 amp dimmers (2400 watts each) that are controlled by two outputs of a dimmer module.

08-2400-01
Analog Output Module -
Provides six independent zero to ten volt contol signals to auxiliary dimmers when not using the Dual 20 Amp Dimmer Module.

08-2130-01
Fluorescent Dimmer Module -
Provides dimming for three independent fluorescent loads with a total capacity of 1800 watts.

08-2200-01
Relay Module -
Provides switching for six independent loads. Inc. and L.V. - max. of 960 watts per load. Fluor. - max. of 1800 watts per load.

08-2220-01
Interlock Relay Module -
Provides three independent motor controls - i.e., curtain control (open/close), screen control (up-down), etc.

08-2700-01
Data In Module -
Provides interface capability of optional equipment - i.e., photo cells, wireless remotes, security systems, etc.

Courtesy of LiteTouch Inc.

4.
Security and Life Safety Systems

Crime in America — are you safe? Nearly 23 million American households, or 24%, were victimized by crime in 1991. Though the estimated rate of 52.6 burglaries per 1,000 U.S. households in 1991 was at or near the lowest level since 1973, the proportion of households victimized has remained fairly constant, at about 25% (1985 through 1989). Add to this the estimated 22 million unreported crimes (rape, robbery, assault, larceny, burglary, motor vehicle theft) and you get a more accurate picture of the true extent of victimization.

How do you keep yourself and your family safe? According to one FBI study, a high-quality monitored security system makes a home 15 times less likely to suffer a successful break-in. But you are not only protecting property. The study shows that in about 13% of break-ins, the robber finds someone home, and half those meetings end in assault. As you can see, if you're concerned about protecting your family as well as your property, you must take extra security precautions now!

PREVENTING BURGLARY

Burglars like to operate on familiar routes that offer a means of easy escape. They often select a neighborhood adjacent to a major thoroughfare, property secluded by woods or adjacent to a park. Homes on cul-de-sac streets are also popular. In a recent study, the frequency of burglaries was highest within three blocks of the busiest roads. According to the study, the probability of a burglary is twice as high if you live within three blocks of a main street. However, an alarm system decreases the chance of being burglarized by a factor of more than two for homes in these areas.

Nearly half of all burglars gained entry to the home through the front door, either because it was left unlocked, had inadequate locks, or was poorly constructed. Burglars' favorite entrances:

- first floor — 79%
- garage — 9%
- basement — 4%
- unlocked — 4%
- storage — 2%
- second floor — 2%

First floor entry was broken down further:

- front door — 43%
- back door — 27%
- window — 29%

Your best defense against burglary is a professionally installed alarm system. Alarm systems do more than detect intrusions. They also deter burglars. However, even with an alarm system, the wise homeowner will employ a full package of other security measures and not rely solely on the alarm.

Roughly 7% of U.S. households have a security system. Yet more people might consider such an investment if they knew that convicted criminals say alarms are the most effective deterrent to theft. Consider these statistics:

- 85% of police officials believe that security systems decrease chances of homes being burglarized.
- 99% of all alarm owners say their home alarms are effective.
- 98% of alarm owners would recommend a home security system.
- 96% of potential alarm owners think a home alarm is effective.
- The average loss from a residential burglary in 1987 was $1,004 (the average home security system cost just $1,672).

AUTOMATED HOME SECURITY

By themselves, security systems deliver the "negative" benefits of protection from burglary and fire. People are afraid of having valuables stolen or destroyed and family members harmed. While home automation systems may be convenient and fun, they are often considered "frivolous" purchases. When integrated, security and home automation systems can deliver the best of both worlds.

Security is the principal building block of home automation. Today, most "smart" home electronic systems include security. Today, alarms and their sensors have been positioned at the hub of home automation. Security sensors have become the eyes and ears of electronic home-control systems. This is because microprocessors must be "told" when people are present, away, or asleep. They do this by discerning the arm/disarm mode of an alarm system or by monitoring interior motion sensors.

Your current home security system may be able to integrate with other automation products and systems. Unused zones in your control panel can be used to hardwire-connect automation products.

X-10 Burglar Alarm Interface

The X-10 Burglar Alarm Interface is the best bet for interfacing home automation with your current security system. It can be connected to the output of a burglar alarm system or alarm panel and will flood the house with light when the alarm is tripped. It can be set to turn on all the lights, flash all the lights, or turn on selected lights and/or appliances. It can be activated by a magnetic window switch, photocell, moisture sensor, motion detector, pressure switch, or anything that gives a dry contact closure or low voltage input.

In some high-tech security/automation systems, synthesized speech has removed the need for touchpads, and many systems can be controlled via touchtone phones. Modern high-tech control panels often resemble sophisticated microprocessor-based controllers, capable of connecting security systems with non-security electronic sensors and auxiliary devices. Some control panels have programmable digital zone inputs, for example, that are capable of detecting dry-contact opens and closures. These inputs enable control panels to respond to environmental conditions such as water/leak detection and gas detection.

Homeowners can check on the status of their home through home automation systems using a touchtone phone. A typical system of this type has a computerized voice that reports the status of such items as inside and outside lights, the condition of the alarm itself, and room temperature. If a homeowner wishes to make changes in one of these areas, these also can be accomplished with a touchtone phone.

ANATOMY OF A SECURITY SYSTEM

All alarm systems consist of three essential components: control unit, sensors, and siren. The control panel/processor is the "brain" of the alarm system; with it you arm and disarm the system. All sensors send signals to the control panel via wire or radio-frequency transmitters. The control unit monitors the sensors, and when it receives signals that indicate an alarm condition, it sounds the siren and relays the alarm to the central monitoring station.

The control panel should be installed inside the house where it is protected from tampering. Typically it is installed in a furnace room or other unfinished portion of the house. The system should have an automatic-recharging battery backup for uninterrupted service during power outages and be equipped with a Digital Communicator (also know as an automatic dialer). This Digital Communicator connects the alarm system, via the phone lines, to the central station and has line a seizure feature, which allows the alarm system to automatically send a signal to the station even if the phone is in use or disconnected. The Keypad/Arming panel is used to arm and disarm the system, as well as signal the alarm. A keypad is usually installed just inside the entrance door or doors that you most frequently use.

Courtesy of Aritech-Moose Security Products.

The Z1100e Residential Security System from Aritech-Moose is typical of professionally installed hardwired home security systems. Courtesy of Aritech-Moose Security Products.

A multi-tone siren should be included, and it should be loud enough to be heard outside the home. The siren should have an automatic reset after 15 minutes as you will have a lot of unhappy neighbors if your alarm blares for several hours while you're away. It should have separate and distinctive tones as to what type of emergency is occurring — police, fire, or medical. Prevention is what alarms are all about. If a would-be burglar knows that he has set off an alarm, he is not going to stick around long.

For a reliable, easy-to-use security system, look for these features:

- Entry and exit delays. These give you time to arm and disarm the alarm system, without triggering it, when you leave and enter your home.

- Switchable instant and delay circuits. Most door and window sensors should be on the circuit that triggers the alarm instantly. You'll want to set the main entry doors on a delay circuit when you're not at home so you have time to get in and out of the house, but you should be able to switch them to instant alarm for protection when you're at home.

- Automatic cutoff and reset features. Your neighbors will appreciate an alarm system that turns off the siren after sounding it for a preset period. But after turning itself off automatically, the system should rearm itself to maintain security.

- Battery backup. Systems connected directly to house wiring should have the capability of switching to battery operation if the AC power fails. When the AC power is restored, it should switch back. In addition, the batteries should be rechargeable to ensure that power is available when needed.

CHOOSING THE RIGHT SYSTEM

Once you've decided on a security system, you need to choose the type of system best for you. There are two main types of security systems — hardwired and wireless. If you choose a wireless system, you must then decide on either a supervised or unsupervised system. A hardwired system is one where the system's components (sensors, control box, siren, etc.) are all connected by electrical wiring. There are far fewer problems with hardwired systems than with wireless ones. A hardwired system is the best type of system that you can buy; it is also the most expensive but its benefits outweigh the higher price.

Wireless Systems

In a wireless system all the components are battery powered and the alarm signal is transmitted to the control unit via radio waves. Wireless systems are fairly cheap and easy to install, which accounts for their popularity. There are, however, several problems with wireless systems. The radio signal from the sensors to the control unit is difficult to align properly, and if not aligned the signal may not reach the control unit. Environments change, which can affect a system's operation. For example, the addition or removal of metal cabinets or appliances, foil wallpaper or mirrors can block or reduce radio frequency transmission range.

Another disadvantage of wireless systems is that the sensors that transmit signals to the control panel are powered by batteries. If a homeowner forgets to change them, his protection is compromised. Some of the newer units, however, signal when the battery starts to get low. If you buy a wireless system get one that is supervised.

An unsupervised system is an alarm system without any built-in system to automatically check the status and working condition of the sensors. With this type of system, a manual battery check must be done monthly and the batteries replaced at least once a year. If you forget to check the batteries and one goes dead, any break-in at the location of the dead sensor will not activate the alarm. Most do-it-yourself wireless systems available at your local hardware store are unsupervised systems.

A system in which the alarm signal is heard and/or seen only in the immediate vicinity of the protected area is known as a local alarm system. You simply cannot rely on a neighbor to make a timely call to the police should your alarm be heard going off. Monitored alarm systems are the preferred type of system. The alarm signal is transmitted to a 24-hour monitoring station, which in turn calls the appropriate agency to dispatch emergency units (police, fire department, ambulance). Monitoring is an ongoing expense, usually about $20 to $25 a month, but one that is well worth it.

An alarm system with a telephone link to a central station provides the most reliable protection. For a monthly fee, the central station monitors your alarm system — 24 hours a day, seven days a week. Whenever the alarm is activated, the system's control unit automatically places a call to the monitoring station, alerting it to a possible problem.

Typically, if the homeowner sets the alarm off by accident, the central station will telephone the home and ask if everything is all right. If you say yes and then give them your secret password, this assures them that it is not a burglar answering your phone, and it doesn't go any further. Systems employing automatic telephone dialers should have a dedicated phone line or cellular backup so that the central station will be notified even if the household phone lines are tampered with.

Your alarm system is only as good as its weakest link. The telephone connection box on the outside of your house is one such weak link. This is because most security systems utilize telephone lines to send the alarm signal to the central monitoring station. Cut the line and no signal can be sent to the monitoring station. To protect yourself, you can install a line interrupt alarm, which sends a signal through the phone line to the central station. If the signal is interrupted, an alarm is sounded at the central station.

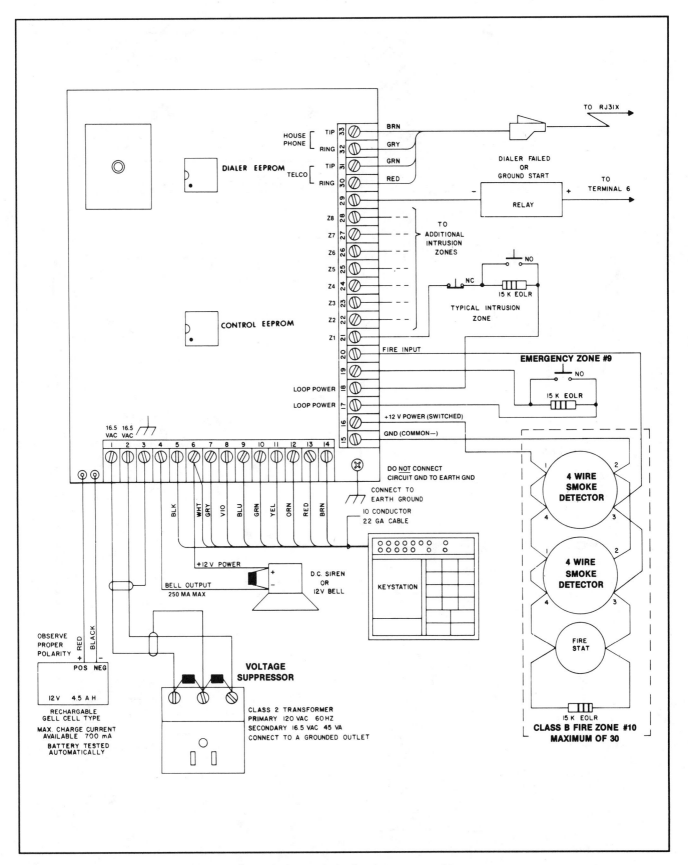

Wiring diagram for a typical ten-zone security system.

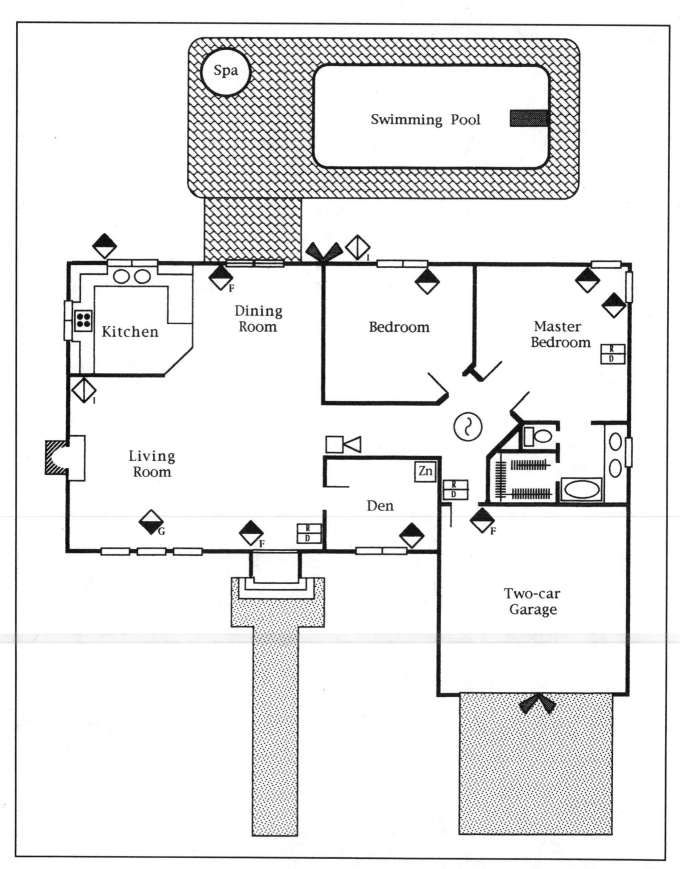

Security range from basic (this page) to sophisticated (facing page).

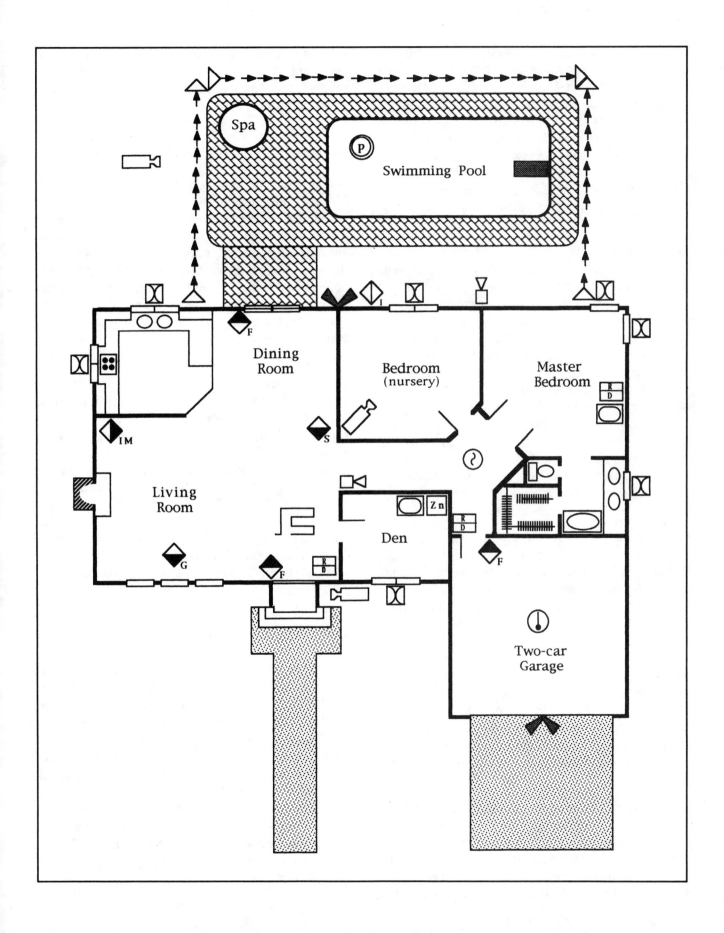

You can also back up your phone line with either a cellular phone connection or a mid-range wireless radio transmitter. The central monitoring station will have to be equipped to receive cellular or the wireless radio for you to be able to use these alternatives. A cheaper option is to have the alarm installers relocate your incoming phone line so that it is not accessible to tampering. Leave a dummy line where the old one was so that a burglar will be fooled into thinking that he has disabled the alarm when in fact it is still in operation.

Levels of Defense

Alarm systems can be set up to provide three levels of defense: perimeter protection, space protection, and point protection. Perimeter protection means equipping exterior doors and windows with sensors to detect unauthorized entry. For space protection, motion detectors or other types of sensors are installed inside the home as a second line of defense to guard specific hallways or rooms. Point protection is used for guarding specific objects or storage areas. The most effective alarm systems usually combine comprehensive perimeter protection with some space protection in areas an intruder is most likely to pass through. Point protection is normally used only in homes that have especially valuable objects, such as expensive artwork or other collections, or potentially dangerous items like guns.

Outer perimeter protection is the first line of defense. The best way to prevent burglary is to scare away would-be intruders before they can do any damage. Motion-detector lights are a good selection for perimeter protection. When motion is detected, floodlights turn on for a preset time, usually five minutes. This lets people know they've been detected, without frightening innocent passersby or visitors. The Dual Floodlight Outdoor Motion Detector from X-10 is perfect for this application. When motion is detected, the floodlights and up to four additional lights (inside and outside the home) are activated. The floodlights can also be turned on and off from any X-10 Controller. By adding an X-10 Chime Module, you will be forewarned when someone has activated the motion-detector lights.

Interior "traps" to detect an unwanted presence inside the house form the second line of defense and are frequently focused on entryways or near valuables. Interior sensors are often freestanding sensors that emit a pattern of micro- or ultrasonic waves and trigger an alarm when the pattern is disrupted. Passive infrared detectors pick up the warmth of a human presence, and pressure pads (flat switches, usually under carpeting) react to a footstep. These can be adjusted for weight, so pets won't trigger them.

X-10 SECURITY SYSTEMS

Automated home security is one of those products, like insurance, that the buyer wishes never to use. It is installed in the hope that, if the owner is ever involved in a fire or burglary, it will prevent or minimize loss of life and property. Beyond that, a security system should give the homeowner a sense of security, of safety and well-being. Unfortunately, many consumers feel the systems are hard to use and produce too many false alarms. A system that is simple to operate and dependable is more than a matter of convenience.

X-10 Protector Plus

The Protector Plus System from X-10, Inc. is just such a system. The Protector Plus is a wireless and self-supervised home security system that provides full home security and protection. It is also fully compatible with the X-10 home automation system. The system consists of a Control Console/Base Receiver as a central supervising unit, Remote Control, Remote Siren, Motion Detector, and Door/Window Sensor. Because it's X-10, no special wiring is needed. Simply plug the Control Console and Remote Powerline Siren into power outlets; and place Wireless PIR Motion Detector and Door/Window Sensors in appropriate locations throughout the house.

The Security/Home Automation Remote Control (model SH624) lets you arm the system in either the "Home" or "Away" mode. This means that signals from the Motion Detectors will be ignored when the system is armed in the "Home" mode, but motion detectors will trip the system when it is armed in the "Away" mode. The SH624 also lets you control up to four lights and appliances connected to modules that are set to the same Housecode as the Console. For greater convenience, add a 16-unit RT504 Wireless Remote Control to your system. This unit lets you turn on and off, and dim and brighten lights individually. To give your home a lived-in look, you can add the MT522 Mini/Timer or CR512 Clock Radio/Timer, which can turn your lights on and off at pre-set times.

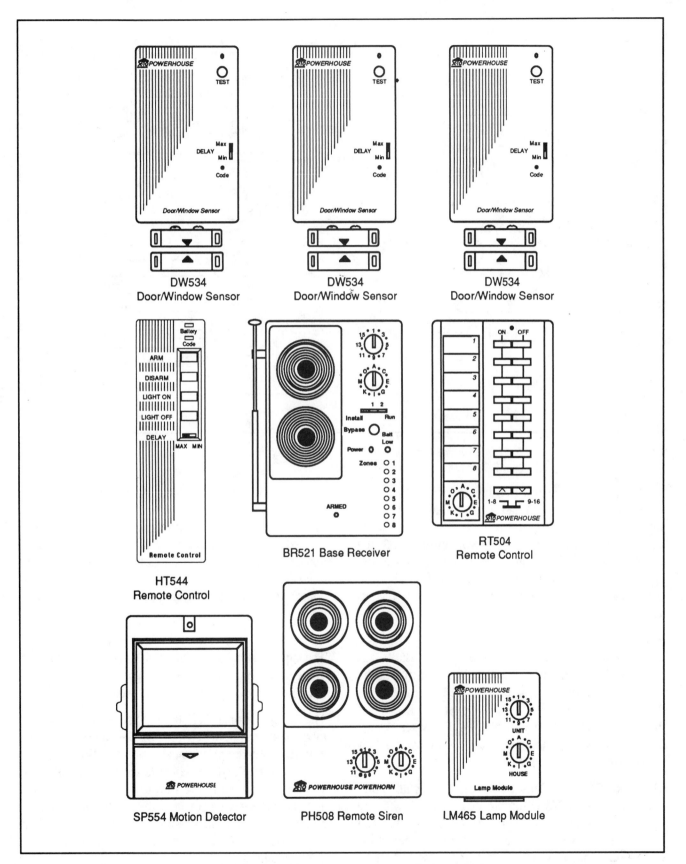

X-10's standard wireless security system. Courtesy of X-10.

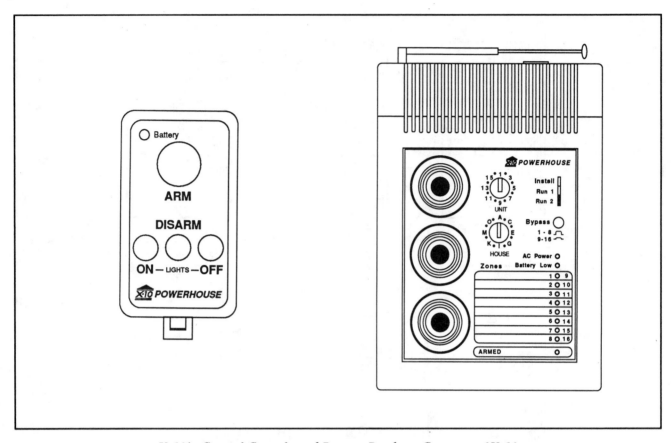

X-10's Control Console and Remote Pendant. Courtesy of X-10.

The Control Console/Base Receiver supervises the whole system (up to 16 zones) and receives radio frequency signals from detectors and sensors. When the alarm trips, the Control Console sounds its built-in (95 dB) siren and sends digital signals over existing house wiring to trip the Remote (110 dB) Siren, and to flash lights connected to X-10 Lamp Modules/Wall Switch Modules.

You can shut off the alarm by pressing the disarm button on the remote control. If you don't press disarm, approximately four minutes after the alarm was tripped the siren will turn off automatically. The lights that were flashing will remain on steadily (to let you know that there has been an intrusion). When the system is *not* armed, you can set it to announce the opening of a door or window with a pleasant chime.

The Door/Window Sensor is compatible with either Normally Open or Normally Closed switches (Normally Closed magnetic switch supplied). Other switches can be used, such as pressure mats, glass-break detectors, etc. Door/Window Sensors can either be set for MIN: instant alarm (normally used for windows) or MAX: delayed alarm (normally used for doors). In the Delayed mode the alarm will trip 30 seconds after the sensor has tripped. This gives you time to disarm the system after you enter the house. If the sensor is set to MAX, you can override this and arm it for MIN by setting the remote control to MIN before arming the system.

The Wireless PIR Motion Detector can also be set to trip the alarm instantly or 30 seconds after it detects motion. The supplied lens covers about 40 feet at an angle up to 90 degrees. Multiple coverage patterns (angle and distance) are available with optional lenses.

The X-10 Personal Assistance System (PA5800) is a medical alert system designed for the elderly and those with life-threatening medical problems. When tripped from the Call Pendant, which is worn by the user, the system automatically dials up to four phone numbers and plays 15 seconds of voice message to call a friend or neighbor for help. The Personal Assistance System can also be used to control lights and appliances by adding Lamp Modules.

CHOOSING AN ALARM COMPANY

Finding a professional alarm company isn't difficult. The membership roster of your state alarm association is a good place to start looking for a reputable alarm company. Although not all alarm companies are association members, membership indicates a commitment to industry standards and professionalism. Also ask friends and business associates who have alarm systems for their recommendations. Then check the alarm company's credentials by asking for references. Employee training also is an important criterion for judging an alarm company. Ask how employees are trained. The more employees who have successfully completed training courses, such as the National Burglar and Fire Alarm Association's National Training School, the better.

Contact your local police department to find out if the alarm companies must be licensed. If so, ask for a list of licensed companies and deal only with those firms. In addition, some localities require that the system itself be licensed. It is also a good idea to find out what constitutes a violation under local false alarm ordinances and what the penalties are for those violations. Many locales fine the homeowner if emergency personnel are dispatched due to repeated false alarms.

As with any major purchase, you need to check out the company and the product to make sure that you are dealing with a reputable organization that is going to install the system correctly and be around to give you service down the road. Once you have decided on the type of system you want and pre-screened several alarm companies, have a salesperson come out and give you an estimate. You're better off getting each company's stated best offer and then choosing the best one to continue negotiations with. Never pay the first price quoted; you can usually get a better price if you are patient.

For professional installation:

- Consult at least three security companies or dealers.
- If you plan to buy a full system, request a list of ten clients from each security firm and randomly contact three references from each list.
- Check with local licensing authorities to see if a permit or license is required for security companies in your community. Check the dealer's reputation with the governing agency and the Better Business Bureau.

- Weigh the initial cost versus the long-term benefits, as well as suitability, flexibility, and the security company's sensitivity to your needs.

For do-it-yourself installation:

- Buy security equipment from a major manufacturer and from a dealer with a long, stable history.
- Buy security equipment that has been on the market for at least a year (so you can be sure the bugs have been worked out) but less than five years (so that the system is technologically up to date).
- Be careful to read the warranty and service/replacement policy.
- Before buying a security system or control panel, read the installation directions to see if they are written clearly enough to follow.
- Make sure that the firm provides technical assistance for problems that may crop up.

FALSE ALARM PREVENTION

False alarms have become a very serious problem for the security industry, the police, and the end user — you, the homeowner. As more homes and businesses install alarm systems, the number of emergency dispatches increases. Nearly 99% of all alarms turn out to be false, according to police agencies. Cities all over the United States have turned to false alarm legislation and fees in their frustration over this continuing problem.

The false alarm problem lies in the fail-safe principle on which alarm systems are based. Because the alarm is designed to go off when current through the protective circuit is interrupted, any accidental break in the circuit will set off the alarm. The three most common causes of false alarms are: an open circuit resulting from a break in the wiring; a bad sensor contact; and improper sensor contact installation or an entry point left open.

Winter's cold temperatures can also play havoc with your alarm system and sensors. The National Fire and Burglar Alarm Association advises to watch for:

- poor foil connections
- PIRs on or facing cold surfaces
- sound detectors made more sensitive by colder air
- inadequate battery backup
- homeowners leaving and lowering the house temperature

While a well-designed system is one key to eliminating false alarms, training is also essential. The National Fire and Burglar Alarm Association claims that user error accounts for 70% of all false alarms. The homeowner should only do business with a dealer who will provide a good instruction manual or video and adequate end user training.

SECURITY SENSORS

PIRs

The most commonly used space sensor is a passive infrared detector. PIRs "see" their environment in segments. Segmented lenses or mirrors, depending on the type of PIR, create "optical zones" that divide the protected area into sections. These lenses or mirrors alternately focus each optical zone onto a dual- or quad-pyroelectric element. The infrared light energy received from the various segments is added together and monitored for any changes that indicate an intrusion. Modern PIRs are not prone to false alarms in environments where the ambient temperature suddenly changes.

Wall-mounted PIRs usually work well when they are installed in the corner of a room. The optical zones of a wide-angle protection pattern typically cover 75 degrees, which is sufficient for most rooms. In addition to wide-angle patterns, the same detector with a different lens can create different protection patterns. A long-range pattern enables the detector to cover long, narrow hallways. A curtain, or barrier, pattern is designed for detection in front of a row of windows or doors.

Wall-mounted PIRs should not be installed above 10 feet, or above 12 feet for ceiling-mounted PIRs. Be sure that the detector's field of view is unobstructed. Objects placed in front of a PIR sensor will diminish its detection capability. PIRs should be installed so each optical zone terminates on a solid object if possible.

Generally, when the temperature in a room is nearly the same as the temperature of a human body, a PIR will respond more slowly than if the room temperature were much warmer or colder. However, even in a room that is kept at nearly the same temperature as that of the human body, the background's infrared light energy level inevitably will be slightly different from a burglar's because the texture and color of a burglar's clothing has a different energy-level output than the objects in the room.

Will the unit's mounting surface be subject to vibrations? If so, false alarms may occur. Install the device on a solid, vibration-free surface. PIRs should not be installed facing windows that are subject to headlights and other sources of infrared light. They should be installed so optical zones do not terminate on known heat sources, such as fireplaces, electric heaters, or steam pipes. Mask zones that point to ceiling fans and mobiles.

A PIR does not actually sense air temperature. It electronically observes the temperature of objects in its field of view. Any difference in thermal energy between background objects and something new entering the detection field causes an alarm condition. A PIR's range is not fixed. It continually changes as room temperature fluctuates. Don't use a PIR that has more than twice the range of the area you want to secure. Otherwise, the sensitivity will be too great, resulting in false alarms. Install a PIR so intruders will likely break its pattern in a crosswise fashion, instead of walking straight toward the unit. Detection will be faster.

Microwave Motion Detectors

Microwave motion detectors detect intruders using radio waves at an ultra-high frequency of 10.525 GHz. Microwave signals can pass through common construction materials, such as drywall, paneling, plaster, and glass. They cannot, however, pass through metal. While detecting through walls can be a plus in some instances, it can cause false alarms in others. Microwave energy can penetrate exterior walls and detect people on the sidewalk. Adjusting the sensitivity will help reduce these false alarms. Microwave detectors use high frequency radio waves to detect intrusion. A transmitter sends and receives radio waves while the detector monitors the reflected energy. An alarm is initiated when the waves sent out have been distorted by someone or something moving in the protected area.

Dual-Technology Detectors

Dual-technology detectors are equipped with two sensing elements that use different detection technologies (usually PIR and microwave). Both sensors must detect motion to trigger an alarm, which reduces false alarms. These devices should be used to secure environments that normally create false alarms when single-technology detectors are used.

Magnetic Switches

The primary device used in perimeter protection is the magnetic contact switch. Each switch has two parts — one is mounted on the inside of the door jamb or window frame and the other on the door or window sash. When the system is armed, the alarm will sound if contact between the two parts of the switch is broken. For ventilation, you can mount an additional half of a magnetic contact elsewhere on the jamb so that the contact on the sash will align with it in the open position.

A magnetic switch consists of two separate units: a magnetically activated switch and a magnet. The switch is usually mounted in a fixed position (door jamb or window frame) opposing the magnet, which is fastened to the door or window. When the movable section is opened, the magnet moves with it, activating the switch.

Recessed magnetic switches are useful when protecting: doors, windows, sliding doors, hinged skylights, gun and china cabinets, file cabinets, and drawers containing valuables such as silverware and jewelry. Plunger-type contact switches are used for tamper control to protect against unauthorized access to a control panel enclosure. Roller-plunger switches can be used under vases, sculptures, and movable safes to detect the movement of the protected object. Cable switches are used to protect nonstationary items like motorcycles, bikes, RVs, and trailers that are stored outside near the home.

Wired Screens

Wired screens, which activate the alarm when they're tampered with, are another option for homeowners who like to keep their windows open. Alarm screens look like any high-quality, fiberglass-type screen, but offer a detective ability. Once the system is plugged in, an alarm will be activated if the screens are tampered with from the outside. Small wires are woven vertically through the screens at 4-inch intervals. Once connected, these wires form a protective barrier. They fit any window, even louvers.

Inertia Shock Sensors

Inertia shock sensors are designed to detect a forced entry before the intruder has gained entry to the protected area or building, not after the penetration has been accomplished. All inertia shock sensors detect the impulse generated by an attempted forced entry. Some of the different materials that shock sensors can be mounted on are: glass, brick, wood, drywall, and sheet metal. The most popular application is for glass. One benefit in using a shock sensor is that it can be mounted on the frame, not necessarily on the glass itself. By frame mounting, the sensor will protect windows that open, without the use of unsightly take-offs or door cords. One sensor can protect multiple panes of glass, which makes it cost effective as well.

Photoelectric Beam Detectors and Pressure Pads

Photoelectric beam detectors use a beam of light projected between two points. Any interruption of the beam, such as an intruder passing through, sets off the alarm. Pressure pads, also known as floor mat switches, are weight-sensitive devices installed under carpets, usually in front of a vault or other valuables. They are a series of thin metal strips separated by a non-conductive material. When enough pressure is placed on any one of the strips, the alarm circuit is closed and an alarm is initiated.

Ultrasonic Detectors

Ultrasonic detectors sense intrusion with sound waves by transmitting and receiving inaudible sound wave patterns. When these patterns are transmitted, they bounce off ceilings and walls, finding their way back to the receiver. The detector compares the sound wave patterns transmitted to those received. An alarm is initiated when the patterns differ. Anyone entering the protected area will cause a change in the sound wave patterns.

Sound Discriminators

Sound discriminators, sometimes called audio detectors, are microphones sensitive to certain sounds and frequencies. They are tuned to pick out or discriminate for sounds of breaking glass and splintering wood while ignoring background noise. A sound-activated installation relies on special microphones used as sound sensors. Their sensitivity is set to let the monitoring center hear into the premises if a noise rises above a certain ambient level or if selected sound discrimination frequencies are present. However, noise from airplanes, some trucks, motorcycles, and thunder will activate the system. Sound-activated systems generally do not interface with existing traditional systems unless there is extensive rewiring and equipment replacement.

Motion-Activated Listen-In Systems

Motion-activated listen-in system components can be easily added to an existing system to make it two-way, even if the equipment brands differ. When a contact switch or passive infrared sensor, for example, triggers an alarm, the system operates as a hands-free intercom between the protected premises and the monitoring station. The central station operator receiving the signal listens to the sounds at the subscriber's premises. Based on the sounds heard, the operator decides whether to call the police.

Vehicle Detection Systems

Another device that can enhance perimeter security is a magnetic field vehicle scanner (typically used at stoplights). Simply bury the 14-inch probe in a location under or near a driveway. When a car moves past it, the detector is triggered. Since vehicle scanner detectors only detect large moving metal objects, there is little chance of a false alarm. Vehicle detectors are ideal for homes with long or remote driveways.

The Vehicle Alert vehicle detection system comes with a weatherproof probe that can be buried 6 inches deep in dirt or 1 inch deep in asphalt or concrete. The probe comes with either 100 or 300 feet of cable, and you can extend the cable up to 2,000 feet. The probe has a circular coverage pattern of up to 22 feet in diameter when the vehicle is moving at 15 mph or faster, slower vehicles must be closer to the probe. When a car drives by, the control module panel beeps for a few seconds.

The AutoTell Vehicle Detection System from Ortner can, upon detecting an approaching vehicle, turn on your lights (up to 2400 watts), activate alarms, turn on CCTV cameras, call up radio paging systems, and open electronic gates. The sensor, when placed alongside a stationary metal object such as a camper, boat, or vehicle will detect any movement of that object and sound an alarm.

In addition to buried type detectors, infrared detectors are available. The Home Driveway Alert System is an infrared alert system that gives you advance notice of approaching guests, service calls, or intruders. Mounted on a tree or post, the infrared sensor detects the heat and motion of approaching visitors up to 40 feet away and sends a signal to the receiver inside the house. The drawback to infrared activated detectors is that any moving object (pets, wild animals, blowing debris) will activate the system, potentially causing a false alarm problem.

ENVIRONMENTAL SENSORS

In addition to security functions, a true whole-house security/automation system is also capable of monitoring your home's environment. Environmental sensors can detect temperature, humidity, water leak, moisture, rain, and gas leak. With today's airtight homes, it is important to monitor your home's environment for potentially dangerous toxins such as carbon dioxide and radon. Studies have shown that radon is the second leading cause of lung cancer, after cigarette smoking.

Temperature Monitors

Digital temperature monitors can control high and low temperatures, and some can activate an alarm or a shut-off device. You can program a monitor and sensors so the temperature range inside a weekend house is maintained between 58 and 62 degrees during the week. If the temperature drops or rises beyond these set points, a relay function can set off the automatic dialer to notify you at your weekday residence. In addition, some sensors support multiple probes that can oversee the temperature in a living room as well as a freezer in the basement.

Winland Electronics offers several temperature sensors. The company's Model TA2-HLD is one of the most reliable, quickest-responding temperature sensors available. It can monitor any range from -67 degrees to 300 degrees F, depending on the probes used.

Water Detectors

Water detectors fit a wide range of applications — from detecting household water leaks to monitoring swimming pool water levels. Many water sensors are designed to be installed around water heaters and washing machines to detect even the slightest amount of water. The Water Watch from Atlantic Hydrokinetics sounds an alarm and turns off the water valve whenever a small leak is detected.

Humidity Detectors

Humidity detectors help avoid problems in attics, basements, greenhouses, and computer rooms. Winland's Model HA-1 humidity detector watches for a user-set level of between 20 and 80% humidity. When that level is exceeded, the relay activates an alarm or a telephone dialer. Winland's DPM-4 humidity and temperature detector monitors two zones of humidity and two zones of temperature.

Gas Sensors

Residential gas sensors can detect either explosive gases, such as propane, butane, or natural gas, or poisonous gases such as carbon monoxide. Industrial Communications and Electronics makes Safe Guard gas monitors, which do more than just detect gases. The company recently introduced a self-cleaning semiconductor model; it can react to the presence of carbon monoxide by turning on an exhaust fan and/or sounding an alarm. Safe Guard monitors range in price from about $70 to $125. PAMA Gas Alarms from A.D.D.M. International Inc. come in plug-in models and models that can be connected to your automation or security system. PAMA Model GHD 2000 detects propane, butane, and natural gas; Model GHD 2001 detects carbon monoxide. Prices start at about $90.

SMOKE DETECTORS

According to the National Fire Protection Association, smoke detector use in the United States rose in 1987 to four-fifths of all homes. But in roughly one-third of these homes, the detectors don't work. This means that more than one-fourth of all American homes have non-operational smoke detectors. Power-source problems, especially dead and missing batteries, are the main reason for non-working smoke detectors. Dead batteries probably reflect the lack of regular testing and maintenance, while missing batteries may reflect a wider range of problems, including frustration over nuisance alarms.

Supervised Systems

A supervised home automation/security system provides the solution to the non-operational smoke detector problem. The automation/security system monitors the detectors and notifies the homeowner when there is a problem such as a dead battery in a wireless detector. If you have standard smoke detectors, the National Fire Protection Association advises you to change the batteries each year on the daylight to standard time change.

Any security or home automation system worth its salt will included smoke detectors (and sometimes rate-of-

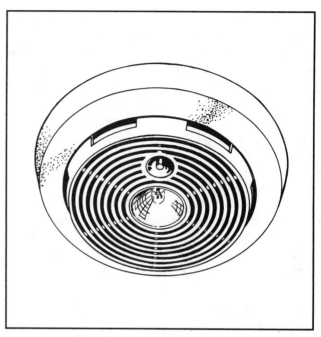

First Alert smoke-fire detector.
Courtesy of Pittway Corp.

rise heat detectors) as standard components. There are several advantages to having your smoke and heat detectors integrated with your security/automation system. First, the detectors are connected (using hardwired or wireless technology) to your system. This allows the system controller to "supervise" the detectors — warning you of potential problems such as dead batteries in a wireless detector. Second, the system protects your home when you're away by automatically activating an audible alarm and sending a signal to a central monitoring station, which in turn notifies the fire department.

Types of Smoke Detectors

There are two types of smoke detectors available for residential use: photoelectric and ionization. Photoelectric smoke detectors sense smoldering fires better than the ionization detectors. Photoelectric detectors work by sending a light beam into a sensing chamber. As smoke enters this chamber, light is reflected off the smoke particles. The detector reacts and initiates an alarm when enough particles are present to reflect a predetermined amount of light. Photoelectric detectors react better to smoldering fires because this type of fire produces larger smoke particles, which reflect more light.

Fast-burning fires are detected more quickly by ionization smoke detectors. They react better than the photoelectric detectors to smaller, less visible smoke particles from rapid burning fires. Ionization detectors use a very small amount of radioactive material to increase the electrical conductivity of air in the detector's chamber. As smoke enters this chamber, the electrical current flowing through the chamber is reduced. A fire alarm is initiated when the reduction drops below a predetermined level. Your safest bet is a combination of photoelectric and ionization detectors, installed where each is needed most.

Both photoelectric and ionization smoke detectors come in battery-powered and house current-powered models. Smoke detectors that operate on batteries tend to take less time and fewer tools to install. Once the battery-powered unit is mounted, the owner simply slips in the battery, tests the unit, and the job is done. In about a year the detector will begin to emit "beeps" every minute or so, and will keep this up for a week or longer, to tell the owner that the battery has begun to fall below a safe minimum of power and should be replaced.

Smoke detectors that operate on household electric current have the power they need to operate as long as there is current in the circuit to which they are connected. However, installation is somewhat more complicated. In the event of a power failure, detectors will become inoperable unless the detector has a battery backup. In most regions, this is a rare event, but if power outages are frequent where you live, you might think twice about depending only on this type of smoke detector.

Heat Detectors

Rate-of-rise heat detectors can be used to supplement your smoke detectors. They send an alarm if the temperature rises more than 10 degrees within 60 seconds, or if the temperature exceeds the set upper limits on the unit. These are normally placed in the attic, by the furnace, and by the water heater. Like smoke detectors, heat detector models are available that can be connected to your security/automation system to provide for detector supervision and faster notification in case of an alarm.

Installing Smoke Detectors

Where and how you install your smoke detectors is very important because an improperly positioned detector may not function properly. You must also be careful to position your detectors so that your entire home is adequately covered. Before you buy a detector make sure that it is UL listed. Read the instructions enclosed

with your smoke detector carefully to find out exactly how and where to install it.

As a rule of thumb, you should position a smoke detector on the ceiling just outside each bedroom and in the escape routes of your home. Make sure you can hear the detector in the hall loud and clear. If there is any doubt, or if you smoke, place an additional detector inside your bedroom. If you have a multi-level home, install a detector on every floor. Place a detector at the top of each stairwell. Hallways longer than 30 feet should have a detector at each end. In the basement, mount the detector on the ceiling at the top of the stairway, not near a furnace exhaust.

The greatest cause of false alarms is improper placement of detectors. The best way to avoid false alarms is not to knowingly place detectors in areas where they will not operate properly. Electrical noise generated by fluorescent light fixtures may cause false alarms, especially in photoelectric smoke detectors. Install detectors at least 6 feet away from such light fixtures.

Avoid very cold or very hot environments, unheated buildings, and rooms where the temperature can fall below the operating temperature range of the detector. Avoid placing smoke detectors in or near areas where combustion products are normally present, such as kitchens or other areas with ovens and burners; in garages or automotive shops where products of combustion are present in vehicle exhaust; within 15 feet of furnaces, water heaters, or gas space heaters. When a detector must be located in or adjacent to such an area, always use a photoelectric smoke detector rather than an ionization smoke detector.

Do not install smoke detectors in excessively dusty or dirty areas. Dust and dirt can accumulate in a detector's sensing chamber and make it overly sensitive, or block air entrances to the sensing chamber, making it less sensitive than required. Be sure to avoid areas where fumigants, fog, mist-producing materials, or sweeping and cleaning compounds are used. These items can sometimes cause false alarms in both types of smoke detectors.

Avoid damp or excessively humid areas and areas next to bathrooms with showers. A tremendous amount of humid air is generated during a hot shower. The moisture in this humid air can collect in the sensing chamber as water vapor, then as it cools, it condenses into water droplets that can accumulate inside the sensing chamber and make a detector overly sensitive.

Also avoid placing detectors near fresh air inlets or excessively drafty areas. Air conditioners, heaters, fans, and fresh air intakes can blow the products of combustion away from smoke detectors, reducing their effectiveness. A smoke test should be conducted to determine the proper distance between such air inlets and the detector. The placement of detectors near air inlets can also cause dust and dirt to accumulate on the detectors more rapidly, resulting in a more sensitive detector.

Dead air spaces at the top of a peaked roof or in corners at the junctions of ceilings and walls should also be avoided. Dead air at the top of a peaked or A-frame type ceiling may prevent smoke from reaching a detector. Side wall mounting is acceptable in such rooms or spaces. Detectors should be located 9-12 inches below the junction of the wall and ceiling. Ceiling-mounted detectors should be located at least 9 inches from the wall.

Watch for insect-infested areas. If a tiny insect enters a detector's sensing chamber, it may cause a false alarm. Take proper insect eradication procedures before installing detectors in such a location. If an insect spray is used, be sure to spray the area before the detector is installed and do not allow the insect spray to enter the detector.

ACCESS CONTROL

An essential function of security, beyond sensors and alarms, is access control. Access control is a system used to protect people and property by controlling who passes through a protected entry location: a door or gate. Locks and keys are one form of access control. While locks provide a certain degree of protection, keys can be easily lost or duplicated, and most locks can be easily picked. Electronic access control enhances security by restricting access to only authorized people. Many home automation systems, such as Unity's Home Manager, offer access control as an integrated function of their overall system.

Access card reader technologies include:

- Bar code — a series of lines forming a code that can be read by a card reader

- Magnetic stripe — a card that has a data-encoded stripe on one face

- Proximity — the card contains a microcircuit that when placed in close proximity to a reader, will activate a reader

- Smart — a plastic card embedded with integrated-circuit chip; a smart card has both a coded memory and microprocessor intelligence

- Wiegand — a card with ferromagnetic wires embedded in it.

Electronic Key Entry

A simple and affordable method of access control is an electronic key entry system integrated with your security system. These low-cost proximity access control systems, such as the AC-100 from ProxiKey, take some of the features found in their larger, more expensive commercial counterparts and greatly simplify the concept. They can be used for outside doors, including the garage door, and on inside doors to protect valuables stored in a security room. For added protection, electronic key systems can be connected to the home's security system to trigger an alarm if a forced entry occurs, or they can be used as an on/off switch for lights.

Systems consist of electronic keys or cards, in a variety of shapes and sizes, from credit card-sized to carry in a wallet, to key-sized to attach to a key ring; a reader for each door, designed to read keys or cards up to several feet away; and a door controller, which is the brains of the system.

Electronic keys and cards are impossible to duplicate. Every key produced contains a small computer chip holding a unique code assigned at the factory. When held near the reader, the code embedded in the electronic key is read and transmitted to the door controller.

If the controller recognizes the code, a message is sent back to the reader, which activates the locking mechanism and unlocks the door. This touch-free convenience makes unlocking the door easy for those who may have difficulty unlocking a conventional lock — children, the elderly, the physically challenged.

Readers are mounted near the frame of a protected door and are linked to the door controller by a hardwire connection. The door controller can be mounted on a wall in a secure place such as a closet (usually next to your security system's control box) to protect it from tampering and vandalism. The door's existing mechanical lock is replaced with either a magnetic lock or an electronic strike installed in the door frame.

Homeowners can customize their systems with the touch of a button at the door controller. The controller can be programmed to permit or restrict access based on time, days of the week, and the user's level of authorization. For example, a maid can be allowed access to the front door from 9 a.m. to 5 p.m., Monday through Friday. If she tries to use her key outside of this time and/or days, the door will not open. Some systems can generate a detailed report, called an audit trail, showing the date and time that the door was accessed and by whom.

If an electronic key is lost or stolen, the homeowner can select the code of the missing key and erase it from the system.

CCTV AND VIDEO INTERCOMS

Most whole-house automation systems offer some combination of closed circuit TV (CCTV), video intercom, and whole-house paging intercom. There are also several outstanding stand-alone residential intercom systems available from such manufacturers as ChannelPlus, Aiphone, NuTone, Telecall, and DFE, Inc. Examples of areas that benefit from being observed via CCTV include front and back doors, yards, pools, driveways, and nurseries.

By combining both video and audio, video intercom systems let homeowners positively identify a caller prior to opening the door. A video intercom has two basic parts: an outside entrance station with a closed circuit television camera and an intercom, and an inside station or video monitor with an intercom. A visitor presses a button, signaling his presence to the occupant. Inside the entrance station, the camera relays the image to the inside station. When a caller announces his arrival by pressing a button, the occupant sees and hears him at the same time. After identification, the occupant gives the visitor access by either opening the front door or pressing a button on his unit, activating an electric door strike.

Video intercoms were once used primarily for apartment complexes and commercial buildings. But they have found their way into residential use as more parents search for ways to protect their latchkey children. Young children alone while their parents are at work can inconspicuously identify callers at the front door without letting them know they're home alone. With multiple stations installed, the system becomes an extension of the parents' eyes. Systems with audio and visual capabilities in one package range in price from $400 to $1,000.

Most intercoms on the market contain at least some of the following features:

- Selective call/all call — This feature allows users to call selected rooms or all the rooms that have substations.
- Monitor feature (listen-in) — This allows someone at a master station to listen-in indefinitely to a room with a substation.
- Privacy button — This allows an intercom station to "shut out" the rest of the system, or turn off the "listen-in" feature.
- Hands-free operation — This feature allows people using the intercom system to reply to a caller without pressing buttons.
- Radio presets — When pressed, these buttons automatically select a radio station.
- Voice override — This ensures a person's intercom message will take precedence over whatever music is being played, so the speaker doesn't need to reduce the volume of the music before it delivers a message.
- Chime tone — A pleasant chime tone is broadcast throughout the intercom system to signal the arrival of a visitor.
- Stereo sound — This is an intercom system designed to accommodate stereo sound.

Video-Door Monitor

The Video-Door Monitor from Telecall is an intercom that can be upgraded to include security and environmental monitoring. After pressing the doorbell button, the visitor's image appears on the large, easy-to-see 5-inch TV monitor inside your home. The homeowner can check out the visitor while ensuring complete safety. By picking up the handset, the homeowner can talk while watching the visitor on the screen. To monitor the entrance at any time, simply press the monitor button.

By adding the security unit, the homeowner can integrate security with the Video-Door Monitor into one system. Intercoms, telephones, security sensors, and home controllers can be added to build your own personal network for communication and burglary and fire prevention. The security unit features: a gas alarm (gas leakage), bath alarm (overflow and temperature), fire alarm, security alarm, and panic button.

Compact video camera. Courtesy of Sony.

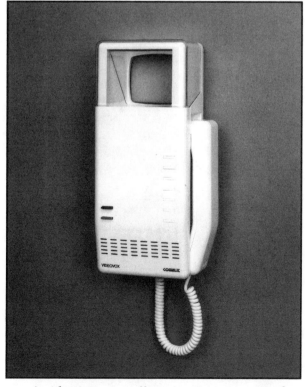

A video intercom allows maximum security by providing positive visual identification of visitors . Courtesy of The Ultrak Group.

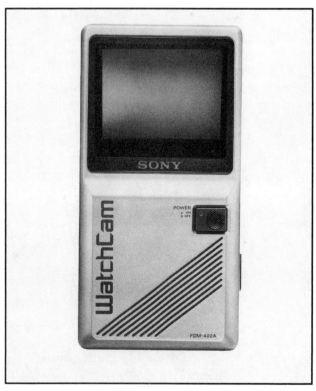

Four-inch video display monitor. Courtesy of Sony.

Radio-Intercom

Another intercom system that is expandable into a home automation system is the NuTone Radio-Intercom. The Radio-Intercom combines NuTone's traditional home communications center (video door answering and whole-house intercom/music) with home control (via X-10 technology) to enhance security, convenience, and energy savings. Adding the Remote Transmitter HC-100T brings you easy, one-touch control of your automated lights and appliances.

Touch N Talk Telephone Intercom

The Touch N Talk Telephone Intercom from DFE Inc. is a residential door answering/access control system. It works in either local mode or remote mode. In the local mode, you can answer your front door from any phone in your home. When your doorbell goes off, simply pick up the nearest phone, press the star (*) button to open the speaker at the door and talk to the visitor. When the conversation is completed, press the pound (#) button or hang up to turn the speaker off.

When nobody's home, you can program the control center to dial a remote number (remote mode). You can, for example, have it dial your office number or a friend who's willing to "house sit" for you. The phone will ring. You'll hear a distinct tone. Press the star button and you can talk to the visitor as though you're at home. The pound button deactivates the system.

Finally, be careful with wireless intercoms; many can cause electromagnetic interference (EMI) on the power line, which can cause problems with X-10 equipment.

5.
Controlling Your Environment

From passive solar design to zoned heating and cooling, the marketplace has always been slow to react to new technology. Consumers won't spend extra money for energy efficiency today, even if it means saving money and scarce resources in the long run. Homeowners will conserve energy if it's convenient and if it saves money. Utility companies around the country are among the biggest supporters of home automation. They realize that their "load management" and "time of use pricing" strategies will only be accepted by customers through the convenience offered by home automation.

According to the U.S. Department of Energy (DOE), the average homeowner in 1987 used 8,930 kilowatt-hours (kw hr) of electricity annually, at an average cost of 7.6 cents per kw hour, or $680 per year. This was an 11% increase over the previous ten years — above and beyond inflation! (Further information is available from the National Energy Information Center at 202/586-8800.)

A well-integrated, efficiently functioning system includes a heat source (probably a furnace or heat pump), a cooling system (air conditioner or heat pump), air treatment products (electronic air cleaner and humidifier), and a zone control system. It provides desired temperatures throughout the home, without hot or cold spots. There's no over-cooling on the first floor in the summer while the air conditioning works overtime to cool the hot upstairs. In the winter, the south side of the house doesn't get overheated while the furnace tries to heat the north side to a comfortable temperature.

Creating the right system for your home requires proper planning. You need to consider your lifestyle, the design of your home, the climate where you live, your expectations, and your budget. A knowledgeable professional heating and cooling contractor should be able to advise you on planning the best indoor comfort system. In addition to helping you plan your system and select proper equipment, an experienced and knowledgeable contractor will be invaluable in installing and servicing the system.

PASSIVE SOLAR AND HOME AUTOMATION

One of the big reasons consumers lost interest in passive solar design is that "passive" is a bit of a misnomer. Most serious passive solar designs require a fairly active homeowner. Blinds and vents must be opened and closed, the furnace thermostat must be regulated, and the homeowner must make decisions based on what kind of weather is expected. For instance, if a cool night is forecast, then he should be "collecting" heat during the day; if a warm night followed by a still hotter day is expected, then he should try to collect as little heat as possible.

This kind of effort is not practical for many homeowners, and is impossible if they are not home most of the day. The effort level involved in "managing" the passive solar home, combined with the fairly wide temperature swings one can experience if trying to minimize use of the conventional heating and cooling system, made passive solar construction unattractive for many homeowners.

Home automation can be used to totally eliminate the burden of day-to-day management of the passive solar home. Blinds, vents, motorized windows, etc., can be opened or closed automatically based on preprogrammed decisions. Comfort levels can be improved, too; the homeowner can establish an acceptable temperature range and the conventional heating and cooling systems could be automatically turned on or off if these limits are exceeded. Zoned temperature management could also eliminate the room-to-room temperature differences often associated with passive solar construction. In short, home automation will allow you to fully and comfortable utilize your home's solar architecture as it was originally intended.

ENERGY MANAGEMENT

The energy industry was greatly and permanently affected by two events in the 1970s: the 1973 oil embargo and the failure of nuclear power as an alternative energy source. Before these events, the industry encouraged consumers to use as much electricity as possible, as it was felt supply could always be increased to meet demand by building additional generating plants. But after these events, it was apparent that the supply of energy indeed had boundaries: natural resources were drying up and becoming expensive, environmental concerns were mounting, nuclear power was not trusted by the general public, and alternative energy sources (such as wind and solar) failed to develop.

The peak generating capacity a utility needs is determined by the amount of electricity the utility will be required to supply during the worst case, "peak-load" times — typically, during weekday summer afternoons when the use of air conditioning peaks. Since large scale storage of electricity is not economically feasible, utilities are faced with the prospect of building generating plants that are used only occasionally, when demand warrants it.

To avoid building these new plants, utility companies are attempting to shift some of the load from peak times to off-peak times (load management), and are offering incentives in the form of varying rate structures and time-of-use (TOU) pricing (they charge less for power at off peak times).

Currently, utilities have little control over how their energy is used. The consumer has control over the heating, air conditioning, and appliance usage. The utility companies can encourage management and conservation, but it is still up to the consumer to implement it. The utilities have tried offering credits to business and homeowners who build energy-efficient structures or install high-efficiency appliances and HVAC systems, but this has met with only limited success. When peak period demand for electricity exceeds generating capacity, utilities must either add capacity or decrease demand.

The situation would greatly improve if utility companies could easily interface with homeowners, allowing each utility's control over the major electricity users in the household. With the customer's consent, they could shift the energy load, cutting back energy use during peak periods and increasing it during the "valleys." This "load management" technique is the energy industry's hope for correcting their current problems.

Automation offers the utilities the ability to control a house's electrical usage from a remote location. Rates could be set to encourage consumers to use electricity in off-peak hours whenever possible. Automation would offer utilities benefits in other areas, such as remote meter reading, gathering data for research, and pinpointing trouble spots within the system. The consumer would get better value for his money, more dependable service, and convenience.

Demand Side Management

Demand side management (DSM) entails selling electricity in the most efficient manner possible. Integral to this is load management, which involves reducing demand for electricity during peak periods and encouraging demand during non-peak periods. Load management is especially helpful in heavily populated areas where energy becomes scarce during peak periods of the day.

DSM encompasses a total system solution that includes high-efficiency smart appliances and intelligent networks that can determine where energy consumption can be delayed or curtailed in the home. The intent is to develop a lower and more evenly distributed demand for electricity, thus allowing utility companies to better utilize plant capacity and to avoid "brownouts."

The National Appliance Energy Conservation Act has instigated the creation of a whole new line of high-efficiency appliances. To date, standards are in place for furnaces, water heaters, refrigerators, freezers, room air conditioners, and fluorescent lights. By the end of 1993, standards should also be set for central air conditioners, heat pumps, dishwashers, clothes dryers, and washing machines.

Distributed Load Control

Distributed load control is a good option for both the utility company and the homeowner. Distributed load control allows the customer and the utility company to share the control of energy management by utilizing two-way communications via a gateway and a home controller. The most cost-effective means of two-way communication is via telephone lines, power line carrier (PLC), and radio frequency (RF). The utility gateway downloads rate schedules to a home controller, enabling the house to determine the cheapest time to run appliances.

If the utility company needs to redistribute more energy during peak periods, a message is sent to the house requesting a specific amount of energy reduction. Instead of the utility company randomly turning off appliances, the house will decide which is the best appliance to turn off at any given time. A homeowner's preferences can be preprogrammed into the home controller for automated usage control.

Current Energy Management Programs

The Electric Power Research Institute (EPRI) has developed a Utilities Communication Architecture (UCA), a universal standard that will allow the electric utilities industry to integrate previously autonomous systems within individual utility companies. UCA will allow for two-way communication between the utility and your home.

CyberLYNX Computer Products, Inc. has developed a Utility Information Gateway (UIG), which provides a communications link between the home and the utility company. CyberLYNX has also developed appliance modules that utilize CEBus (called CAM-CEBus Appliance Modules). These developments have been incorporated into a series of prototype homes called the Energy House in Columbia, SC. The project is a collaborative effort between CyberLYNX, Duke Power Company, South Carolina Energy Research and Development Center, and Clemson University.

The Demand Side Management program at Energy House works as follows: the utility company will use a Utility System Control Center to send, via telephone cable, a transmission to the home's pole-mounted UIG. The UIG acts as an interpreter between the utility company and the home, converting the digital telephone signal to the CEBus protocol. The signal is then transmitted to the home's automated meter via power line. The meter allows the utility company to remotely read electric, water, and gas usage, update time-of-use or real-time pricing of electricity, obtain a customer energy usage survey, and request an energy reduction or redistribution from the home. This information is then forwarded to the home's Energy Management Unit.

The Energy Management Unit is basically a PC that analyzes power rates and load distribution requests to determine the home's most efficient energy usage based on the homeowner's preprogrammed preferences. It then issues commands to the CEBus appliance modules (CAMs) to perform required functions. These range from simple on/off commands to more complex functions such as monitoring and changing hot water temperatures. The Energy Management unit can also analyze appliance use data and give the homeowner an itemized record of energy consumption. This will allow the homeowner to determine optimum energy usage.

NetComm, Southern California Edison's new remote electronic communications network, is in use in more than 1,000 Valencia-area customers' homes. The homes are connected to the utility's computers. The system delivers services such as remote meter reading, remote connect and disconnect, meter/billing information requests, and actual energy usage and cost of usage measurements.

The PDI Energy Management System (EMS), developed as part of the SMART HOUSE L.P. consortium, is designed to reduce energy consumption through automated coordination of appliances and heating, ventilating, and air conditioning systems (HVAC) within a SMART home. The PDI EMS controller's primary objective is to manage energy use in the home based on preferences preprogrammed by the homeowner. This enables the homeowner to monitor energy use and status to date, and to program SMART appliances accordingly. (For more on SMART HOUSE see Chapter 8.)

The Utility Consumer Network (UCNet) developed by GE Meter & Control and Ericson GE Mobile Communications gives utility companies two-way communication with their customers, demand side management, and load distribution automation capabilities. The UCNet

System is unique because it is the only system that integrates both voice and data as one system.

The UCNet System allows utility companies to offer flexible time-of-use rates, real-time pricing, direct load control, and interruptible service control and monitoring services to their customers. A UCNet Pilot System has been installed in 100 coastal homes serviced by the Mississippi Power Company.

Genesis from Itron, Inc. utilizes an effective and flexible two-way multimedia communications network for remote data collection, control, and monitoring. The system supports demand side management functions such as variable pricing, load control, and Automatic Meter Reading (AMR).

The Meter Minded System from Interactive Technologies, Inc. (ITI) provides automatic meter reading, usage disconnect, and security functions such as intrusion detection, fire detection, and environmental monitoring. Meter Minder incorporates either hardwire or supervised wireless technology and is monitored by an ITI CS-4000 Central Station Receiver.

Integrated Communication Systems' TranstexT Advanced Energy Management (AEM) System provides both utilities and their customers with progressive demand side management capabilities. Integral to the system is TranstexT ComSet, which converts incoming telephone communications to power line communications for distribution though the home's existing wiring. TranstexT AEM enables both the utility and the homeowner to automatically control central heating and cooling, electric water heaters, and appliances.

For further information on at-home energy management, contact the following companies:

CyberLYNX Computer Products, Inc.
2885 E. Aurora Ave., Suite 13
Boulder CO 80303
(303) 444-7733

Electric Power Research Institute (EPRI)
3412 Hillview Ave.
Palo Alto CA 94303
(415) 855-2000

GE Meter & Control
130 Main St.
Somersworth NH 03878
(603) 749-8126

Integrated Communications Systems, Inc.
1000 Holcomb Woods Pkwy., Suite 412
Roswell GA 30076
(404) 641-1551

Interactive Technologies, Inc.
2266 Second St. North
North St. Paul MN 55109
(800) 777-1415

Itron, Inc.
15516 East Euclid Ave.
Spokane WA 99215
(509) 924-9900

PDI Corp.
180 Admiral Cochrane Dr. #215
Annapolis MD 21401
(410) 224-2130

ZONING

More than any other feature of an automated home, zoned heating and air conditioning offers the most dramatic energy management benefits: it can actually increase comfort at the same time it is saving energy. According to 1988 data from Honeywell, using a single ten degree setback per day, heating savings were from 9 to 18%; using two setbacks daily, 18 to 30% savings were realized. Cooling savings were 7 to 18% with a single five degree setup, and 11 to 33% with two setups.

Most existing and new homes have a passive duct system that cannot respond to hot and cold spots in the home. With a passive duct system, all areas of the home — hot and cold — receive the same kind of air. The system can only determine the average temperature of the home; it cannot read hot/cold problem spots. As a result, these areas don't receive the air they need, while expensive air is dumped needlessly into unoccupied areas.

By dividing your home into as many as four zones (or up to eight in the case of larger homes) and placing a thermostat in each area, you can preset the temperature you desire in each zone, taking into account your use of the zone, the season of the year, and the path of the sun each day.

Air ducts leading to each zone are equipped with motorized or air-activated dampers. Zone thermostats and damper control outputs are connected to the zone control

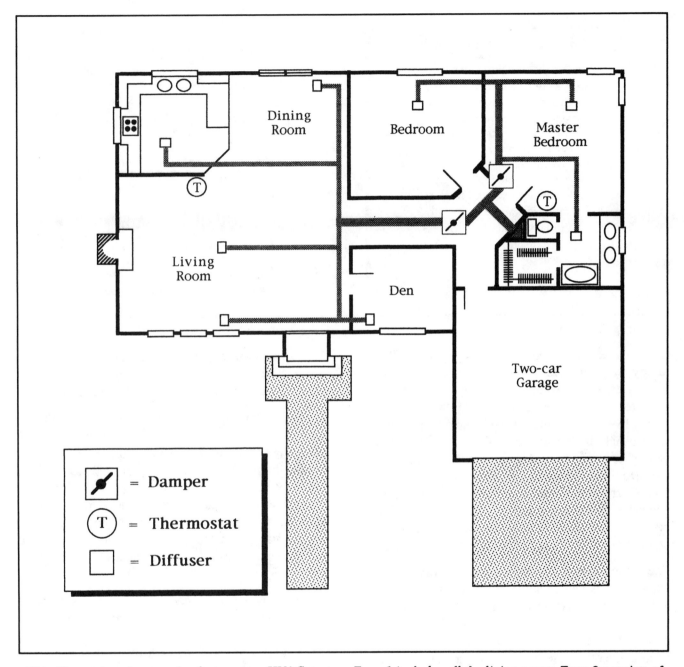

This illustration shows a simple two-zone HVAC system. Zone 1 includes all the living areas; Zone 2 consists of the sleeping areas. This simple system allows the homeowner to automatically shut off unused areas (the living areas at night and the sleeping areas during the day) to save energy.

panel, which contains the logic relays or electronics. When a zone thermostat calls, two events occur: the central heat air system starts and all dampers serving the non-calling zones close.

There are several criteria influencing how to zone an existing home: duct layout, living patterns, and floor plan. Existing duct layout has a direct impact on zoning

options. If the home has a duct running from a central plenum to each room, options are unlimited. Ducts can be grouped together to make a zone including whatever rooms you want. A home with two or three large trunk lines that progressively branch into smaller ducts may make grouping certain rooms together impractical. However, placing one damper in the trunk line can offer an economical way to control all the downstream ducts.

Inflatable Dampers

- Most applicable for retrofit
- Easy retrofit installation
- Each damper costs approx. $25
- Most effective for homes with many ducts (4-20)
- Partial opening not possible
- Not self contained--system requires additional hardware
- Can puncture, affecting operation
- Impervious to dirt and corrosion
- Virtually silent operation
- When inflated, air leakage is near 0%

VS

Motorized Dampers

- Most applicable for new construction
- Retrofit requires cutting into duct
- Each damper costs approx. $100
- Most cost effective in homes with few ducts (1-4)
- Can allow for partial opening/closing
- No additional hardware required
- Does not puncture
- Can corrode and accumulate dirt, affecting operation
- Can produce noisy creaks
- When closed, leakage is 5%-15%

Living patterns are important to consider as well. If your family uses the den, kitchen, and living room at the same time and these rooms are connected by a duct, then make these rooms one zone. If most of the day is spent primarily in one room, such as the home office, it may be wise to make it a separate zone. Creating a "slave zone" is another common zoning method. A slave zone is a room, rooms, or an area that is infrequently used. A slave zone thermostat located in the slave zone area guards against temperature extremes by instructing the dampers to open or close air flow. This thermostat does not control the central heat and air system.

The home's layout also affects zoning. A typical two-story home is much warmer upstairs than downstairs. The solution: make the upstairs and downstairs two separate zones. Another common layout is a single level home with all the bedrooms at one end and all the living areas at the other. The solution: divide the home into a living zone and a sleeping zone.

Dampers

An HVAC system can be zoned using conventional, motorized dampers or inflatable dampers. The following comparison chart between motorized and inflatable dampers will help you determine what type of zoning is best for your home (see chart above).

Despite its benefits, electronic HVAC zoning systems have been mostly confined to new construction using motorized dampers. These dampers can be put in as the ducts are being installed, and zones can be determined in advance and ducts grouped accordingly. To maximize airflow, ducts should be oversized by one inch.

In existing homes, the duct system is already in place behind walls, ceilings, and floors. While installing motorized dampers in each duct is possible, doing so would require cutting into walls, ceilings, and floors. This would be time consuming and expensive. Inflatable dampers were designed for multi-duct retrofit applications. These dampers are flexible so they can be inserted directly inside the existing ducts — through the plenum, through register grills, or by cutting a small hole in the duct.

Based on signals from thermostats, switches, sensors, motion detectors, or other devices located throughout the home, motorized and inflatable dampers will either stop air flow or allow air to pass to different zones. When the thermostat tells a motorized damper that a certain room needs more air, the metal plane inside the duct opens. When enough air has reached its destination, the plane simply closes. An inflatable damper works in much the same way, except that it inflates like a balloon to close the duct and block air, and deflates to allow air to pass.

Potential Problems

Neither motorized nor inflatable dampers are trouble-free. Over time, metal dampers can begin to creak and rattle, and pivot points can fail as motors accumulate dirt and corrosion. Because inflatable dampers are impervious to dirt and corrosion, they are less noisy; however, the urethane material can be punctured, slowing operation.

Zoning a forced-air system can cause other problems as well. It may increase the noise at registers. When you shut off half the ductwork, you're moving basically the same amount of air through a smaller volume so you may get increased noise. The solution? Install a bypass — a duct with a barometric damper to connect the supply and return plenums directly. That way excess air can be routed there.

When you close off rooms with dampers, you create back-pressure on the system. There has to be enough airflow going through the system to protect the equipment from freezing (air conditioning) or overheating (heating). Failure to do this can cut the life of HVAC equipment in half. To prevent this, ductwork and HVAC equipment must be sized correctly — preferably by a heating/cooling contractor with an engineer on staff. A bypass duct can also be used to solve this problem.

If your system includes a heat pump or an air conditioner, a wise precaution is to install an evaporator-coil temperature-limit switch. This optional device keeps the evaporator coil from freezing: it opens all dampers and turns off the compressor anytime the coil temperature drops too low.

Zone Perfect

The Zone Perfect, a new single fully integrated zoning system from Bryant, Day & Night and Payne's (BDP), provides heating and cooling control of up to four independent zones for as little as $400 per zone. The system includes programmable thermostats for each zone and two-position motorized duct dampers. Central humidifiers and electronic air cleaners can also be added to the system.

Zone Perfect features an equipment safety device that monitors and maintains proper air flow and temperature control. It also has an optional setback feature that allows the homeowner to program temperature settings in any zone at any time of day. Zone Perfect operates with one heating and cooling system, making it more efficient and less expensive to install, operate, and maintain than conventional dual-system zoning installations. A properly designed Zone Perfect system can save as much as 30% on monthly heating and cooling bills.

Airzone

The Airzone Home Zoning System from Enerzone Systems Corporation has been ranked by the U.S. Department of Commerce as one of the top energy-related inventions (savings of 25 to 50% can be expected). The key to the system is its FlexDamper air control inserts. They have no motors or gears, no electrical or lubrication requirements, no noisy metal parts. They incorporate a unique flexible engineering material from DuPont, called Hytrel polyester elastomer. FlexDamper inserts fit neatly inside existing ducts.

When activated, each FlexDamper insert flexes to fill and seal off the duct in which it has been placed. It forms a completely snug seal inside the duct. There's no leaking air, no noise, no wasted energy escaping through the duct into unwanted areas. When deactivated, the FlexDamper insert simply flexes back into its original open position, sending warm or cooled air into selected areas of the home. FlexDamper inserts operate independently in each zone of the home, responding to the comfort settings established for each zone.

Total Zoned Comfort

The Total Zoned Comfort system from Carrier is a whole-house integrated HVAC system. The Total Zoned Comfort system uses either a Carrier high efficiency central air conditioner or a Carrier heat pump, plus the proper Carrier indoor fan coil or furnace, and damping devices to control the flow of air to each area of your home.

The optional access monitoring system known as Assured Comfort links the Total Zoned Comfort system directly with the dealer's computer by means of a telephone line. Your system can be electronically analyzed for proper performance directly from your dealer's place of business.

SETBACK THERMOSTATS

Automated electronic thermostats let you "set back" your heating and cooling system when you're not home, saving you money on the biggest energy user in your home. Setback thermostats can be used in conjunction with zoned HVAC systems or as stand-alone units that replace your existing thermostat. Most setback thermostats are easy to install, program, and operate. They are a very cost-effective way to control your heating, ventilating, and air conditioning system.

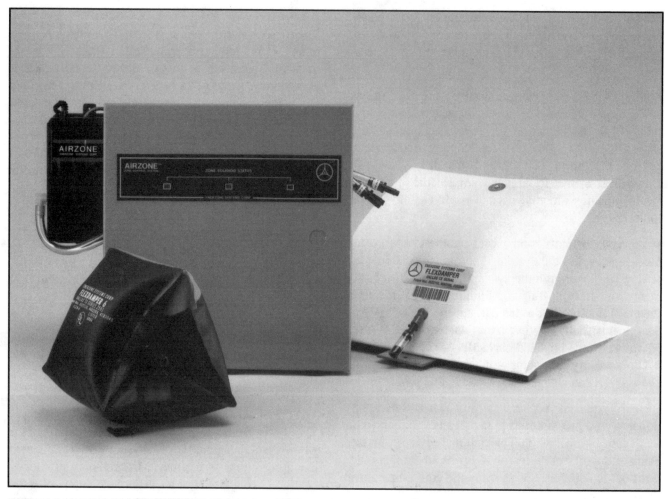

The Airzone Home Zoning System is easy to install, simple to use, compatible with home automation systems, and produces immediate energy savings. Courtesy of Enerzone Systems Corporation.

If you're building a new home, your best bet is to have a professional HVAC contractor design and install a proprietary zoned energy management system. These systems are available from such companies as Carrier, Unity, and Honeywell. While these systems are generally more expensive than traditional HVAC systems, the energy savings and convenience features more then offset the price difference.

X-10-Compatible Thermostats

For those who want their setback thermostat to be controlled by their X-10 system, there are several manufacturers, such as Clark & Co. Inc., offering X-10-compatible setback thermostats.

Clark & Co., Inc. manufactures a stand-alone X-10-compatible setback thermostat. Clark thermostats connect to your HVAC system the same way as any other setback thermostat. The main difference is that Clark models are fitted with an extra set of contacts. These contacts allow you to override the setback and turn up the heat (or air conditioning) from any X-10 Mini, Maxi, RF, telephone, or computer-interface controller.

The Clark Comfort/Setback Thermostat is always ready to save energy. It permits comfort whenever needed, yet it will automatically set back if the room is vacant. Once the user sets a desired room temperature on the thermostat, he must push a button on the control to activate a "comfort cycle." This cycle can be preset to last from 30 minutes to 12 hours. When the preset time period elapses, the thermostat automatically lowers or, in the case of air conditioning equipment, raises the room temperature either 9 or 18 degrees to conserve energy. If a person is still in the room when the time elapses, he activates the comfort cycle again. The Clark is easy to retrofit and costs about $90.

ESTIMATED SAVINGS FROM USING A SETBACK THERMOSTAT

A. Enter your total annual gas/electric/oil bill $_____

If you heat the house and water with the same fuel,   x 0.8

multiply by 0.8 to get your annual heating bill   (1) $_____

If your house is all-electric, multiply your electric   x 0.7

bill by 0.7 to get your heating bill.   (1) $_____

B. Hours per day you plan to keep thermostat

at lower setting   (2) _____ hrs.

C. Hours furnace will run at normal setting

24hrs - (2) _____ hrs   = (3) _____ hrs.

D. Furnace running time at normal thermostat

setting during a typical 1-hr. period   = (4) _____ min.

E. Furnace running time at lower setback thermostat

setting during a typical 1-hr. period   = (5) _____ min.

F. Total furnace running time with no setback

(4) _____ x 24 hrs   = (6) _____ min.

G. Total furnace running time at lower setting

(with setback)   (5)_____ x (2)_____   = (7) _____ min.

H. Total furnace running time at normal setting

(without setback)   (4)_____ x (3)_____   = (8) _____ min.

I. Total furnace running time (with setback)

(7)_____ + (8)_____   = (9) _____ min.

J. Furnace running time saved per day

(6)_____ - (9)_____   = (10) _____ min.

K. Percent savings   (10)_____ ÷ (6)_____   = (11) _____ %

L. Estimated annual savings

(11)_____ % x (1) $_____   = (12) $_____

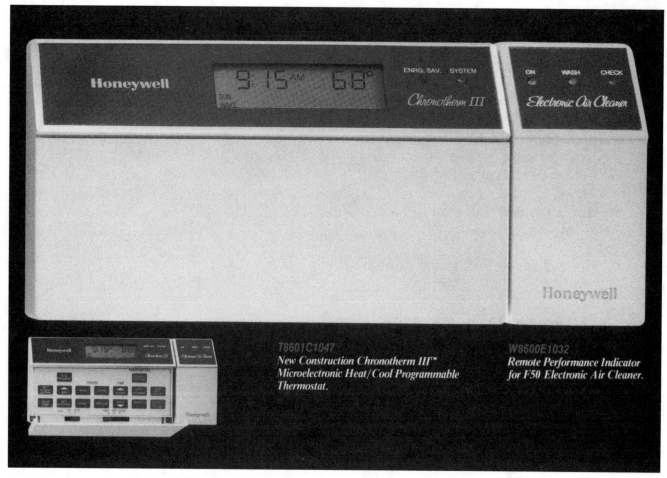

Chronotherm III programmable thermostat. Courtesy of Honeywell.

With the Setpoint Thermostat, available exclusively from Home Automation Laboratories, you can set a setback temperature and activate it via X-10 signal. The setback mode is triggered by closing two electrical contacts on the thermostat using an X-10 Universal Module or any other dry contact closure. For normal thermostat operation, just press the up/down buttons to select the desired temperature. The Setpoint Thermostat has separate temperature settings for heating and cooling and the microprocessor-controller keeps this temperature within 1 degree F.

Chronotherm III

The Chronotherm III Setback Thermostat from Honeywell automatically operates your heating and cooling system according to your schedule. Adaptive Intelligent Recovery maximizes energy savings. The thermostat chooses the optimum time to start gradually returning to the next comfort temperature setting. You save energy

for a longer period of time, yet you're comfortable when you want to be. The Chronotherm III will save from 9 to 30% on your energy costs.

The Chronotherm III Thermostat comes already programmed for nighttime energy savings. And you can easily set it to fit your own energy savings schedule — up to four different heating/cooling time periods (WAKE, LEAVE, RETURN, and SLEEP) in each daily schedule.

WINDOWS AND BLINDS

Even owners of moderately priced homes are finding that the use of advanced window technology is convenient and cost effective. Electronically controlled window treatments — curtains, blinds, shutters, etc. — are, for the most part, readily available, but automatic control for the windows themselves is less common. There are companies that produce electronic controls for draperies, vertical and horizontal blinds, shades, Roman

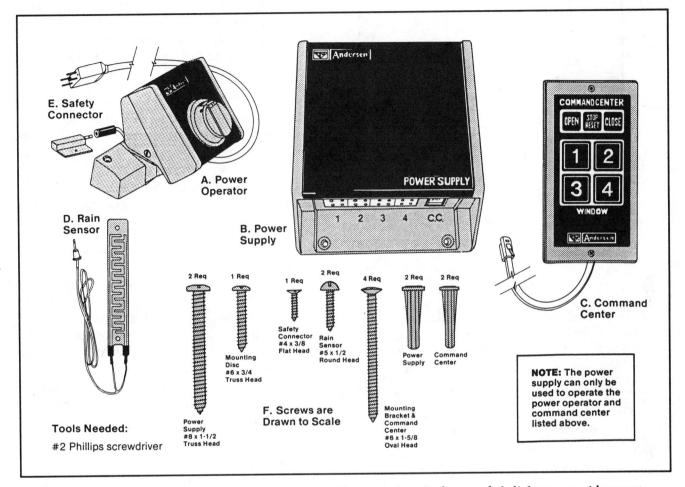

The Andersen Electric Window Opener can be retrofit to existing windows and skylights to provide remote-controlled motorized operation. Courtesy of Andersen Windows.

shades, Austrian puffs, and window quilts. These controls include switches, remotes, timers, and temperature sensors.

Electronically controlled window treatments not only add to the environmental comfort of a home but can also enhance security. Automatically opening and closing draperies, shades, and blinds makes a house appear occupied when no one's home.

Rain and Temperature Sensors

But the homeowner has more to choose from than just a wall switch. Andersen Corporation offers a rain sensor that when connected to a motorized opener will close the window when it detects moisture. Bramen Co. Inc. has a temperature sensor that will open windows when a room gets too hot and close them when it gets too cold. The homeowner can set the window to open and close at

certain temperatures, and best of all, the motor is solar powered. The solar-powered opener not only saves energy, but installation is a breeze.

Rain and temperature sensors work well to increase the environmental comfort of a home, but the windows opening and closing without the homeowner's knowledge can produce a security risk. Security screens solve this problem and are a good idea even if you do not have motorized windows. Security screens are custom-made to look like normal insect screens, but they have small, virtually invisible wires woven into the fiberglass mesh. The wires are connected to the home's security system like any other security sensor.

Window Controls

Nearly all automation equipment can be retrofitted onto existing windows and window treatments. Most of the

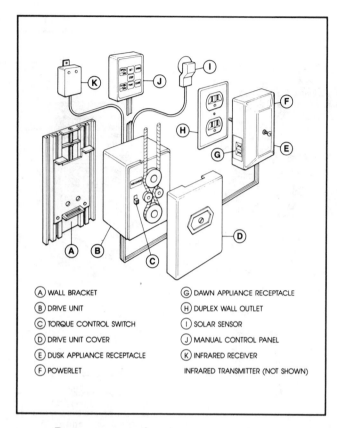

A WALL BRACKET
B DRIVE UNIT
C TORQUE CONTROL SWITCH
D DRIVE UNIT COVER
E DUSK APPLIANCE RECEPTACLE
F POWERLET
G DAWN APPLIANCE RECEPTACLE
H DUPLEX WALL OUTLET
I SOLAR SENSOR
J MANUAL CONTROL PANEL
K INFRARED RECEIVER
INFRARED TRANSMITTER (NOT SHOWN)

Drapery control system component parts.
Courtesy of Solar Drape.

electronically controlled window treatments can be integrated into a home automation system. For example, Mastervoice's Butler-in-a-Box whole-house automation system can control window treatments by interfacing with an infrared controller. Unfortunately, electronically controlled windows from Andersen Corp. and Bramen Co. Inc. do not easily fit into a whole-house system and work best with their own controls.

Windows can also be electronically controlled. Andersen Corp. and Velux-America both market systems to open and close windows. The most popular type of window to be electronically controlled, however, is the skylight. There are several reasons for this: its location on the ceiling makes manual operation difficult; since heat naturally rises, opening and closing skylights is an excellent way to control ventilation.

A retrofit motorized window package with hardwired remote command center is available from Andersen Corp. The Electric Window Opener can be added to most installed Andersen venting awning and roof windows manufactured in the last twenty years. Installation

is easy with a screwdriver and a little time. The Electric Window Opener will remotely open one window sash. Additional power operators and extension cords can be purchased to open and close up to four windows from one command center.

Windows can be programmed to open or close to any desired position, and by adding the optional rain sensor the window will automatically close when rain is detected. In emergency situations, the window can be manually opened or closed by using the flip-up crank located on the power operator. Also included is a safety screen connector, which allows automatic operation only when the screen is in place.

Marvin Windows has developed a prototype system that provides whole-house control of motorized and electronically locked windows. The system uses two-way infrared communication with a handheld remote control. Window status, such as "locked," "25% open," etc., is indicated on a liquid crystal display on the remote. Using the system, a homeowner could control an attic window, for example, from anywhere in the house. Since the windows are operated electronically, controlling them by such devices as rain, wind, or light sensors is easily accomplished.

Solar Drape

The Solar Drape system from Solartronics, Inc. utilizes built-in timing devices, remote control, and solar sensors to trigger the opening and closing of drapery. The drapery units are available in two models: the DM-100, or basic model, and the DM-200, which comes equipped with a security feature that allows you to time the operation of add-on appliances (lamps, radios, television) to create a "lived-in" look. Both models offer standard powerful motor controls that can pull up to 100 pounds of window coverings. Remote control is offered in addition to the standard wall-mounted control panel for ease of operation and convenience.

Solartronics Solar Drape skylight system utilizes a unique remote-controlled solar power source combined with a pleated or Duette shade to cover a skylight or sloped glazing area. Solar Drape has a unique power track for remotely and automatically opening and closing the skylight shade via light control or handheld remote control. To motorize pleated and Roman style shades, Solartronics offers the SD-1000 (pleated shades) and SD-2000 (Roman shades).

All entrances of this home are completely protected by insulating security shutters, forming a formidable barrier against intrusion and severe weather. Courtesy of Roll-A-Way Insulating Security Shutters.

X-10 Drapery Puller

The X-10 Drapery Puller allows you to add convenient automated control to your draperies, and keep your existing draperies, rods, hooks, and pull cords. This heavy-duty drapery puller motor exerts 22 pounds of pull, enough to handle 66 pounds of drapery weight. It also has a built-in rocker switch for manual override or full manual operation. Since you will keep your existing drapery hardware, installing the drapery puller is easy. Just mount it on the wall, run the existing pull cord through the patented three-pulley tension guide system, and adjust with an ordinary screwdriver. Then plug the AC power cord into any AC outlet, and plug the AC control cord into an X-10 Appliance or Outlet Module. To operate, just press ON from any X-10 console to open the draperies or OFF to close them.

Serena Window Transformations

Lutron's Serena Window Transformations is a decorator-styled motorized window and projection screen covering. Serena holds up to four surface covering materials, ranging from pastel plaid to Oriental floral fabrics, on inside top and bottom rollers. Using the wall-mounted control, a homeowner can scroll from one window covering to the next to match the home decor. Sunblock and sunscreen coverings are also available, allowing the homeowner to control the amount of sunlight entering the house.

Rolling Security Shutters

Coastal residents know the benefits of rolling security shutters. For years they've used security shutters to protect their homes from hurricanes. When fully closed, rolling shutters deter break-ins and form an insulating dead-air barrier between the shutter and the opening (door or window) that dramatically improves the R-factor of the opening. Rolling shutters stop radiant heat from escaping in the winter and eliminate solar gain through the windows in summer. When rolled down, there is complete privacy from the outside, sounds are blocked or reduced, and inside lights are blocked from view.

Rolling security shutters are similar in principle to the roll-down shutters used by businesses to protect their stores, but they're much more attractive. Roll-A-Way Insulating Security Shutters is one of the larger American shutter companies. They manufacture manual and remote-controlled electric-operated rolling shutters. These are available in several different styles including: jamb mounted, face mounted, soffit mounted (concealed), and ShutterPrime (combination replacement window/rolling shutter). All can be installed during either construction or retrofit and make an attractive as well as practical addition to your home. Rolling shutters are available from other manufacturers such as Pease Exterior Rolling Shutters and European Rolling Shutters.

Shutter Timers and Controls

The Digital Timer from Somfy allows you to simply and effectively automate your shutters. The Digital Timer is the only currently available dual-direction timer for shutter motors. There are two models available: 24-hour or full seven-day programming. The timer also comes with separate programs for weekdays and weekends. An override button allows you to raise or lower your shutters without affecting the preset program. Use the Digital Timer to raise your shutters automatically to bring in morning sunshine and then to lower them automatically before the sun heats up your home.

Somfy's IGC (Individual-Group Control) allows your home automation system to interface and control your home's motorized shutters, screens, and awnings. The IGC also offers remote control capabilities via Somfy's IR and RF Remote Controls. Somfy products are only available from third-party manufacturers of shutters, screens, and awnings such as Pease Rolling Shutters and Roll-A-Way Insulating Security Shutters.

ENVIRONMENTAL CONTROL

Atmosphere Manager

The Atmosphere Manager from Norm Automation Corporation gives users the ability to choose and control a room's atmosphere including indoor temperature, humidity, air pressure, wind speed, fragrance, volume of exchanged fresh air, and light through a two-way touchscreen remote control.

Twelve sensors constantly monitor indoor and outdoor temperature, humidity, and air pressure. The high speed computer uses an artificial intelligent database to generate the optimum climate. With the built-in human sensors (not motion detectors), fresh air flow can be directed to follow up to six people.

The theory behind the Atmosphere Manager is modulation. Instead of keeping environmental factors, such as temperature, humidity, light, and fragrance constant, the Atmosphere Manager has adopted a revolutionary and dynamic approach. The temperature, humidity, and light-

The Atmosphere Manager from Norm Automation.
Courtesy of Norm Automation Corporation.

ing are constantly and automatically modulated and adjusted. The Atmosphere Manager achieves perfect modulation using a high speed computer and sophisticated mathematical modeling. The advanced ventilation, optic electronics, ultrasonic wave, infrared ray, and radio frequency technologies make total automation of atmosphere management a reality.

For energy efficiency, built-in sensors activate the Atmosphere Manager as you enter the room and turn it off as you leave. You can also preset the operating times and climates in advance. The Atmosphere Manager's air conditioning capacity is 10,000 Btu (British Thermal Unit), while the heating capacity is 13,440 Btu. The Atmosphere Manager has a suggested retail price of about $4,000, or as much as a standard central heating/cooling system.

X-10 Controls
You can use X-10 technology to automate plug-in wall- and window-mounted air conditioners. To control standard air conditioners designed to plug into 220 volt 20 amp outlets, use X-10 Appliance Module HD245. You must use an X-10-compatible controller to switch the HD245 on or off. To control units that plug into 120 volt 20 amp outlets use the Leviton Single Wall Receptacle Module, which is a wire-in module.

Greenplug
Want to save money on your electric bill? Just plug a Greenplug from Boulder, CO-based Green Technologies Inc. into your wall outlet. Then plug an appliance (refrigerator, freezer, or air conditioner) into the Greenplug. You can immediately reduce the appliance's energy consumption by 5 to 30%.

The magic behind Greenplug is the "Ideal Voltage Controller" circuitry that instantly reduces the incoming load of electricity to the appliance's "ideal operating voltage." Most outlets receive 120 volts of electricity. But appliances seldom require that much juice. The Greenplug gives the appliance the amount of electricity it needs to run efficiently and no more.

Square D Breakers
A residential electrical system is no better than the circuit breakers used to protect individual circuits. Square D circuit breakers trip faster than breakers from other manufacturers. When you protect your circuits with 15 and 20A single pole Square D breakers with QWIK-OPEN protection, you have a breaker that will trip within 1/60 of a second. With Square D's TRILLIANT Home Power System, you get more than just the traditional residential circuit breaker box. Square D incorporates a plug-in Surgebreaker Secondary Surge Arrester that fits into a standard breaker space and a Ground Fault Circuit Interrupter (GFCI) Branch Breaker for GFCI protection, which is required by the National Electrical Code.

6.
Home Theater

You may have heard the term "home theater" recently. A home theater is an integrated audio and video system that brings you sound and images that are as close to real life as possible. You are a *participant*, not a viewer.

When we speak of home theater, we are talking about more than a VCR hooked to a 25-inch color television. We are talking about sophisticated audio/video systems that combine such elements as a large screen (up to 120" or more diagonal), high quality video components, surround sound audio, remote control, and perhaps even customized lighting systems and acoustically designed surroundings.

Once you have decided to install home theater, you have three choices: buy a manufacturer's prepackaged home theater system; hire a professional designer/installer to assemble a system; or design and install a system yourself.

A packaged system will eliminate much of the initial work of designing the system but is less flexible than a custom-designed system. Packaged systems are offered by companies such as Mitsubishi, Pioneer, and Fisher. A custom-designed system may be the easiest way to obtain the home theater that is truly desired, but it is also the most expensive.

Just what does a home theater cost? If you wanted to dedicate an entire room to a home theater, complete with controlled lighting, screen and draperies, perhaps even a projector that lowers from the ceiling, and the very best audio and video equipment, the cost could run well over $100,000. A more reasonable, yet still impressive, home theater can be obtained for around $10,000. If corners are cut and some quality sacrifices made, a serviceable system can be assembled for $5,000 or less.

Creating your own home theater doesn't have to be expensive or complicated. Generally speaking, starting with your existing equipment, you can obtain greatly enhanced sounds and images with the addition of just a component or two.

If you already have a stereo and two speakers you're happy with, you can save some money by buying an add-on surround processor. It works in tandem with your existing stereo, providing surround decoding and the additional amplification for the center and surround speakers.

GETTING STARTED

The first step in creating a home theater is to choose the best space. Room dimensions are crucial for good sound reproduction. Most experts suggest a rectangular space. The Custom Electronic Design and Installation Association (CEDIA), a trade group of home-theater installation professionals, suggests an approximate ratio of 1.0 to 1.6 to 2.5. Since most homes have a ceiling height of about 8 feet, an approximate room for a home theater would be about 13' wide X 20' long.

Theatre Design Associates (TDA) offers a line of modular, ready-to-install units dubbed "Dream Palaces." These ready-made theaters can be installed in rooms ranging in size from 12' by 14' to 18' by 24'. (Larger dimensions generally require custom work.) All units include the theater itself — walls, columns, curtains, lights, dimmers, and seats — and start at $15,500. Electronic equipment is not included in the packages, although TDA works with suppliers to create a total sound environment. Theatre Design Associates operates 15 showrooms around the U.S. and in Canada.

The ELAN Home Theater Sound Package turns your home into a cinema with the thundrous theater-quality sound of Dolby Pro Logic from International Jensen. Courtesy of Square D Company.

For more information, call (800) 786-6TDA or (718) 398-3874.

The key to obtaining the right system is first to decide which features are most important to you, then decide on a budget, eliminating the features that are desired but not affordable. When deciding which features are desired, it is important to remember that audio and video are almost always completely separate entities as far as home theater is concerned. They may originate from the same source, but once the system receives the signal from the tape, disc, or broadcast medium, the audio and video portions are sent in entirely different directions.

In setting up your home theater, don't overlook a carefully designed seating area. Comfort is important. Proper lighting, screen size, and speaker placement will give you a theater quality system that can fit into a home environment.

First, ask yourself the question professional A/V installers ask their clients: What kind of experience are you

*Courtesy of SoundTrack/Patrick Farson,
copyright 1993.*

*Courtesy of SoundTrack/Patrick Farson,
copyright 1993.*

seeking? Where you like to sit when you go to the movies will best answer this question. Do you go up front, where you're drawn into the action, or do you like a more removed perspective?

Video Monitoring Component

The first choice should be the type of video monitoring component to use. There are three major categories to choose from: direct view, front projection, and rear projection.

Direct view is best represented by the common, self-contained sets most of us have in our homes. Direct view offers, in general, the best picture, but true home theater size is not available. Models offering high quality 32- to 35-inch pictures are available from many manufacturers for $2,000 to $3,000. Large direct view sets may be attractive to those who have space limitations, as they take up less space than either a front- or rear-projection model. Also, in a smaller room, the viewing distance is smaller and large screen size becomes less important.

If you sit the correct distance away from a properly color-adjusted set, direct view works well. Measure the distance from your main seating area to the screen. CEDIA recommends seating distance be twice the size of your set. If the distance is less than seven feet, try a 20- to 27-inch set. If you sit between seven and 15 feet from the screen, pick a 31-inch to 35-inch direct-view set. If your seating is 15 feet or more from the TV, you should move up to a bigger screen size, at least a 52-inch model, via a rear-projection set.

Screen

Rear-projection systems can offer a bigger picture than direct view, but the size of the picture is limited by the amount of space available behind the screen, where the image is projected. Rear-projection TVs come in 40-, 46-, 50-, 52-, and 60-inch sizes, usually in the $2,000 to $3,000 price range. To get a really large image, the screen may have to be placed several feet from the back wall. These systems can produce large images, such as Mitsubishi's 120-inch custom-installed unit, but most units settle for screens in the 40- to 60-inch range. The picture quality does not match direct view in brightness or sharpness, but the drop-off is compensated for by the increase in screen size.

If a true big screen experience is desired, front projection is the most popular choice. Front-projection sets are two-piece systems with a projection unit, mounted on the floor or ceiling, and a retractable screen. Most cost $3,000 to $5,000. Since the screen can be mounted flush against the wall, room size has less importance than with rear projection.

A fairly large room is needed, since there must be considerable distance between the screen and the projector to obtain a large image, but almost the entire room can then be used as a viewing area. There are several options for placement of the projector. It can be ceiling mounted, placed on a table top, or even hidden away in a coffee table. Care must be taken that the viewers not block the image from the screen.

Keep in mind one consideration before choosing a front-projection system: ambient light washes out the images on the screen, so such a system works best in a dark room. If the viewing room is sunlit during the day, or if the system is going into a multi-purpose room rather than a space dedicated to the home theater, a rear-screen system will prove more practical.

Position the screen so that it is visible to anyone who wants to view it. There's no reason you can't place the set in a corner on the diagonal. Make sure that the proposed area behind the screen is not overly bright. Otherwise, the picture will look dim by comparison. Windows and lamps are common causes of screen glare.

Some of these systems come with their own screens, others do not. There are different types of screens available. For example, if you want the best out of your surround sound system, a screen that is acoustically transparent (one that does not distort or muffle sound produced behind it) is desirable.

Also, the screen can be mounted a number of different ways. It can be mounted directly on a wall, so that it is always down, or a roll-up version can be installed. Some designers prefer curved screens, as they work better in soft light, but they offer a far more limited optimum viewing area, and are also more difficult to hide when not in use.

Lighting

Perhaps the most ignored aspect of home theater is lighting. Movie theaters are dark, with little ambient light. Homes tend to be bright, with windows and interior lighting. Darkness is a necessity in the home theater setting. If there are windows, they must have heavy curtains. No skylights allowed! The wall behind the screen should be white or light gray, with no accent colors. A gray-shaded light should be placed behind the screen, at about 10% of the screen brightness. The picture then needs to be adjusted, black and white levels need to be calibrated, the gray scale set, and the color, tint, and sharpness adjusted.

Audio

Once a video monitor and screen are chosen, the next question is how to connect the video portion of the presentation to the audio portion. This takes place at the audio/video receiver. For true home theater sound, the A/V receiver offers surround-sound capability. A true sur-round-sound receiver will feature Dolby Surround processing capability, four or more amplifiers, a video monitor connection, and two or more video source connections.

The basic function of the surround-sound receiver is to separate and distribute the soundtrack of the movie to speakers around the room. This is done by the Dolby Surround Processor. It is designed to place the sound in proper relation to the action on the screen. Voices will seem to come from the screen, while sound effects may come from beside the screen or even from behind the viewer.

A good home theater's sound flows seamlessly around the room — left, center, right, back — while dispensing a smooth blend of the sound from the "main" and "surround" speakers. You get that effect by putting the main speakers fairly close to the TV screen and aiming the surround speakers so their sound bounces off a room's surfaces.

Most speakers sound best when the tops of their enclosures are at or near ear level, with no furniture blocking the sound paths. Experiment with "aiming" speakers. Some speakers sound best when angled in so that the sound is centered in the primary listening area. Others sound best aimed straight ahead. Find where the speakers sound best, then move them just far enough away from those positions to make the room workable.

Low bass tones, which come from the speaker system's large woofer cones, can project around most obstacles. Bass tones are strengthened by reverberations off nearby walls and floors. For this reason, bass sound will be maximized if you place your speakers on or in front of the room's most solid wall. Minimize excessive, boomy bass by mounting the speakers on stands, well away from any walls.

In a Dolby Pro Logic setup, the center speaker, responsible for all dialogue, should be wired for placement just above or below the video screen. The left and right speakers should be wired to flank the screen at least 5 to $6^1/_2$ feet from each other (inside edge to inside edge). They should also be lifted to a seated ear level position (usually 44 to 45 inches above the floor), and at least 2 feet from the outer walls. The rear left and right speakers should be placed 6 to 8 feet above the floor, firing toward the room center (primary listening position) from the side walls behind listeners, from the back wall, or down from the ceiling behind listeners.

For the front two or three speakers, it is generally agreed that top of the line loudspeakers should be used. Not only are these needed to meet the demanding sound of movie soundtracks, they are necessary if the consumer wishes to use the system for audio programs.

When considering rear-channel speakers, the best strategy may be to install high-quality rear speakers only if budget permits. Many designers feel that speakers and amplifiers of limited ability are adequate for the task, claiming the function they perform will never use the upper potential of higher-priced units.

Although the center speaker has a very important job, delivering dialogue, music, and some special effects, you don't need a huge speaker. Pro Logic has the ability to redistribute center-channel frequencies below 100 Hz (bass) to the left and right speakers. This takes the load off the center speaker, so you can use a relatively small speaker and amplifier with no loss of bass or loudness. A good rule of thumb: the center speaker's power should be about equal to that of the right and left speakers.

One important feature to look for in a center speaker is magnetic shielding. This enables you to place the speaker directly below or on top of the screen without affecting the picture. If your TV has a built-in speaker, you may be able to dedicate it as the center speaker. If your right and left speakers are small, you may want to add a subwoofer to carry all the bass. Make sure the subwoofer will interface properly with its satellite speakers. Keep in mind that most freestanding subwoofers are active (have their own dedicated power amplifiers built in). Some have adjustable crossovers that let you select points where the subwoofer leaves off and the satellites take over.

A popular speaker choice for home theater installations is in-wall or "architectural" speakers. These blend into the background so well they can be practically invisible. While there are many brands that deliver high-quality sound, it is generally agreed that they cannot match top-of-the-line free-standing speakers.

Another possibility is the subwoofer, which will add bass punch to almost any system. A subwoofer is a speaker that reproduces only the lowest frequencies. It will increase the bass response of the system and can be used to augment smaller main speakers. Since the low frequencies produced by subwoofers are not localized by the human ear, the subwoofer can be placed anywhere in the room. Often, a subwoofer is built into a wall or hidden in a coffeetable.

Acoustics

Sound reproduction is affected by many variables, including floor and wall surfaces, furnishings, speaker placement, and seating arrangements. Floors should be covered with some sound-absorbing material like carpeting to absorb the "hard room" sound.

Nothing corrects problematic acoustics in a room more efficiently than the judicious addition of surfaces that absorb, reflect, and scatter or diffuse sound. Upholstery, rugs, and curtains are sound absorbers. Windows, mirrors, and bare plaster walls are sound reflectors. Irregular surfaces, such as shelves full of randomly sized books and knick-knacks, diffuse sound. The question is whether you have the right numbers of these elements in the right spots.

If too many sound reflectors are your problem, carpets or rugs will help cut reflections from bare floors. Pleated draperies reduce sound reflections from windows; bookshelves can break up reflections from walls. Hanging decorative rugs on the wall can also help. If, however, you have too many sound absorbers, you need to either take away absorbers (like the ones listed above) or add reflectors (such as small, glass-covered pictures) or diffusers (bookshelves).

You don't want hard reflective surfaces on the side walls between you and the speakers. Although you should put your speakers where they'll sound best and your TV screen where it's easiest to view, you can place your other equipment almost anywhere you find convenient.

Video Source

Once a suitable system is assembled to reproduce the sights and sounds of a favorite movie, one last component is needed: a video source, or something that actually plays the movies. VHS format videocassette player/recorders are the most common type in use today, but other types should be considered. While VHS does offer the most available titles, the picture quality is somewhat lacking when displayed on a home theater's large screen.

Selecting the source components, better known as VCR and laser disc players, is even easier than choosing the monitor. The list of necessary features for a home theater VCR is a short one: hi-fi stereo sound is the only real "must have," incorporating four video heads (as opposed to two), which gives you better special effects.

Although some home theaters are based on multiple sound components, the most practical choice is an audio/

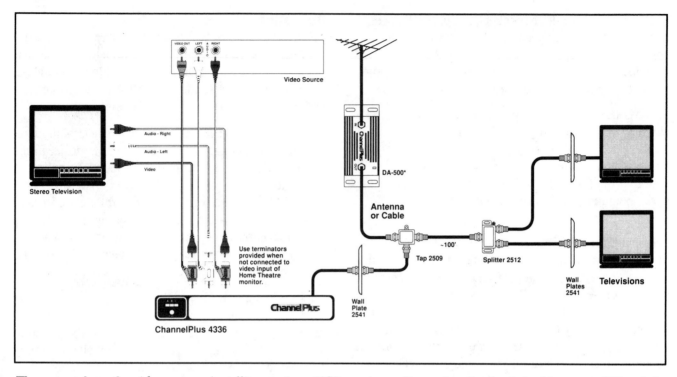

The output from the video source (satellite receiver, VCR, etc.) supplies a signal to both the big screen TV and the modulator. The 4336 modulator has a high input impedance to maintain a 75 ohm impedance match. Expand to 4, 8, or 16 televisions using additional splitters and amplifiers. Courtesy of ChannelPlus.

video (A/V) receiver. This is the heart of your home theater, the place all the components are connected and selected. A/V receivers provide power for all four surround channels.

Most major releases on VHS or laser disc are recorded with four different audio tracks (channels) embedded in the sound. A stereo VCR plays the four of them crunched down into two — a left and right, for stereo. Once you have a Dolby Surround Sound system, you can play back all four channels, which are actually routed to five different speakers.

Laser disc is the fastest growing alternative to the VCR. It uses technology similar to a compact disc (CD) player, digitally storing the movie's audio and video information. The digital electronics give laser discs excellent picture quality and sound comparable to CDs. With laser discs growing in popularity, the number of titles available is rapidly increasing. Also, many laser disc movie titles are available in a "letter box" format. This places black bands above and below the picture, so that the width-to-height ratio is the same as in movie theaters.

With a complex home theater system, remote control is a necessity. Not only is the usual advantage of couch

control multiplied by the increased number of components involved, but remote control allows adjustments to the surround sound system to be made from the viewing position, which is a major convenience.

Instant Home Theater

Hooking up and configuring a multiple-component home theater system can be confusing, and with loads of wire, quite unattractive. Mitsubishi has introduced a product that can eliminate a lot of complicated home theater wiring. Mitsubishi's Instant Home Theater (HTS-100) has built-in Dolby Pro Logic Surround Sound. By plugging it into any television with stereo audio outputs, the TV can produce Dolby Pro Logic sound. Unlike traditional A/V receiver setups where the receiver is the center of the system, the HTS-100 acts as a stand-alone add-on to your television. You don't have to rewire the entire system. The connections of your TV, VCR, and cable hookup remain the same.

Operation of your television also remains exactly the same. When the HTS-100 senses the presence of an audio signal from the television, it automatically turns on and turns off when it doesn't. The HTS-100's remote

The Instant Home Theater system HTS-100 from Mitsubishi makes installing a home theater simple.
Courtesy of Mitsubishi.

can be taught to operate most any remote-controlled component in your system; it replaces all the rest. One button turns on both the HTS-100 and your TV. The HTS-100 sells for $600.

OTHER CONTROLS BUILT IN

Another home theater trend is systems that offer more than just A/V functions, such as home control, yet are still extremely easy to use. The FroxSystem and Media Magician from User Interface Technologies Corp. are two examples. Like the FroxSystem, the Media Magician makes programming A/V components a breeze through interactive control. Users refer to pop-up menu selections overlaid on the TV screen, and make their selections by remote control. The FroxSystem remote, FroxWand, utilizes only one button; the Media Magician control remote is multi-buttoned.

While FroxSystem incorporates a proprietary video transmission technique called Active Pixel Control, Media Magician control is CD-ROM based. Media Magician does not have FroxSystem's high resolution/line doubling capabilities, making it much less expensive—approximately $5,000 compared to FroxSystem's

$10,000-$50,000 price tag. In addition to A/V control, Media Magician feature bi-directional X-10 for control of lighting, security cameras, Jacuzzi, etc.

Media Magician and Tel-a-Magician (included free with Media Magician) provide custom interactive control of multi-zone/multi-source audio/video, lighting, mechanical systems, and automation. Standard features include on-screen and telephone control (with Tel-a-Magician) of nine zones (144 max), 200 A/V sources (3,200 max), three RS-232 ports (32 max) for interfacing with AudioAccess, AudioEase, LiteTouch, Lutron, etc., lighting, timers, mechanicals, and seven relays and eight contact sensors.

The Tel-a-Magician provides full access to Media Magician's power. Tel-a-Magician's customized voice prompting literally reads Media Magician's menus over the phone. Thousands of voice menus are stored on CD-ROM (voices are recorded, not computer synthesized). Or you can use the Tel-a-Magician's speed dial feature to control A/V, lighting, pool and spa, draperies and blinds, doors and gates with the press of one button. The Tel-a-Magician allows you to use your TV in conjunction with the phone to provide full access to the on-screen menus.

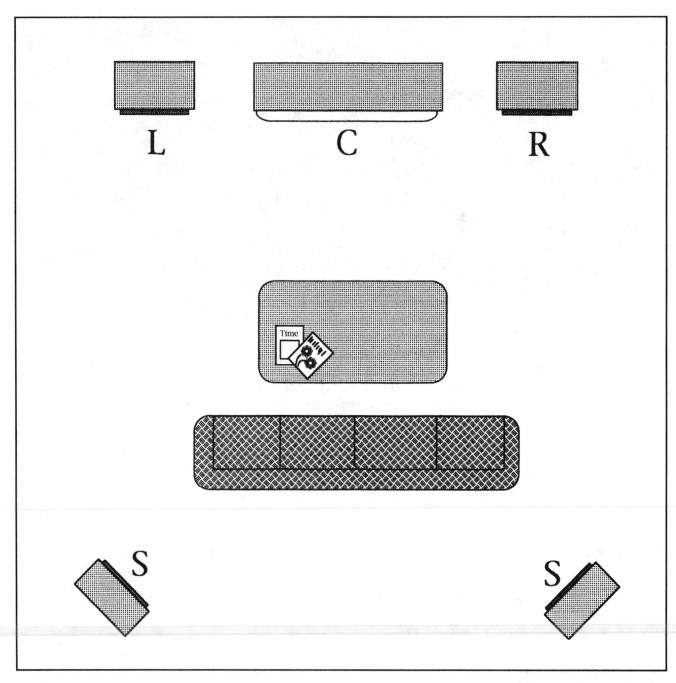

This illustration shows the proper speaker positioning for surround sound: L — Left, R — Right, C — Center (either above or below the viewing screen), S — Surround Sound Speakers.

SURROUND SOUND

Dolby Surround sound is a multi-channel technology that has been used in movie theaters for years. It recovers all the sound effects that have been encoded on a movie film and directs the sounds to the appropriate channels. What this means is, if a train is approaching on screen from the left, you hear its whistle from the left of the theater. With Dolby Surround sound, you hear the movie as it was meant to be heard for a three-dimensional sonic experience.

There are basically two ways to get Dolby Surround sound in the home: through a passive decoding system (fixed matrix) or an active decoding system (variable/ adaptive). Of course, you can hear the entire soundtrack of a Dolby stereo movie in regular two-channel stereo, but you'll miss all the exciting effects — intriguing dialogue bursting from the center of the screen, race car engines exploding from the sides, and crickets chirping from behind.

A Dolby Surround sound decoder is a passive decoding system. It recreates cinema sound by restoring the vital front-to-back dimensions, and steering the sound in the appropriate directions — to the left, right, and surround speakers — for an effect not possible with conventional two-channel stereo playback.

Passive decoders are also equipped with circuitry to improve the surround separation. Basically, they prevent predominant front-channel sounds (conversations, etc.) from leaking into the surround channels. Dolby Surround sound decoders are easily built into home stereo video systems. According to the Custom Electronic Design and Installation Association, a recent trend is eliminating the outboard decoding unit and instead integrating it within the system components — stereo TVs and VCRs, receivers, amplifiers, and preamplifiers.

Dolby Surround Sound System
• Stereo TV and stereo VCR or laser disc player
• Dolby Surround decoder (if not already built into existing components)
• Left and right surround speakers

Dolby Pro Logic Surround Sound System
• Stereo TV and stereo VCR or laser disc player
• Dolby Pro Logic decoder
• Center speaker

Optional:
• Full-range, high-quality left and right loudspeakers
• Separate subwoofers
• Separate amplifiers
• Self-powered surround loudspeakers if additional amplification is needed

Although Dolby Surround sound heightens your sense of "being there," there is one missing element — a distinct center channel. In a basic Dolby Surround system, center sound, like on-screen dialogue, is reproduced as a "phantom" channel that seems to emanate from a point between the front left and right speakers. "Phantom" redistributes all center-channel information

to the sides (to right and left speakers). This method of signal distribution makes proper placement of left and right speakers and a central seating position essential.

To create an effective "phantom" center channel, left and right speakers should be placed relatively close together (flanking each side of the screen), and you must sit in the center of the listening area, between the two front speakers. Otherwise, important dialogue moves off the screen. The effect: the speaking character is in one location (the movie screen) and the voice is coming from another location (a rear speaker). Ultimately, the entire presentation is ruined.

A Dolby Pro Logic (active) decoder separates and sends sound to a true, visible center-channel speaker placed close to the screen. With dialogue firmly anchored at center, you perceive the movie more accurately. No matter where you sit in your home theater, the dialogue is projected directly toward you, just as it would be in a real-life conversation. Especially if your home theater consists of a large projection screen with widely-spaced front speakers, a center speaker becomes essential.

An exciting development currently in the works is a home version of Dolby's new AC-3 multi-channel digital coding technique. The format, called Dolby Stereo SR*D, will bring six discrete channels (left, right, center, left surround, right surround, and subwoofer) of digital sound to home theaters, hopefully by 1994. With Dolby AC-3, it will also be possible to play multi-channel stereo or even mono, and to tailor dynamic range to the noise level of the specific listening environment.

GLOSSARY OF HOME THEATER TERMS

A/V RECEIVER — Component much like a receiver within a stereo system, but it accepts video signals, with many featuring surround sound processors.

CEDIA — CEDIA is the Custom Electronic Design & Installation Association. It is a trade association for designers and installers of high-end audio/video and automation systems.

DEDICATED ROOM — A room whose sole purpose is the viewing of a home theater system. Such elements as lighting, drapery, and furniture arrangement are all designed with this in mind.

DOLBY PRO LOGIC — Advanced surround sound system for the home. Adds fifth speaker for dialogue and "logic steering," which increases the apparent separation between channels.

DOLBY STEREO — Sound reproduction standard used in most theaters. Uses a minimum of six channels.

DOLBY SURROUND — System designed to duplicate Dolby Stereo in home. Uses three channels and four speakers.

HIGH DEFINITION TELEVISION (HDTV) — A standard that will dramatically increase the number of HRLs (see below), providing a much sharper picture even if the image is several feet wide. HDTV requires signals broadcast in HDTV format.

HORIZONTAL RESOLUTION LINES (HRLs) — The lines across the television screen that create the picture. The greater the number of lines, the sharper and more defined the picture.

IMPROVED DEFINITION TELEVISION (IDTV) — A system that electronically doubles the horizontal resolution lines, producing a picture somewhere between HDTV and current broadcast television. IDTV uses standard television signals.

INTEGRATED ROOM — A room containing a home theater system but used for other purposes by family members.

LASER DISC — Disc with digital video images encoded into it, much as a compact disc stores digital audio information. Generally considered the best source for video reproduction currently available. This improved quality can be especially important in home theaters using larger screens.

SUPER VHS — Player that, when combined with compatible S-VHS tape, will produce image featuring an increase in horizontal resolution lines, and produce a sharper picture.

SURROUND SOUND — A system that separates the various components of the soundtrack then disperses them to speakers placed around the room. For example, voices could come from behind the screen, while other sound effects could come from beside or even behind the viewer. Four to five speakers are generally incorporated, and a surround sound processor is used to create the effect.

THX — Movie sound enhancement technology that incorporates Dolby Pro Logic. THX is designed to maximize dialogue intelligibility. It is dedicated to movie sound reproduction and cannot be used for straight audio. It is being licensed by Lucasfilm to various manufacturers.

UNIFIED REMOTE CONTROL — A remote that can control all elements of a home theater system, including audio and video, and sometimes even extend to functions such as lighting and draperies.

7.
Whole House Audio/Video Systems

A multi-room, multi-source A/V system (distributed audio/video) allows users to watch and listen to any media room source (VCR, laser disc, CD player, stereo, etc.) in the bedroom, den, bathroom, patio, or anywhere else they desire, all at the same time. Most distributed audio/video systems are custom installed by audio/ video professionals. This is not to suggest that you cannot install a whole-house A/V system yourself. You can. But do-it-yourself installation requires some basic skills in order to run all the wiring necessary, install speakers, and set up A/V components.

For those of us who are all thumbs, custom installation is the way to go. Manufacturers have developed systems that combine all the A/V switching, modulation, and infrared extension necessary for multi-room, multi-source A/V in one complete, pre-configured package. These packaged systems generally provide greater multi-sourcing capabilities than individually assembled multi-room systems.

At the hub of a multi-zone network is a master controller. All of the primary and secondary room components are interconnected through it, sending instructions to one another via a combination of relay control, IR control, and computer control. The master controller receives independent user commands and sends them to the appropriate primary room units. It then transmits a signal to secondary room components located in several zones throughout the house.

The master controller is basically the brains of the system, receiving information, making a decision, and directing the operation of many pieces of equipment. Examples of multi-zone systems are Simul*source from Soundstream Technologies, Niles Component Commander from Niles Audio Corporation, MRX Controller from Audioaccess, and Sony Digital Signal Transfer (DST) from Sony.

Moving up the ladder of whole-house entertainment sophistication are computer-controlled systems. Unlike multi-zone systems in which functions are predetermined, computer-controlled systems' functions are totally customized by inserting pre-configured computer cards/ROM chips into controller components. Plug-in computer cards make these systems extremely flexible, easy to upgrade and install, as well as able to integrate with other home control systems. Examples of computer-controlled systems are ELAN HD from Square D, AXCESS from AMX Corporation, and The AudioEase System from AudioEase.

ELAN

ELAN starts with a single, open-wiring format that integrates most of the audio, video, and telephone systems in your home. With ELAN, music from your existing stereo system can flow seamlessly, from room to room, over high quality Jensen or Advent wall, ceiling, or outdoor speakers. Each room features its own volume control for your listening comfort. The optional IR remote control allows you to control your equipment from any room in the house. ELAN also offers door chime and paging over system speakers.

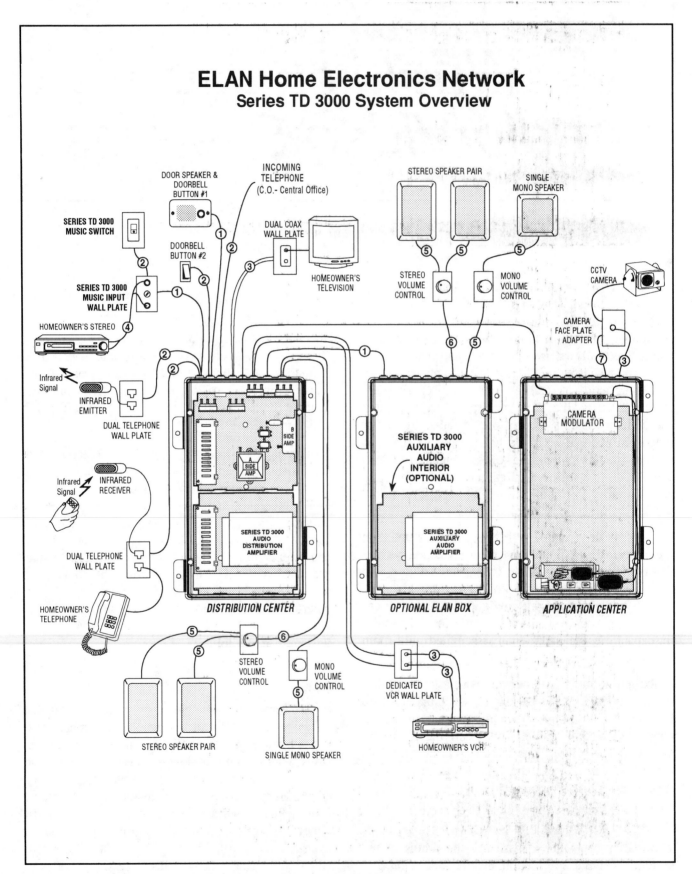

ELAN Home Electronics Network
Series TD 3000 System Overview

Courtesy of Square D Company.

The ELAN Series MD Home Electronics Network from Square D features handsome rack-mounted modular components that work with a homeowner's existing stereo, video, and phone to perform a variety of functions, including whole-house audio, video, and telephone distribution, paging, closed circuit cameras, and more. Courtesy of Square D Company.

You can watch videos or cable television channels from any TV set in the house, no matter where your VCR and cable hookup are located. ELAN can even use your television as a security monitor. Place the closed circuit cameras in the baby's room, at the front door, by the pool, wherever surveillance is important. Then simply switch to the appropriate television channel and you'll see and hear what the camera sees and hears from any television in the house.

The surround sound provided by ELAN Home Theater package upgrade turns television and video viewing into an experience. With five specially matched and placed Advent in-wall speakers, a subwoofer, a surround sound processor, and your own TV and VCR, ELAN gives you the ultimate in home entertainment.

The ELAN Series TD is a whole-house audio, video, and phone system for new homes. The ELAN Series TD changes the way new homes are wired to allow your TV, VCR, phone, and stereo to work together and give you a whole new world of convenience. ELAN Series TD provides single-source, multi-room distribution of audio and video signals, as well as phone integration. Designed to be an integral part of your new home, both hardware and installation can be included as part of your mortgage.

ELAN Series MD is designed for installing whole-house audio and video distribution in existing homes. Instead of the built-in wiring distribution hub found in ELAN's Series TD, the Series MD uses modular rack-mounted units that can be mixed and matched to suit your needs. The main components are the single-zone, multi-room Audio Distribution Amplifier, which powers up to 16 wall and ceiling speakers, and the Video Distribution Amplifier, which sends video signals throughout the house so that any TV in the house will work from one VCR or cable input.

The audio amp also integrates the doorbell and telephone, allowing the doorbell chime and house-wide paging via the phone to be heard over the system's speakers. You can also add the optional closed circuit camera package and the home theater sound package.

Also designed for retrofit applications, the ELAN Series HD allows the user to simultaneously send a compact disc signal to the living room, a tape deck signal to the kitchen, and an FM tuner signal to the bedroom.

Sony

Sony's Digital Signal Transfer (DST) System allows you to bring audio and video signals to any room in your home at the touch of a button. The DST is the first digital, multi-room, multi-source transmission system. Because the Sony DST multi-room system transmits audio signals digitally, each of up to 16 extension rooms can have the sonic quality of the main media room. Located in the media room, the Digital Master Control Center accepts signals from up to six audio-only sources and three audio and video sources. The Control Center can simultaneously transmit three different audio signals and a single video program anywhere in your house. You can access the system via Digital Link Touch Panels, which mount on the wall, or the easy-to-use handheld DST Remote Commanders.

US Tec

The Sight 'n Sound system from US Tec is a pre-wired wall receptacle system that gives the homeowner the convenience of running electricity, cable TV, telephone,

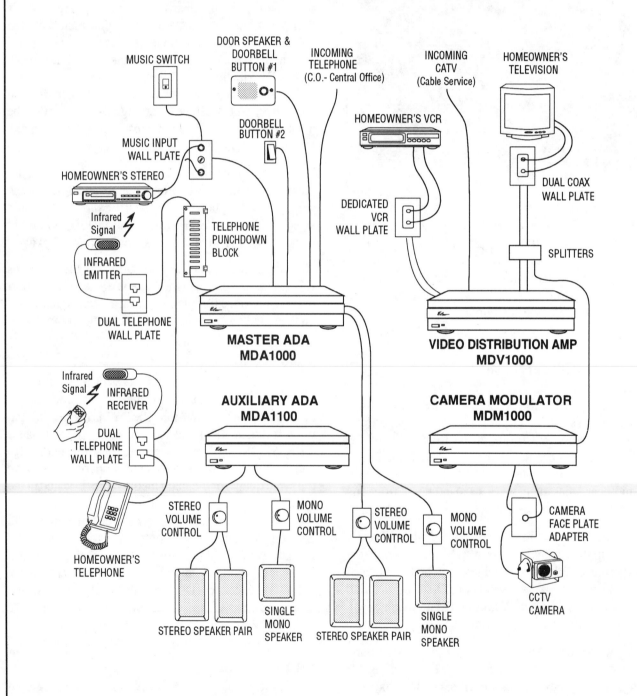

ELAN™ Home Electronics Network Series MD System Overview

Courtesy of Square D Company.

The ELAN Series HD Home Electronics Network from Square D is the first component-based multi-zone, multi-source system for housewide audio, video, and telephone distribution. Courtesy of Square D Company.

ELAN Series HD components are designed with preprogrammed, plug-in cards that control specific functions and allow installers to easily customize systems to meet individual needs and tastes. Courtesy of Square D Company.

stereo sound systems, VCRs, and security cameras from the same wall plate.

The Sight 'n Sound system eliminates the unsightly tangle of wires and pockmarked walls often associated with audio and video systems by putting combination plates in opposite corners of key rooms.

US Tec estimates that pre-wiring a new home should cost only $200 to $300 more than a normal wiring operation. Retrofitting a home built after 1950 with eight wall plates will cost about $1,000 for the rewiring, including materials and labor. The control box sells for just over $700, putting the total cost for a user-ready system at less than $2,000. US Tec sells kits containing eight wall plates, the controller, and cable for $1,460, not including labor.

Niles Audio

The RVS-6, from Niles Audio, is an X-10-compatible infrared remote control speaker selector, volume controller, and infrared repeater. It can distribute one amplifier to up to six pairs of speakers. The RSV-6 is installed at the main equipment location. The user can control the volume of any or all of the rooms connected to the RSV-6 using its front-panel pushbuttons, or by remote control from any area equipped with wall-mount, ceiling-mount, or tabletop sensors. In addition, any wireless lighting controller that uses the X-10 standard can be used to control the RVS-6. Simply plug an X-10 remote console into any AC wall outlet, and remote operation of the RVS-6 is possible from those areas not equipped with a remote sensor.

Multiplex Technology

A whole-house video system enables the homeowner to see high quality entertainment and CCTV signals on any TV in the house, no matter where they originate. With a ChannelPlus modulator from Multiplex Technology, you can watch a video tape, laser disc, or other video source on any TV in the house, simply by switching to a certain channel.

What is modulation? Every TV station starts with the electronic signal we call "video." A method is needed to deliver the signals from a lot of stations to a television set, allowing the TV's owner to choose which "video" he wants to watch. Each TV station adds its video signal to a high-frequency carrier. This is called modulation.

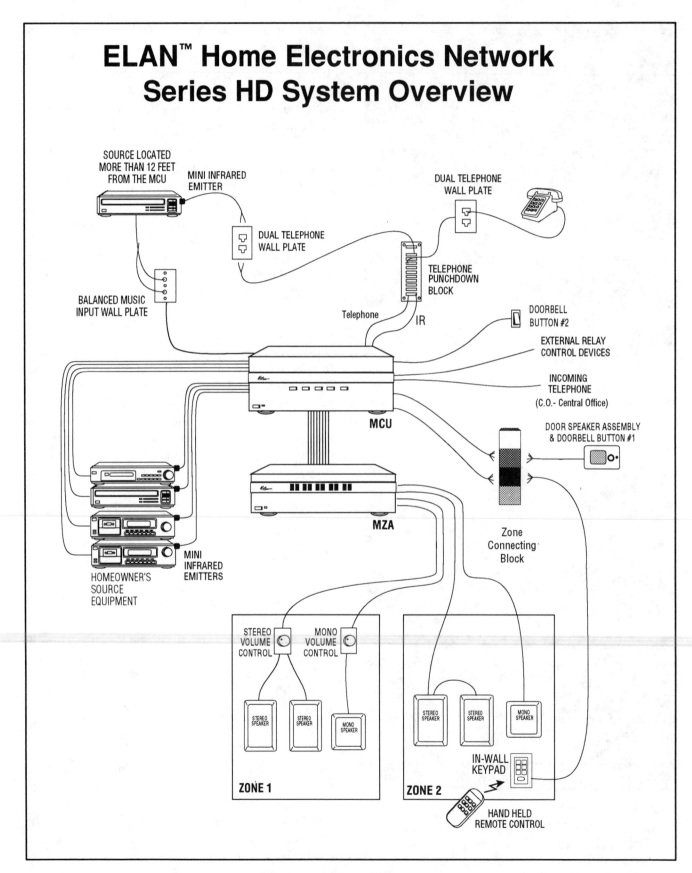

ELAN™ Home Electronics Network
Series HD System Overview

SOURCE LOCATED
MORE THAN 12 FEET
FROM THE MCU

MINI INFRARED
EMITTER

DUAL TELEPHONE
WALL PLATE

DUAL TELEPHONE
WALL PLATE

BALANCED MUSIC
INPUT WALL PLATE

TELEPHONE
PUNCHDOWN
BLOCK

Telephone

IR

DOORBELL
BUTTON #2

EXTERNAL RELAY
CONTROL DEVICES

INCOMING
TELEPHONE
(C.O.- Central Office)

MCU

DOOR SPEAKER ASSEMBLY
& DOORBELL BUTTON #1

MZA

Zone
Connecting
Block

HOMEOWNER'S
SOURCE
EQUIPMENT

MINI
INFRARED
EMITTERS

STEREO
VOLUME
CONTROL

MONO
VOLUME
CONTROL

STEREO
SPEAKER

STEREO
SPEAKER

MONO
SPEAKER

STEREO
SPEAKER

STEREO
SPEAKER

MONO
SPEAKER

IN-WALL
KEYPAD

ZONE 1

ZONE 2

HAND HELD
REMOTE CONTROL

Courtesy of Square D Company.

The different TV stations are assigned different carrier frequencies. All these carriers are transmitted from the TV station antenna to yours. Your TV set contains circuitry that will select a carrier and retrieve the video signal from it. This is called de-modulation. Similarly, a cable company takes many different video signals and modulates each one to a different TV channel. The only difference is that cable companies transmit on cable, rather than through the air.

A local modulator such as ChannelPlus will allow the user to create a carrier with a video signal on it (maybe a front door camera or a satellite receiver). Viewers select the video signal at any TV in the house just like any other TV channel.

The modulator takes the output (signal) from a video source, puts it on an unused channel, and transmits it via coax to any and all TVs tuned to that channel. For example, if VCR output is dedicated to Channel 42, by turning your TV to Channel 42, you can watch a videotape that's playing in the media room. A different channel can be assigned to each video source, including closed circuit television (CCTV) cameras.

A typical multi-room video system with the modulation and wiring for three dedicated entertainment channels, two CCTV cameras, amplification to split and adjust the signal, and a remote control extender costs around $3,000.

SPEAKERS

Installing speakers in several rooms, or surround sound in any room, can lead to a space problem. You may have trouble finding places to put all the speakers unless you build some into the walls. Ideally, a room's main stereo speakers should be directly across from the primary listening area, 6 to 10 feet apart and mounted at the listener's ear level (44 to 45 inches from the floor). Surround-sound speakers should be mounted 2 or 3 feet in front of the listener on the room's side walls. The speakers shouldn't go on the back wall, where listeners near that wall won't hear them. Surround speakers may also be mounted in the ceiling.

Surround-sound speakers, especially the main (front) ones, should be at least 2 feet from the ceiling, floor, or nearest side walls to prevent boomy or uneven bass and distracting reflections in the upper frequencies. Both speakers of a stereo or surround-sound pair should be the same distance from the ceiling, floor, and side walls so one won't have more bass than the other.

In-wall speakers must be installed between wall studs. Installation is easiest if you're building from scratch or have the walls torn apart for major renovation. With everything exposed, you can install a speaker's mounting brackets easily and run wires freely. Speakers are harder to install in exterior walls, especially in existing construction. Exterior walls may have double drywall or drywall over plywood and usually are packed with insulation.

Most in-wall speakers are two-piece systems. A bracket mounts in the wall, and a baffle screws to the bracket from outside the wall, clamping the wall between them. In new construction, you want to mount the frames early, so the drywall installers can cut around them. Enclosing the rear of the speaker will give you better bass. Walls leak and resonate, reducing bass and coloring the sound. Typical drywall construction resonates in the mid-bass range — about 150 Hz.

Most in-wall speakers are small, so they don't reproduce bass well. Adding subwoofers, extra speakers that play only low frequencies, will give you more and better bass. If you hook up in-wall speakers through a crossover, which routes all bass to the subwoofer and is usually provided with it, the small speakers will be able to play louder without the strain that comes from handling low frequencies.

The sound from in-floor subwoofers enters the room through standard heating/air conditioning vents. Subwoofers can be mounted almost anywhere but will sound most natural if they are at the same end of the room as the main speakers.

Keep in mind that a wall cavity is not necessarily an empty space; it can hide lots of surprises. Don't just start drilling. Try to open up a hole first to see what's there. Be alert for plumbing pipes, sewer vent stacks, gas lines, electrical wire, and firebreaks. To improve performance and reduce sound transfer through the wall to another room, you can pack fiberglass insulation behind in-wall speakers. Avoid placing the speakers right in a corner; the bass notes will distort and sound boomy.

At a live concert, most of the sound you hear reflects off the walls, floor, and ceiling. Only a small percentage of the sound reaches your ears directly. This combination of reflected and direct sound is what gives live music its full, rich spaciousness. Bose patented Direct/Reflecting speaker technology re-creates a natural balance of reflected and direct sound, which allows you to experience the realism of a live performance in your home. Plus, you can enjoy the freedom to sit almost anywhere in the room and still hear full stereo. Direct/Reflecting speakers range in price from about $270 a pair for a 2.2 speaker system to $1,500 a pair for the 901 speaker system with equalizer.

A look at the back of your receiver will tell you exactly how many speaker pairs you can hook up to it, by the number of pairs of speaker output connectors in the back — usually two, labeled A and B. What if you want to add a third, fourth, or fifth pair?

If you piggyback more than one set of wires onto one speaker output, you run the risk of blowing up your receiver. Receivers and speakers are designed to operate at a certain impedance, usually 8 or 4 ohms. Piggybacking lowers the impedance, sending a dangerously imbalanced current through the speaker lines.

A speaker distribution system installed near your receiver will take the output for one set of speakers and split it into several lines, feeding sound to as many as 12 pairs of speakers, depending on the particular component. Protection circuits keep the line signals in and out of the receiver in balance at a safe level of resistance.

Systems come in a variety of configurations, including options of manual or automatic engagement of the protection circuits. (If you frequently use just one pair of speakers, the manually engaging circuitry is preferable, as the protection circuits cut the volume output slightly when engaged.) The box requires no AC power connection, but it does need to be installed with its ventilation holes clear.

For multi-room installations, include "in-line" volume controls in the remote rooms. This lets you adjust the volume in the room where you listen to music, no matter how far away your equipment stack is. If the system is in a bedroom, consider installing an in-wall headphone jack. To do this, you just run speaker wire from an amplifier or a receiver to the volume control, and then to the speakers (the control affects only that set of speakers).

If you want more than two speakers, you can't just connect them to your amplifier directly. Doing so could overload the output with too low an impedance and

damage the amplifier. To correct this problem, you can install an EZ-Match Volume Control near each pair of speakers (up to eight pairs of speakers can be wired in parallel to your amp). The EZ-Match provides both in-room volume control and on/off switching plus built-in impedance matching.

Volume controls housed in unobtrusive, freestanding boxes cost about $120; in-wall controls cost about half that. The dial on the box will give you about a 30-decibel volume control in ten steps of three decibels each. The last step cuts the volume completely.

To add remote control to your audio/video system, mount an infrared receiver in the room with your remote speakers. Receivers can mount in-wall (in a single gang electrical J-box) or be hidden behind speaker grills or placed on a shelf. Receivers connect with three telephone wires back to your stereo location, where they are connected to IR emitters that emit the signal to your components. Emitters can be placed directly in front of, attached to, or across the room from your components.

To control each room (or zone) independently, you'll need a separate audio receiver for each zone. In addition, you'll need a Zone Controller, from Video Link, to route control signals from Zone 2 to the Zone 2 amplifier. You'll also need a Distribution Amplifier for each source component (VCR, CD, tape, etc.) so it can connect without loss to all zone audio receivers. This setup allows you to play one source (like a tape) in one zone while playing the same or a different source (like a CD) in a different zone. This provides whole-house audio distribution at a fraction of the cost of professionally installed systems.

Wiring Tips

Wiring the speakers is as important as installing them. Typically rated in the hundreds of watts, speakers require a large wire. Experts recommend using 14 gauge or larger (larger wires have smaller gauge numbers). Anything smaller and you risk damaging your equipment. For runs of up to 80 feet, 16-gauge wire is the minimum for good sound. For longer runs, use 14- or 12-gauge wire. It's more difficult to pull heavier wires through wall cavities.

Buy speaker wires with round insulation jackets. Run speaker wires through their own holes in the studs. Don't use holes that are or will be used for electrical, phone, or

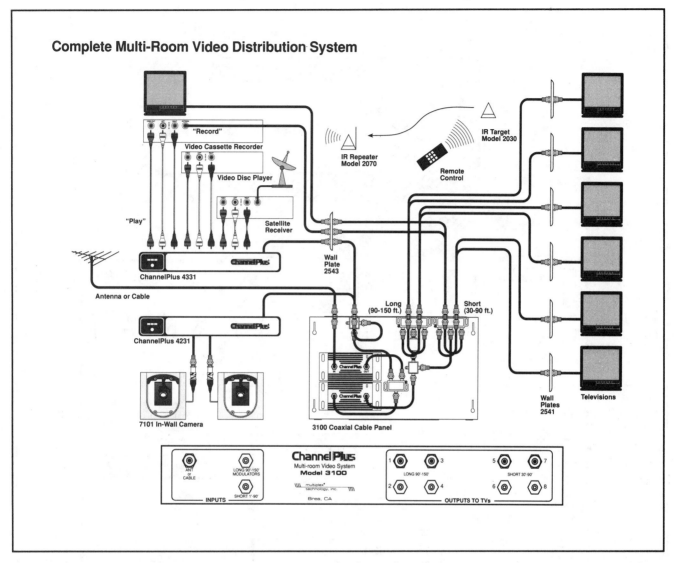

Complete Multi-Room Video Distribution System

The model 3100 Coaxial Cable Panel balances, combines, amplifies, and compensates for different frequencies and cable lengths. With this system, the homeowner can select from the VCR, laser disc player, satellite receiver, two cameras, or the normal cable or off-air programs, by just changing the channel on any TV. He can control the video sources from any TV location. Courtesy of ChannelPlus.

intercom wires. Those wires can cause electrical noise in nearby audio cables. If you must run your stereo-signal wires near electrical cables, don't let them run in parallel for more than 2 or 3 feet, and if possible cross them at 90 degree angles.

Take great care when wiring; one wire hooked up wrong could blow your speakers or receiver. Use wire in a sheathing rated at least CL-2. This designation, which is a fire hazard-reducing electrical code standard, is printed directly on the sheathing. Regular speaker wire is flammable and can act as a fuse. Twisted pairs may be shielded or unshielded. Shielded wires have a foil wrap-

ping around them, which ground out electrical interferences. Wires with a 100% foil shield are the most effective.

When running wire in a crawlspace, get it off the ground, as required by code. Hanging it from floor joists protects it from water as well as from rodents. Don't run wire where you can walk on it; you could rub away the insulation, which could cause a short and blow up your system or start a fire. Give yourself slack on the wires so you can slide components out of the stack when necessary.

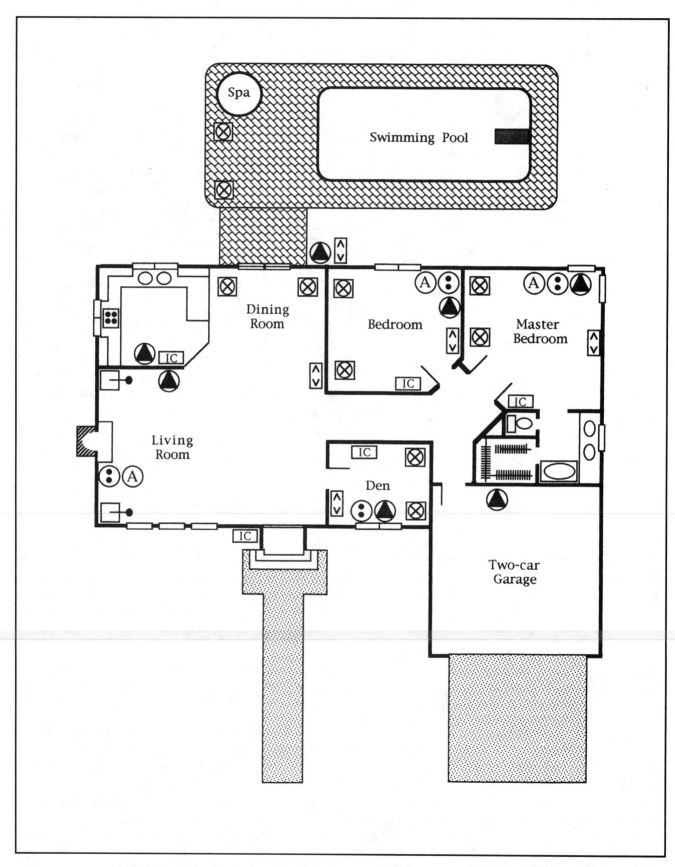

A typical whole-house distributed audio/video system layout. (See key at right.)

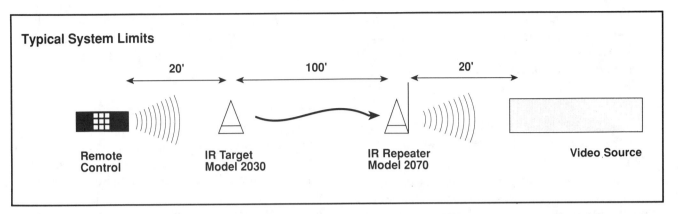

Courtesy of ChannelPlus.

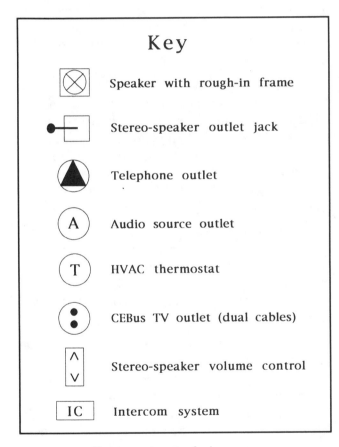

Key to system on facing page.

Identify your wires as you go. Marking them helps make sure you get your final connections right and ensures that the code inspector won't refuse to pass your house because of unidentified wires on the plans.

Experts recommend RG-6 coaxial cable for a stronger signal than the commonly used RG-59. The slightly larger and only slightly more expensive RG-6 has a foil wrap that grounds interference. To maximize the efficiency of RG-6 dual coax wiring, excessive splitting should be avoided. Signals lose strength each time they are split or divided into separate locations. Serious loss can occur when splitting into four or more outlets. To prevent loss, install an audio/video amplifier before splitting.

Installing 75 ohm terminators at each unused outlet also reduces signal loss and interference. The terminators act as resistors, absorbing the signal rather than reflecting it back through the system, which is a common tendency of unattached cables.

MEDIA STORAGE POINTERS

Measure your components before you buy or build. Be sure the shelves are deep enough for your TV and that the doors will close. Allow enough space around components for ventilation. Check your owner's guide to find out how much air space is needed. Look for a pull-out swivel shelf to set the TV on so you can see it from different parts of the room. Be aware that older sets are very heavy. If the TV throws the unit off balance, anchor the unit to a wall. For easy viewing, put the TV screen 30 inches from the floor if the audience will be seated, and 50 inches from the floor if you'll watch it from your bed. Put the VCR and TV in the same compartment so you'll have to open only one door to operate both via your remote control. To accommodate wiring, get a unit with an open back, large holes in the shelves, a triangular hole cut in the back corner of each shelf, or a built-in power strip of plug-ins.

Any armoire or cabinet you plan to use for audio/video storage requires the following:

- Holes for running wires. A tangle of wires connects to the AC plug and hooks the components together. Be sure you can drill holes if they are not provided. Remember that a vintage armoire takes a cut in value when you make a cut in it.

- Air circulation space. To avoid overheating, plan for breathing room around each element in the system. Check owner's manuals for each component's requirements.

- Unblocked speaker locations. Placing speakers behind closed doors defeats the purpose. One alternative? Replace wood doors with a frame stretched with an open-weave fabric.

- Wire-hiding tips. Speaker wires can be run along baseboards, fastened with staples, tacks, or clips. Wires can also hide behind moldings — crown moldings installed near the ceiling are good for this purpose. An 18-gauge lamp cord (available by the foot) works fine as speaker wire and is available in several colors or can be painted to match your molding color.

REMOTE CONTROL SYSTEMS

Early remote controls could only operate very basic functions, such as on/off, up/down volume, and up/down channel. Over the last fifteen years, as technology changed from ultrasonic to infrared, the penetration of remote-controlled devices has increased substantially. Today 75% of all TVs sold have remotes and 68% of all existing TVs are remote controlled; virtually 100% of all VCRs sold have remotes, and 55% of all existing VCRs are remote controlled; nearly 100% of CD players are sold with remotes and 12% of all existing CD players are remote controlled; 45% of all cable TV boxes are remote controlled.

Remote control units operate using one of two different technologies, radio-frequency (RF) or infrared (IR). Products with simple on/off controls use RF signals and typically have a range of about 100 feet. Garage-door openers are one common example of RF technology. Appliances with more complex controls than a simple on/off switch, such as a stereo, typically use IR signals. Unlike RF signals, IR signals require a straight, uninterrupted path to the receiver.

To permit one consumer product to work in the presence of others, manufacturers vary the different parameters of remote design — IR modulation frequency, transmission protocol, data modulation scheme, and finally, the actual data representing the command. Research has uncovered over 100 fundamentally different designs, over 500 code sets, and over 16,000 data representations for the different buttons on remotes.

Universal Remotes

Remote control clutter in the living room or family room and the problems with replacement of lost or broken remotes have led to the development of the universal remote. All the separate IR codes required to operate the various products in the home can reside in one universal remote. Properly employed, universal remotes can make the process of controlling home entertainment products and household appliances as easy as pushing a button from your easy chair. There are two competing technologies used in the production of universal remotes: learning and preprogrammed.

The learning technology was introduced by General Electric in 1985. GE holds patents on this technology and licenses it to other manufacturers. Learning remotes memorize the codes, one by one, from an original remote. Learning is a complex process and can take 15 min-utes or more per original remote. Memory requirements to store codes are high. And while most codes can be learned, not all can.

Learning technology was the first universal remote technology developed. Its weaknesses present serious difficulties for use in home automation. The learning remote is expensive to manufacture. Sophisticated electronics are required to provide the learning technology and to guide the user through the learning process.

The learning remote is also a difficult one for the average consumer to master. The learning process is time consuming and error-prone and some codes are simply unlearnable. But most important, a working original remote is required for the learning process. As a result, learning remotes cannot provide the product features most required in home automation — ease of use and a truly integrated solution for home entertainment and home automation.

Preprogrammed remotes already contain the codes for a number of home entertainment devices. Consumers select their home entertainment devices by searching the internal library or setting codes. One method utilizes small switches found in the battery compartment. You look up the switch settings for your TV or VCR (provided) and set the switches accordingly. Another approach uses a three-digit code that is entered by the consumer into the remote using a keypad. A code book contains a cross reference between manufacturer's models and codes.

Preprogrammed remotes have several key advantages over learning remotes. Since an original remote is not required for setup, a preprogrammed remote can replace lost or broken remotes. Codes for the most popular home entertainment products are installed at the factory. Preprogrammed remotes also cost half as much to manufacture as do learning remotes.

Universal Electronics, Inc.

The One-For-All Universal Remote by Universal Electronics, Inc. has developed a complete library, incorporating the codes for virtually every remote-controlled home entertainment product. Their universal remote control technology used in conjunction with this approach accommodates a changing and growing library. It uses a memory that can be easily changed or updated and includes a serial port that permits updating by downloading new codes from any IBM-compatible computer. Remotes can be reprogrammed as often as necessary; the actual time required for transferring a new set of codes is only about half a minute.

The One-For-All remote is ready for CEBus communications; as soon as the CEBus infrared commands are finalized, Universal can add the new codes to their library. Remotes programmed from this library would then be CEBus compatible. Universal has also pushed directly into home automation with their One-For-All Command Center.

The command center is essentially an X-10 minicontroller that sits on top of the TV or other convenient location and receives infrared commands from the One-For-All remote, and retransmits these as X-10 commands via the house wiring. Thus, the same remote used for the television and VCR can control lights and appliances. Up to 16 units can be controlled as well as ALL LIGHTS ON/ALL LIGHTS OFF commands.

The One-For-All 12 remote replaces twelve separate remotes, controlling TVs, VCRs, cable boxes, CD players, stereo receivers, laser disc players, satellite receivers, stereo tuners, and more.

The One-For-All 12 allows you to turn on a number of IR devices with the touch of one button (macros). The Audio and Video keys can reduce a number of routine

control commands to a single keystroke. Even complex audio/video systems can be powered up with a single key that saves time and adds convenience. You can get all this for less than $100, plus an additional $35 for the Command Center.

The X-10 Infrared Mini Controller (Model IR543) allows you to turn on up to eight lights and appliances anywhere in your home using the same Universal Remote Control (the One-For-All 12, for example) that you use for your TV, VCR, and cable converter. You program the Universal Remote to transmit signals that can be recognized by the Infrared Mini Controller. In addition, the Infrared Mini Controller has the same features as found in an X-10 Mini Controller.

Extenders

If you have a component that came with a remote control — most likely your CD player, although other new components also have remote capability — you can easily extend its sphere of influence to any room in the house. All you need is a pair of infrared "extenders," which come in the shape of pyramids, black boxes, or built-in wall plates.

You place a transmitter unit in any room where you listen to music, and a receiver unit within sight of your equipment stack. When you point your remote control at the transmitter, it converts the remote's infrared signal into a radio frequency signal (like a garage door opener) and transmits the command to the receiver, which turns the signal back into infrared and relays it to the component in the equipment stack.

Avoid placing transmitters where they would face windows, light bulbs, or fireplaces. These light and heat sources can give off enough infrared energy to block out the weaker signal from your remote control.

Powermid

The Powermid from X-10 is a whole-house infrared remote control extender that allows you to control your audio and video components from anywhere in your home. You simply plug the Wireless Receiver/Infrared Emitter (Model RE549) into any AC outlet in an unobstructed location in front of your TV, VCR, stereo, or cable converter. Then plug the Infrared Sensor/Wireless Transmitter (Model ST539) into any AC outlet in the room where you want to use your remote control.

The ST539 senses the infrared signals from your existing remote control and converts the signals into wireless transmissions. The wireless transmissions are then received by the RE549, which converts the wireless signals back to infrared signals and sends them to your TV, stereo, or cable converter. You can add additional sensors and emitters to control all your audio/video components from any room in the house without running wires. The price is also right (about $60 a pair).

Infrared remote control makes operating electronic components such as compact disc and cassette players much more convenient. Because opaque materials block IR signals, shelves housing stereo and video equipment have always needed to be designed either with no doors at all or with glass doors that enable the remote unit to "see" the components.

Hidden Link

A device called the Hidden Link now offers new cabinet-design flexibility: it bypasses solid objects by redirecting remote-control signals. With Hidden Link you can use solid materials on the doors of an entertainment center, yet still operate the equipment without opening the doors.

The Hidden Link system comprises an AC/DC transformer, an infrared receiver that's about 1 inch high and 3¹/₄ inches wide, and an emitter, which transmits the IR signal from the receiver to the components. This basic setup controls one component. For controlling more components, you would need a control box that can handle up to four emitters, one for each component. Hidden Link works with any remote-controlled electronic equipment, including stereo receivers, tape players, VCRs, and CD and laser disc players. The basic Hidden Link system costs about $60. Multiple-component control boxes cost $25; emitters are $12 each.

X-10-Compatible Controllers

It is also possible to control your IR components with X-10-compatible controllers. The IR Trigger allows you to send up to 16 different infrared commands to your audio/video system, triggered from an X-10 signal or any button, switch, or relay. Any of the trigger inputs can be programmed to initiate a sequence of up to ten separate infrared functions, which are stored in a separate 48-code auxiliary memory. The IR Trigger is an advanced learning microprocessor that can memorize up to 16 infrared commands from your existing remote controls.

Think of the possibilities: you could program your X-10 Timer or Enerlogic to wake you with your favorite station playing at just the right volume. Or you could turn your audio/video system on or off while in bed, taking a bath, or answering the phone in the kitchen.

Bose Lifestyle Music System

The Bose CE-1 Control Expander links current infrared remote controllable components to the keyboard-sized Bose Lifestyle Music System (includes a CD player, AM/FM tuner, and RF remote control). This RF configuration enables users to power their rack of audio and video components from any room in the home, through walls, around corners, even through closed cabinet doors. The user simply enters a three-digit code to tell the Lifestyle system the brand of the connecting unit. The CE-1 then translates key commands from the Lifestyle RF remote to the appropriate infrared commands for these components. The CE-1 retails for about $99.

SmarTouch

SmarTouch by Crestron Electronics, Inc. is a completely self-contained wireless touch panel control system complete with IR learner and emitters and an easy-to-use graphics design program. SmarTouch provides a menu-driven "Control Smart" interface to allow you to create control panels just the way you want with an on-board drawing system. SmarTouch requires no special knowledge or computer skills to design your own custom control system. User-defined menus allow quick selection of the control screen so you only view the equipment controls you need.

To further enhance its capabilities, SmarTouch has a complete selection of economically priced interface modules available for control of volume, lighting, screens, draperies, power, computers, temperature, and other environments. These modules include IR detectors that receive the powerful IR signals generated by SmarTouch.

8.

Water Management

Smart water management means employing automation technology to utilize this precious resource more productively. Automating your home's water systems (domestic water, yard/lawn watering, indoor plant watering, pool/spa) will enable you to conserve water and energy and reduce the amount of time needed for routine tasks such as watering the lawn, garden, and indoor plants, and cleaning the pool or spa. Automating these mundane and time-consuming chores frees you to pursue more enjoyable activities. Isn't that what automation is all about?

In this chapter you will learn how to automate your indoor plant watering, yard and lawn watering, pool and spa care, and your home's bath — even the plumbing itself. Many of the systems described in this chapter are relatively inexpensive ($100 to $500) and most are X-10 compatible or can be controlled with X-10 modules and controllers. Some are stand-alone products; others can be interfaced with your whole-house automation system.

INDOOR PLANT WATERING SYSTEMS

Plants are good for our emotional and physical health. It has long been known that plants have a calming effect on us and are good for our well-being, and they are an excellent natural air filter system, turning carbon dioxide into fresh oxygen and water vapor. Research has determined that plant leaves, roots, and soil bacteria are all important in removing trace levels of toxic vapors associated with indoor air pollution, sometimes called "sick building syndrome." But along with these benefits, plants also bring one problem: the time-consuming care required. While some people consider plant care an enjoyable hobby, many others are either unwilling or unable to put their time and energy into this task. People who travel a great deal are especially concerned with this problem. But now, new technology in the home automation field has given the plant owner an alternative to watering plants manually.

Precision micro-irrigation systems are engineered to provide fully automated service. These systems are designed to consistently maintain user-selected, optimum levels of moisture for each plant, providing a proper balance of moisture and oxygen around the roots at all times. Frequent, gentle irrigation cycles, with moisture concentrated at one or two zones of application, are now shown to be the preferred watering method for maintaining healthy indoor plants. Watering in this manner allows moisture to diffuse throughout the soil mass between irrigation cycles without starving the roots of oxygen or causing undue soil dehydration. This balance of moisture and oxygen levels most closely resembles conditions found in the native rainforest environments of most interior plants.

Aqua/Trends
The Mirage Series from Aqua/Trends is a fully-automated, multi-plant central system designed for watering interior and patio potted plants. The Mirage system makes use of electronics and hydraulics to control water flow and is primarily geared to the needs of plants in commercial and residential settings that require low irrigation volumes and precise water placement. Centralized plant irrigation systems can function as stand-alone units or as networks that permit complete site coverage. Techniques have been developed to interface micro-irrigation capabilities with the microprocessor-based automation systems of "smart" buildings, including X-10 control.

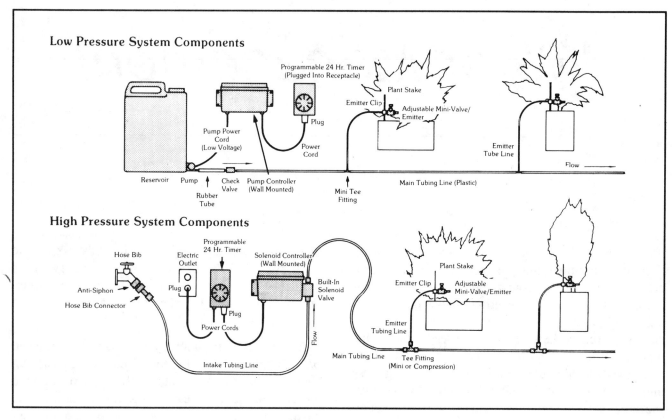

Plant watering systems. Courtesy of Aqua/Trends.

Irrigation systems can be integrated into new construction or retrofitted into existing homes. Systems range in complexity from do-it-yourself kits to complex contractor-installed systems. Installation kits and components are available for interior as well as exterior uses. Automated irrigation systems not only make plant care easier, they change the way the plants are watered. Instead of receiving large amounts of water and then being allowed to dry out, the plants receive small amounts at close intervals, so the moisture level remains constant.

Types of Irrigation Systems

There are two types of irrigation systems, low-pressure and high-pressure. The difference between the two lies in the method of creating the pressure that causes water to flow through the system. Low-pressure versions use a heavy plastic reservoir with a small mounted pump to motivate flow. They are used when connections to a cold water pipe are not readily available. Because the reservoir must be periodically refilled, a low-pressure system cannot be accurately considered fully automatic.

A high-pressure system connects to the home's cold water plumbing and relies on home water pressure to

create flow. With access to a continuous water source, this type of system is fully automatic and can operate indefinitely without much attention. Both systems use short pulses of water flow, only ten or twenty seconds in duration, which is just enough to furnish the limited amount of moisture plants need. In the average home installation, this is repeated twice daily, at regular intervals. Indoor plants require much less water than their outdoor counterparts, because lower light levels slow a plant's metabolism.

For most systems, independent time switches are used to power the equipment according to programmed schedules. These timers provide "windows of power" just long enough to activate the controllers that run the pumps or solenoid valves and cause water to flow for the designated periods. Some models have electromechanical and electric timers built in, but most use external timers. The advantage of these more common types is that timerless controllers make it easier for a micro-irrigation system to interface with the home's central control system.

Another common element is that both versions use special centrally located controllers that power the activating elements — pumps or solenoid valves — for very short periods. Control centers can be mounted in central locations for easy access, while water distribution networks can be routed from the central controller to all existing and potential plant locations. Tubing is installed in a manner to hide it from view, in much the same way as wiring and plumbing are routed through walls. The tubing is generally small-diameter, flexible PVC, polyethylene, or polybutylene. Polybutylene tubing is used in partitions and other enclosed spaces, as it meets most local plumbing codes and does not require soldered fittings.

Various flow devices, such as check valves, are installed in the tubing lines to control water flow volume, pressure, and direction whenever necessary. Of these devices, check-valves are the most useful. They are particularly helpful in keeping the tubes full of water and free of air, eliminating the need for air purges at the beginning of each irrigation cycle. The emitter tubing used at the plant location is small in diameter and generally made of clear plastic, to make it less visible. Pigmented, opaque tubing can be used where algae growth is a problem.

Adjustable mini-valve emitters are located at each plant to allow for fine tuning of the water flow. This precise control permits the watering of small, dry-loving plants to be serviced at the same time as large plants needing greater amounts of water. It also provides system flexibility by permitting a station to be closed down when a plant is removed, or to provide a watering station for future use. A number of plants can be fed water from each emitter tub, by branching them off and using an adjustable mini-valve at each plant. Tube branches of this type can traverse 50 feet or more.

Special irrigation receptacles have been developed by Aqua/Trends to access tubing lines routed through walls. Like electrical outlets, they are mounted on wall surfaces at convenient points around the room. Emitter tubes that feed the plants (up to 50 feet) are connected to the outlets. By branching the tubing, up to 15 small to medium-sized plants can be serviced from a single receptacle. These tubes can be hidden under carpet edges, behind furniture or decorative molding. Inactive receptacles are simply plugged until needed.

Installation of Aqua/Trends Mirage is quick and easy, requiring no special tools or expertise. Full instructions are included with all units. Most tubing fittings are slip-on or hand-tightened compression types. Tubing is plas-

tic, easily cut with sharp knives. Electrical connections are common plug-in types and require no special knowledge or skill. Controllers are mounted on the wall inside of utility rooms, closets, cabinets, or garages, behind furniture and planters, or in other out-of-the-way places where they can be hidden. Timers are plugged into 24-hour electrical outlets. Main tubing lines are laid toward the farthest planter locations. At each plant a cut is made into the tubing line, a mini-tee connector is inserted, and a short piece of tubing is run from it to the planter pot.

An adjustable mini-valve/emitter is fitted to the end of the short tube and secured in place with a special clip and plant stake. Tubing that cannot be hidden under carpeting can be hidden in metal or plastic "wire-mold" affixed to the baseboards. Plastic baseboard cove molding is also effective. Plumbers can install "small-bore" copper tubing into walls, floors, and drop-ceiling plenums during construction to facilitate easier installation.

The specific moisture requirements of individual plants vary, depending on an array of factors, including plant size, growing medium porosity, ambient temperature, light levels, airflow conditions, growth cycle activity, the use of mulch, and container composition. Adjustments in irrigation applications, based on these criteria and others, are needed to ensure that plants receive the proper moisture levels. Most adjustments are made during the first six weeks of system operation, as plants adapt to their new conditions. Some modifications may be also needed later, however, due to changes in plant needs or site conditions. Experience has shown that most common sizes and varieties of container plants used indoors require roughly one-half ounce to two ounces of water, dispensed twice daily.

Plants with special watering needs can be accommodated by making adjustments in the application amounts, the application frequencies, or the types of equipment used. For example, plants that prefer dry conditions, such as cacti, can have their needs met by adjusting irrigation volumes to very small increments. Similarly, large plants or those that have greater moisture requirements can have their needs met by applying water more frequently or by using larger or multiple emitters.

While no technology is capable of completely replacing human plant care, micro-irrigation systems provide a number of benefits: Because these systems seek to maintain an optimum balance between root zone moisture and oxygen levels, many plant problems, such as root rot and moisture stress, can be minimized. In addition, these systems cut waste in watering. Because plants on properly adjusted systems are kept from drying out between waterings, the need to apply greater amounts of water to rewet them is eliminated. Soil surface tension does not have to be overcome. Runoff and overflow are eliminated, too. Proper planning and installation can provide an automated plant care system valuable not only for maintaining attractive plant life, but also enhancing the home's indoor air quality and overall livability.

For further information on automated indoor irrigation systems, I suggest *Building Interiors, Plants and Automation* by Stuart D. Snyder. Mr. Snyder provides a complete understanding of automated, precision micro-irrigation systems, representing state-of-the-art interior irrigation technology. Everything is thoroughly discussed, from uses, recommended equipment and techniques, to system design, installation, and operation. Mr. Snyder is also the founder and president of Aqua/Trends, Boca Raton, FL.

YARD SPRINKLERS

For some, yard care is a hobby, but for others it is simply another dreaded weekend chore. Automation provides "upon demand" yard watering that will water your lawn, trees, shrubs, and flowers only as needed, leading to a drastic reduction in the amount of time and money you need to spend tending your yard. Automation can be as simple as one or more inexpensive programmable timers connected directly to the sillcock or a full-blown intelligent system tied into your whole-house automation system. Automated lawn systems are available from such manufacturers as Rain Bird and WeatherMatic.

Automatic timer models are convenient, inexpensive, and easy to use but are not truly automated unless they allow for intelligent decision making. An automated system will utilize information gathered from attached sensors such as rain, moisture, humidity, and wind to determine when the yard needs watering and to turn off sprinklers automatically if it starts to rain or the wind comes up. Drip irrigation systems for your trees, shrubs, flowers, and garden can also be controlled by an automated system, providing for complete hands-off, worry-free maintenance of your home's landscaping.

A "smart" water management system incorporates a programmable timer, to allow for an efficient watering schedule, and sensors that monitor weather conditions, such as current temperature, wind speed and direction, humidity, barometric pressure, and daily precipitation. These systems adjust the programmed watering schedule according to soil conditions and weather data fed into its microprocessor-based controllers by various sensors, such as soil moisture sensors and rain sensors. Soil moisture sensors measure the amount of water present in the soil. If the moisture is above a certain level, the sensor will send a message to the main controller to cancel the scheduled watering in that zone until the soil is dry again. Rain falling into the open mouth of a rainfall sensor make a electrical connection that sends a signal to the controller to shut off the watering.

POOLS AND SPAS

Wouldn't it be nice to arrive home after a long day at work to take a hot, relaxing dip in your spa? The problem is that in order to keep the spa heated and ready whenever you are, the spa must be kept on at all times — quite a costly proposition. By automating your spa and pool, you can automatically program your system to turn on and off to suit your own schedule. Automation allows you to remotely control your pool or spa from any touchtone phone, including your car phone. When you're on the way home from the office, just pick up your car phone and call home to turn on the spa. When you arrive, your spa will be heated to perfection and ready for that soothing dip.

Pool Management Center

The Pool Management Center (PMC) from American Products allows you to control pool functions, waterfall functions, backyard security lighting, and more — from anywhere in your home or yard. Because the PMC is X-10 compatible, installation is easy. With the PMC wireless remote, operation of your pump, heater, valves, lighting, and other control functions is right in the palm of your hand.

All the electric circuitry required to activate the system's various lights, motors, and valves is safely located in the PMC's control center. The control center contains a master clock and timers that automatically control the filtration and cleaning systems for your pool and spa. An automatic cool-down feature protects your heater by running cool water through it after the spa has been turned off. Systems are available with up to eight remote control functions and are equipped with American Products exclusive Seal Saver feature, which automatically monitors water flow to the pump for optimum protection. You can choose from a host of options including freeze protection for the circulation system, SMART Dual Speed Motor Control, plus interfaces for solar heaters and cleaner pumps.

Autospa

Another choice in pool/spa remote control is the X-10-compatible Autospa IV from Chardonnay. The Autospa allows you to control up to two jet pumps, one or two air pumps, and spa and pool lights (500 watts each). Autospa provides filter pump time-clock bypass, pool cleaner disable, heater thermostat switching (LO/HI), and OFF (without stopping spa circulation). You can easily integrate the Autospa with your existing X-10 system of controllers and modules, allowing complete control from anywhere inside or outside your home.

Aquabot Turbo

Imagine relaxing on a chaise longue, by the pool, with a cold glass of lemonade in your hand, while "cleaning" your pool. Just a dream? The Aquabot Turbo from AquaProducts, Inc. can do all this and more. The Aquabot Turbo is a fully computerized automatic pool cleaner requiring no installation or supervision. Each Aquabot is equipped with its own step-down transformer that converts standard 110V to 24 volts. Simply plug it into any standard 110V grounded outlet and it's ready to go. It is preprogrammed to cover the bottom, walls (including the waterline), and steps of most pools: vinyl, gunite, fiberglass, or concrete. Onboard computers direct the Aquabot to move in a random preprogrammed forward, reverse, and lateral pattern allowing the unit to clean up to 3,000 square feet per hour. Aquabot automatically shuts off after seven consecutive hours of operation, eliminating overcleaning.

Aquabot will scrub, vacuum, and filter out all types of debris and dirt, including algae growth and other particles down to two microns in size, in its own reusable filter bag. This eliminates the need for frequent backwash of your pool filter and therefore saves thousands of gallons of water each year. By mixing the cold and heavily chlorinated water off the pool bottom with the warm and chlorine-starved surface water, it saves up to 30% of your pool chemicals, as well as raising the pool temperature by approximately 5 degrees. AquaProducts, Inc. also offers the Aquabot Turbo Remote Control,

which enables you to steer the Aquabot directly to any visible dirt in your pool with the touch of a button.

DOMESTIC WATER AUTOMATION

Automate your plumbing? Even though you may not have considered your domestic water system as something that can be automated, there are several functions that would benefit from automation. For starters, automatically fill your bath to the perfect temperature, without worrying about overflow, so that it's ready and waiting when you get home (much as you would your spa). Automation allows you complete control of your home, lights, audio/video, and HVAC (you can even answer the front door!) while relaxing in that hot bath. Water leak sensors alert you and automatically shut off the water line upon detecting a leak. You can even automate your sump pump to prevent water flooding the basement.

Ultraflo

Ultraflo offers an automated plumbing system that replaces your conventional plumbing system. Ultraflo's "pushbutton plumbing" system replaces regular faucet controls with several buttons to control water temperature and flow rate. With Ultraflo, you only need one pipe instead of the standard two. The water is mixed to the desired temperature at a central valve unit near the water heater and then delivered to the faucet. The Ultraflo system is priced comparably to standard plumbing and offers energy-savings economy.

Autofill Bath System

Kohler, the long-time plumbing fixture manufacturer, also offers an automated bath product, the Autofill Bath System. This system allows the user to program the bath to fill at any preset time and to a preset temperature. The Autofill Bath System can be used in new installations as well as retrofitted to tubs with the appropriate Kohler hardware.

Ambiance System

Perhaps the ultimate in bathroom automation currently available is American Standard's Ambiance System. When used in conjunction with the Sensorium whirlpool, this multi-function control allows users to control their environment, both in the bath and throughout the house.

The Ambiance system is controlled by a wall-mounted unit and a remote control. These allow the whirlpool to be programmed to fill up to a day in advance, or the tub can be told to fill over a telephone interface. The user also has control over the bathroom's lighting and audio/video systems, five remote devices throughout the house, and a security camera. Doors can be locked or unlocked from the tub and the handheld remote contains a touchtone phone with a number of advanced features. At $25,000, the Ambiance system is aimed at the high-end market.

Basement Watchdog

Sump pump problems are perhaps the most traumatic of all household dilemmas. In most cases, you don't know that the sump pump isn't working until it's too late and the basement is flooded. Help is finally here with the Basement Watchdog, a unique microprocessor-based, AC/DC sump pump system. It can be used as a main sump pump or as a battery backup system to the main pump. Basement Watchdog continually monitors itself, checking battery and pump status every day. It displays the number of hours it has pumped, and sounds an alarm if there are any problems. In the event of a power failure, Basement Watchdog automatically switches to battery power. When there is too much water for the primary pump to handle, the Basement Watchdog automatically begins pumping.

9.
Whole House Automation

Integrated whole-house automation systems provide enhanced capabilities, compatibility with future home automation standards, and greater economy and value. Integrated systems are also easier to operate than individual systems. Such systems relieve the homeowner of the mundane tasks of arming/disarming security, setting up lighting, and activating the answering machine. An integrated system can initiate a whole set of unrelated commands with the touch of a button or two. Because it's easier to use, an integrated system is more likely to be used.

Homeowners who want to add home control features to their current security system can do so with gateways (interfaces) that link one system to another and have them operate as a single system. Most of the whole-house automation systems are capable of interfacing with your current security system.

Whole-house integrated home automation systems are, for the most part, sold through a network of authorized dealers trained to install and maintain the systems they sell. Because these are integrated systems, there is no need to worry about system compatibility and duplication of function. A basic whole-house system typically starts at about $2,000 and goes up from there.

However, do-it-yourselfers can achieve many of the same results with on- or off-line microprocessor-based or PC-based system controllers for less than $500. These controllers are easy to install (most simply plug into an AC outlet) and program (most are very user-friendly). They control your home's functions via X-10-compatible modules. (The next chapter on PC-Based Home Automation includes a more detailed explanation of these controllers.)

In this chapter, all of the whole-house integrated home control systems currently available are outlined (in alphabetical order). All the whole-house systems listed can control a home's basic functions, such as security, HVAC, entertainment, lighting, and appliances. All have microprocessor-based master controllers, which are the brains of the system and control all the various subsystems. Most systems can be controlled via touchscreens, keypads, touchtone phones, or handheld remote controls, and can respond to situations and preprogrammed or timed events.

AMX

The AMX home automation system is a powerful, software-driven central processor designed to consolidate all electrical controls into one simple operation. Draperies, skylights, and other decor elements can be adjusted for any occasion. The spa can be programmed to switch on or off and lighting levels can be adjusted throughout the entire home or by individual room.

The AMX system can be linked interactively with your master security panel, allowing you to send a signal to arm or disarm the entire system, as well as manipulate the closed circuit cameras. By interfacing the AMX system with the heating and cooling controller, you can adjust whole-house or zone temperatures for different times of the day, providing centralized comfort control with a single command. For home entertainment centers, the AMX master control system provides fingertip

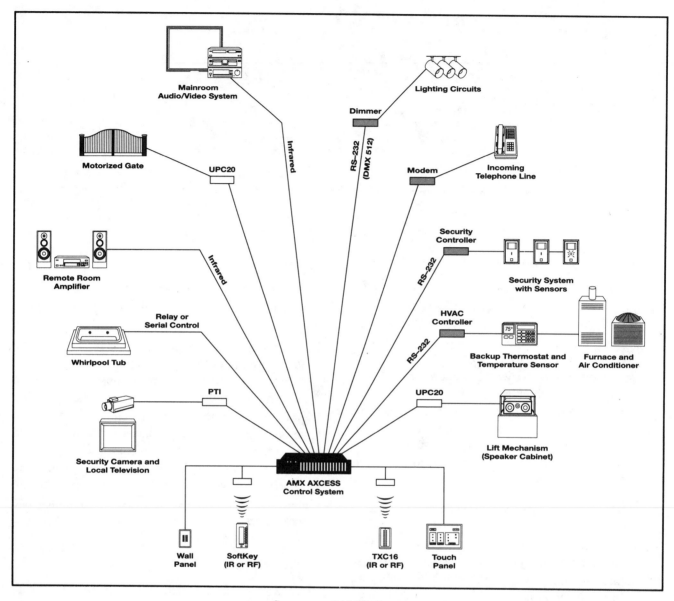

Courtesy of AMX Corp.

control of every element whether you have an elaborate home theater or a complex assortment of electronic components.

AMX offers two systems to choose from: the AXCESS and the AXCENT. The AXCESS system is capable of infinite expansion through its modular card slot design. It is ideal for those who desire "whole-house" control. The AXCENT system, although not expandable, is specially designed for smaller applications with more limited control requirements, such as a home theater.

The AXCESS System is modular in design, so all components can be configured to meet your precise

specifications. The AXP-EL Touch Panel features simple pull-down menus that allow you to change functions, resize, relabel, and add images, which may also be personalized. You can even program the system using your own personal computer, and access can be limited to certain functions.

The AXCESS CardFrame is the foundation of the AXCESS System. The CardFrame is easy to install and accessible from the front, so expansion and equipment changes are as easy as adding or changing cards. Occupying only $3\frac{1}{2}$ inches of a standard 19-inch rack space, the frame has slots for one or two AXC-M Master Cards, one AXC-S Server Card, and 16 device cards. The

AMX TiltScreen Touch Panel. Courtesy of AMX Corp.

AMX Axcess CardFrame. Courtesy of AMX Corp.

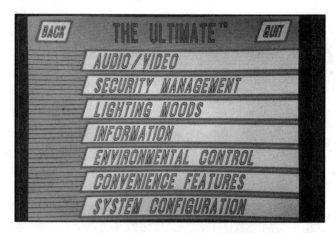

Examples of touchscreen commands for The Ultimate.
Courtesy of Custom Command Systems.

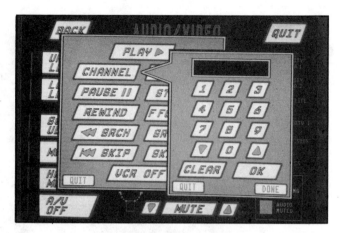

Examples of touchscreen commands for The Ultimate.
Courtesy of Custom Command Systems.

system can also expand to accommodate as many devices as required by the application.

AXCESS peripherals include PC1 and PC2 power controllers, which provide easy, affordable remote control of AC power. Typical applications include turning on/off film projectors, fluorescent or incandescent lights, slide projectors, and audio systems. The MC1 peripheral is a low-voltage control device designed to operate high-voltage bi-directional motors. It is compatible with most motorized screens, draperies, blinds, etc.

Compatible with the entire line of AXCESS control panels, AXCENT offers the same power and programmability as its big brother, but is intended for use in smaller applications. AXCENT offers a broad range of equipment control options and provides front panel switches to allow simple modification of communication parameters.

CUSTOM COMMAND SYSTEMS

The Ultimate by Custom Command Systems combines all of the electronic subsystems in your home: security, audio/video entertainment, lighting, HVAC control, telephone/intercom, plumbing, and information control in one unified package. Custom Command offers five types of control devices, including full-color touchscreens, touchtone telephones, handheld remotes, voice recognition, and touch switches. Though The Ultimate is very sophisticated, it is very easy to use.

The touchscreen uses a full-color, high-resolution video monitor and incorporates state-of-the-art resistive thin-film technology to provide accurate, long-lasting per-

formance. In addition to being used as a control device, the touchscreen can be used to display digitized graphic artwork, the picture from a security camera, or a program from your TV or VCR.

Detailed floor plans of the home make it easy and convenient to operate audio, video, security, heating/cooling, and other subsystems using the touchscreens. Custom Command was the first to use touchscreens that feature "lift-off" technology. With lift-off, the selectable area you are touching highlights immediately but activates only when you lift your finger from the screen. Lift-off technology greatly reduces "false touches" on displays that have many selectable areas.

Custom Command systems are based on a modular design and open architecture, which allows for future expansion and ensures compatibility with a wide variety of products and subsystems. Interfaces allow the Custom Command system to monitor and control every feature of subsystems, such as security, distributed audio/video, HVAC, etc. The system controller manages the operation of the subsystems, each of which can also operate independently. This means that if something happens to the Custom Command System, you can still operate subsystems using their own controls.

The Ultimate is capable of advanced security functions including video security monitoring, driveway monitoring, outdoor security monitoring, remote door locking/unlocking, gate controls, access logging, and much more. Lighting can be programmed to turn on when you enter a room and off after you leave. Scene lighting is also possible, as well as vacation and random security modes.

The Ultimate can interface with your home theater or whole-house audio/video system and provides CD Library Management and entertainment following. With entertainment following, you can have music follow you as you move throughout the house. Motorized windows, skylights, blinds, draperies, fans, and doors can also be controlled. In short, The Ultimate can control nearly every home function imaginable.

The Ultimate starts at about $60,000 and goes up from there. The Entertainer and The Guardian include the features of The Ultimate having the widest market appeal, but can be designed and installed more quickly and less expensively. The Guardian is primarily a home security system and starts at $40,000, and the Entertainer is for home entertainment. Both systems can be upgraded to The Ultimate.

DOMAIN 6000

The Domain 6000 by Intelligent Systems Inc. is a touchscreen-based control system unique in that it uses fiber optics for communications between the central controller, sensors, and appliances. Fiber optics, "light pipes" not prone to the electrical interference that can affect common copper wiring, are considered the current state of the art in communication systems. A completely installed system is about $9,300.

The touchscreen features high resolution color displays and is customized to show the house's floor plan, with icons or pictographs for devices controlled by the system. Types of screens include a Weather Center Display, Security Trace Display, and a Thermostat Program. The system can support up to four separate touchscreens located throughout the house. You can also use a personal computer to program the touchscreen.

The Weather Center Display gives you current meteorologic conditions around the house. The Thermostat Program shows any sensor and displays temperature settings by specific date and time. The Security Trace Display records the date and time for any sensor that was tripped by an intruder. Schedules can be created for nighttime and vacation operations.

The Domain 6000 uses a UL-rated Power Module to control the home AC power line. When the module receives a fiber optic light signal, it switches the line (in less than 0.2 seconds). The line is activated from the touchscreen, three-button module, or keypad. The sys-

tem is also capable of controlling X-10 devices (up to 256). For each half hour of operation, the line can automatically be turned on based on motion, outside light intensity, combination of motion and light intensity, temperature, time of day, and random on/off.

HOME AUTOMATION, INC.

The Model 1503 version 2 Home Control and Security System by Home Automation, Inc. integrates security and home control to provide an affordable system that controls security, temperature, lighting, and appliances. Each system is customized for the user's individual lifestyle and needs. The average system costs $3,000 to $8,000 installed.

The system has 22 zones (expandable to 80) for burglary, fire, and emergency protection and can control 64 (expandable to 128) devices using X-10-compatible control modules, direct wire relays, or temperature sensors. A built-in digital communicator reports alarm events to a central station. A solid state voice dialer is also available.

Lights, appliances, heating and cooling systems, and the integrated security system can be scheduled by time and date, by darkness, or by event, using the console keys and display. Security sensors can be used to activate lights and relay outputs, even when the security system is off. Control programs can be conditioned by darkness, time, or the status of an input. Multiple control outputs can be activated using one command. Homeowners can manually override the system by turning lights on and off as they normally would.

The system has "modes" of operation, such as HOME, AWAY, and ASLEEP that determine the level of security required as well as the indoor temperatures and light levels. Homeowners can easily select the desired mode using a control panel. Special modes can be configured for entertaining or going on vacation.

Model 1503 v 2 systems include Telephone Access, a feature that allows the homeowner to use any touchtone phone anywhere (inside or outside the home) to control his home. This feature is used to check the status of the system or to change settings of security, temperature, or lighting.

The Model 1503 v 2 is UL listed for Grade A Residential Burglary, Fire, Home Health Care, and Digital Communicator. It has numerous features to prevent false alarms,

The Home Manager by Unity Systems controls heating, cooling, security systems, lights, and appliances from a single touchscreen.

including an inside sounder and lights that activate before the outside siren. Home Automation, Inc. systems are professionally installed, serviced, and monitored 24 hours a day by independent security dealers.

HOME MANAGER

The Home Manager from Unity Systems Inc. is a fully integrated home control system that provides room-by-room security and multi-zone temperature control, as well as centralized scheduling and control of a home's lighting and appliances. Unity Systems is the best-selling automated home control system on the market with a network of 175 dealers and over 2,500 installations nationwide.

The system utilizes a sophisticated computer and a wall-mounted touchscreen that displays each home's unique floor plan and simple, step-by-step instructions enabling the homeowner to set up the home's actions to comple-

ment his lifestyle. The homeowner simply touches the screen to activate room-by-room heating and cooling schedules; arm and disarm security zones; set up security access privileges; or schedule appliances, outdoor equipment, and lighting.

The homeowner can also use a personal computer mouse or keyboard to step through the same instructions that display on the touchscreen. An Expansion Module is available for adding control for customers wanting to expand their current systems cost effectively.

The Home Manager provides great security capability, protecting up to 24 individual zones, including fire and smoke detection devices. The homeowner may instantly assign separate passcodes for cleaning, repair, or delivery people, limiting their access to specific times, days, and security zones. Unity's Home Manager accepts most standard sensors including infrared, ultrasonic, microwave, mechanical, magnetic, vibration, pressure, and screen circuits.

The touchscreen provides a log (location and time) of security zone activation and current status. Up to eight remote keypads can be included with each system for added convenience. In addition to arming/disarming the security system, keypads can scan outside and inside temperatures and conveniently turn on/off lights and appliances. The system has a backup power supply and a voice synthesizer and telephone interface for remote operation and control from a touchtone telephone or remote personal computer.

Home Manager controls up to 72 power line (X-10) modules or relays over your home's existing wiring. Any relay not used for temperature control is available to control hardwired low-voltage electrical devices such as yard sprinkler systems. The system accepts up to 96 sets of user-defined instructions based on time, temperature, or security trip events.

Climate control is achieved by using solid state temperature sensors and motorized dampers to control the HVAC system in each zone. The homeowner may define individual temperature settings for every room in the house, then vary those schedules based on weekdays, weekends, or vacations.

Unity's Home Manager is UL listed for household fire, burglary, and process management and can be installed in new or existing homes. A typical installed system costs between $6,000 and $15,000 depending on the size of the home, options, and installation specifications. Case studies of actual residences and buildings controlled by Home Manager have demonstrated energy savings of up to 60% over a year's time.

Unity's new Universal Controller is designed to provide homeowners with convenient, automated control of room-by-room temperatures, lights, appliances, home security, and other home automation applications. In its initial versions, the primary application for the Universal Controller is zoned heating and cooling control. Upgrade options will be available to provide automatic scheduling of indoor and outdoor lights, home security, appliances, and other home control applications. Unity estimates the installed cost of a Universal Controller to start at less than $5,000 and to go as high as $20,000, depending on options chosen by the homeowner.

The Universal Controller system consists of a main control panel and Universal Touchpad for day-to-day operation. The touchpad has only six keys and a multi-line LCD display panel providing simple and easy-to-follow menu choices. A PC is needed for initial configuration but is not necessary for ongoing operation (a PC may be used as an optional user interface). Expansion options include additional Touchpads and networked Universal Controllers, specialty application cards, and sensors and dampers for multi-zone HVAC control.

Each Universal Controller can provide up to 12 individual temperature zones and can control nearly any type of HVAC equipment. Different temperature settings can be scheduled for every zone, varying between house modes (different temperatures for each room during Sleep, Wake, Vacation, etc.) as desired to maximize comfort and energy efficiency.

Examples of products Unity plans to interface its new system with (via application-specific communication cards) are home security systems, lighting control systems, entertainment control and distribution systems, keypads and color touchscreens, and products designed to communicate between utility providers and the home. Unity plans to develop communication cards to support CEBus, Echelon, Honeywell's HBus, and other standards as they emerge on the market.

MAESTRO

Maestro, from CSI, controls your home via a computerized, microprocessor-based control unit using If ... Then logic. The Remote Control is used to enter commands and manipulate all Maestro functions. Commands are displayed on your television for easy setup and modification via handheld RF remote or touchtone phone.

Modular cards (System, Zone, Relay, Phone, Video, RF, Powerline Interface) administer Maestro's many functions. System cards interface with and control the HVAC system. Zone cards control the motorized or flexible duct dampers, allowing for zoned heating and cooling. Relay cards act as switches and have two positions — open and closed — to control various devices, such as fans, sprinkler systems, etc.

Phone cards allow commands to be implemented through any touchtone telephone via local or remote phone. The Video card allows Maestro to be displayed on your television. RF cards receive the radio frequency signals from the Remote Controller. The Powerline Interface interprets the signal sent from Maestro, which controls the power line carrier devices.

Mastervoice's Butler-in-a-Box is an affordable X-10-compatible voice-activated home control system. Courtesy of Mastervoice, Inc.

Courtesy of Mastervoice, Inc.

Maestro uses sensor input to tell the system what's happening and allow it to manage your home. Maestro uses both digital and analog sensors (32 each). Digital sensors monitor the open or closed status of a switch. Analog sensors monitor range of conditions (light/dark, hot/cold, wet/dry) by converting the resistance of the sensor to a number between 0 and 4096. Through these sensors Maestro: "sees" light, dark, and motion; "feels" temperature and moisture.

Maestro software has two main features: Homeowner and Setup. The Homeowner feature is composed of four applications: Genie, Climate Override, Event Report, and Display. The Setup feature is composed of three applications: Genie, Climate Control, and Miscellaneous Functions. Each feature has applications with individual functions and its own set parameters. The applications are accessed through commands using the Remote Control and displayed on easy to read screens through your television.

The Command Mode (Genie) allows you to control any device with the touch of a few buttons. Up to ten different commands may be controlled. The Climate Override application allows the user to manually access

and control specific functions of the Climate Control such as temporarily changing a zone's setpoint, activating the Vacation mode, or changing the System Mode. Maestro automatically logs events as they occur and displays them on the Event Report screen (up to ten different events may be defined). The Display application shows the status of the digital and analog sensors, power line carrier outputs, and relay outputs.

Maestro is designed to incorporate new technology into its system as advances occur, which means that new technology won't render the Maestro system obsolete.

MASTERVOICE

The Butler-in-a-Box home automation system from Mastervoice Inc. is a two-user voice-activated control system with speech output that allows the user to operate all appliances, lights, and telephones through four modes of operation: time, touch, voice, and situation. The system uses the existing household wiring to remotely control devices by using carrier current modules (X-10).

The most unusual aspect of the Butler-in-a-Box is that it responds to voice commands and answers with speech of its own. The system recognizes any language or dialect, and operates (with the noise cancellation feature) in a room full of household noise from up to 20 feet away. It's both speaker dependent and independent. The Butler must be trained for each command by each person in the house. Once trained, the system recognizes specific words. The user trains certain categories of words in sections, such as Commands, Devices, Phone, and Alarm.

The system also has a built-in telephone that is totally hands free and allows the user to remotely dial, answer, and speak on the phone. To allow more flexibility, "macros" will allow several preprogrammed devices to complete several functions. Macros can work by voice or time or through Remote Telephone Access. The system has 99 "smart" timers that allow any chosen appliance to be turned on or off at specific times of day.

Remote Telephone Access allows (through touchtone phone) access to control devices from inside or outside the home. The system also has a built-in alarm system that can detect intruders and request that they identify themselves by giving the correct password.

Voice Mouse is a memory resident program that will allow communication between any Mastervoice system, via the system's serial port, and your personal computer, via the communication port (COM). Voice Mouse will recognize the appropriate ASCII characters and translate them into a series of keystrokes that will enable voice commands recognized by your Mastervoice system to be interpreted and expanded into keyboard commands. This allows you to run nearly any computer program you wish by voice command.

Mastervoice can interface with Memorex infrared remote controls and Remote Control Extender to allow you to operate your remote control equipment — VCR, cable TV, stereo, CD player, draperies, etc. — from any room in your house. The Extender is also compatible with your existing remotes or Universal remotes.

By connecting the SPC-8 Sprinkler Controller to a Mastervoice home automation system, the SPC-8 can be controlled by voice. Or you can use the Mastervoice system's "smart timers" to operate the SPC-8 at the most convenient time possible. When used with the electric Moisture Sensor, the system will conserve water automatically by not watering when the ground is too wet or when it is raining.

Mastervoice has several versions of its original Butler-in-a-Box, which is priced at $2,995 suggested retail. The Series II is a four-user version that includes all the features of the basic Butler-in-a-Box and has a suggested retail price of $3,995. The Environmental Control Unit (ECU) is a single user version, suggested retail $1,795. The Intelligent Home Controller (IHC) is a version of the original Butler-in-a-Box home automation system but without voice recognition capability. The Intelligent Home Controller retails for $1,195.

SAMANTHA

Group Three Technologies' SAMANTHA Gold, or Security And MANagement Through Home Automation system allows you to control the essential functions of your home. With the simplicity of a touchtone phone, SAMANTHA automatically monitors home communications, lighting, appliances, security devices, temperature, and more. At a basic system price of $1,495, SAMANTHA offers a value that's hard to beat.

The Personal Home Director (PHD) is the nerve center of the SAMANTHA system. This master unit houses:

- the central processor electronics
- a battery for retaining critical data during power outages
- dual cassette drives for storing voice messages and certain customized menus
- a backlit super-twist LCD display for displaying time, phone numbers, and menu prompts
- a keyboard for entering commands and data
- a phone handset for phone conversations
- a sensor to measure room temperature
- a microphone/speaker that can serve as a speaker phone or intercom
- circuits to communicate with other system components

The PHD supervises all system functions, provides synthetic voice throughout the system, and bridges the system to the local telephone network. All program and synthetic voice is stored on a user-accessible ROM card, making future upgrades and options easy. The PHD is installed by inserting the power cord into any available outlet and the telephone cord into a standard telephone jack.

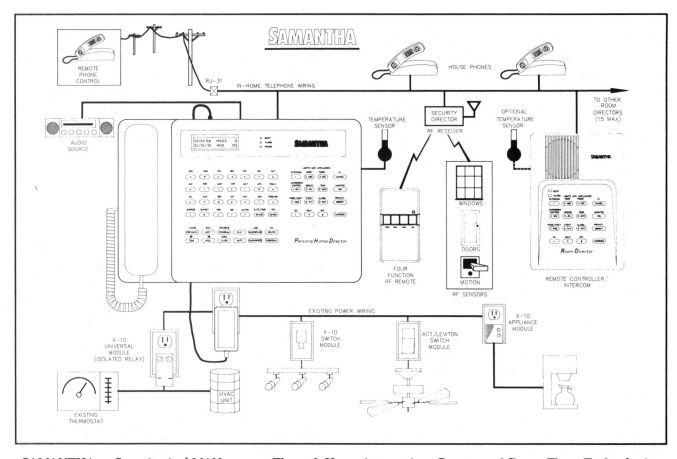

SAMANTHA — Security And MANagement Through Home Automation. Courtesy of Group Three Technologies.

Room Directors can allow you to control SAMANTHA's features from up to 15 rooms in your home. The Room Director communicates through existing telephone wiring and contains a speaker and microphone for audio/voice communications, a 16-key keypad for entering commands, and optional temperature sensors. Installation is easy: just plug it into any AC outlet and telephone jack, then enter the unit's assigned address into the SAMANTHA PHD.

SAMANTHA Gold interfaces with Ademco's XMP Security Panel to provide complete security protection. The XMP can provide up to 64 two-wire multiplex or wireless zones and supports two-wire smoke detectors. The XMP can be programmed via downloading, through a keypad console, or via the SAMANTHA Gold PHD. SAMANTHA also provides light and appliance control (up to 128 modules) via X-10-compatible modules.

SAMANTHA can also function as a speaker phone for hands-free use or conferencing. A built-in memory dialer stores numbers by any alphabetical code you key in. SAMANTHA also operates as an answering machine with beeperless remote operation, tollsaver, date/time stamping, and call screening.

SAMANTHA offers a unique approach to energy management. While not a true room-by-room zone control, which requires damper installation, SAMANTHA improves on a single thermostat by allowing optional temperature sensor installation in any room with a Room Director. SAMANTHA averages temperature readings to determine if the heating or cooling system should be turned on or not. By averaging temperatures in several different rooms, extreme temperature swings can be avoided.

SMARTCOM 2001

SmartCom 2001, from Telestate International, is a powerful communications system designed especially for the home, featuring Infrared Remote Operation. SmartCom 2001 provides security, hands-free intercom, multi-line telephones (3 line, 16 station) with music hold, message center, door intercom, emergency dialing, and

Courtesy of Group Three Technologies.

management subsystems. Ports may be converted via a single line interface card to accommodate standard or wireless phones (up to three per port).

The SmartCom 2001 provides standard security features with up to 16 security zones, call screening, emergency dialing, and in the future Incoming Call Identification (ISDN). By combining the SmartCom 2001 with DSC's PC1550, PC2550, or PC3000 Security Systems, all of SmartCom 2001's phones become remote security keypads that allow full security system access. In addition, the SmartCom 2001 features:

- direct station dialing
- direct dialing (by name)
- hold
- hold recall
- remote answering and forwarding
- last number redial and more

The SmartCom 2001's remote control gives you features not available in any other home communications system. With the remote control, you can answer the phone when it rings without leaving your chair, even through the phone is located on the other side of the room. You can answer the doorbell and unlock the door from any location in the house.

The SmartCom 2001 is also a monitor system for any room in the house. Just add a SmartCom phone station

(up to 16 stations) to any room you want to monitor. Remote monitor is also a standard feature and is activated from a different site by calling in and using the programmed access code.

The Smartcom 2001 also allows your existing single line phones to be used in this system. Your existing cordless phone becomes a three-line phone with many of the SmartCom 2001 features accessible to you anywhere on your property without wires to limit you.

SOPHI

The Sophisticated Home Control System from Digital Technology, Inc., Sophi for short, is a comprehensive, integrated security system, access control system, telephone answering machine and voice mailbox system, lighting control system, home heating and air conditioning control system with multiple zone control, and energy management system.

Sophi is hooked to the existing cable TV wiring in a home and displays its status on an unused cable channel. It is controlled by a standard remote control that also controls the TV, VCR, and audio system. The TV screen displays a series of easily understood menus and the user is guided by a series of voice prompts from the TV's speaker. Operation from the telephone is also aided by voice prompts from Sophi's built-in speech system.

A basic Sophi system consists of: a main control box, four room modules, a control module, a remote control, and a cable TV modulator. The main control box is mounted in a closet, basement, garage, or other out-of-the-way place and communicates with all modules over existing power or spare telephone wires.

Room modules are small, inexpensive plug-in decorative boxes that resemble digital clocks and display time and temperature. Room modules sense the temperature, light levels, and humidity (optional) and allow easy access to Sophi from any room in the house by receiving infrared signals from any handheld remote control. These remotes are also used to control the TV, VCR, or audio system in this area.

Room modules have a unique "ID," or address, and they communicate with the main unit over the existing AC power line. This communication is two-way and uses a protocol similar to that used by office computer networks. (It does not use the X-10 format.) A basic Sophi

PRODUCT COMPARISON CHART

Feature	AMX	CUSTOM COMMAND	DOMAIN 6000	HOME AUTOMATION INC	HOME MANAGER	MAESTRO	MASTERVOICE	SMARTCOM 2001	SMART-REDI	FULL-SMART	SAMANTHA	SOPHI	SQUARE D - ELAN	TOTALHOME
Standard Lighting Control	▨	▨	▨	▨	▨	▨	▨	▨	▨	▨	▨	▨		▨
"Scene" Lighting Control	▨	▨	▨		▨	▨	▨	▨		▨				▨
Home Security System	▨	▨	▨	▨	▨	▨	▨	▨	▨		▨	▨	▨	
Access Control		▨			▨		▨			▨				
Temperature Control	▨	▨	▨	▨				▨	▨	▨	▨	▨	▨	▨
Programmable Thermostat	▨	▨	▨			▨				▨				▨
Dampered HVAC Control		▨								▨		▨	▨	▨
Intercom		▨	▨	▨	▨			▨						▨
Distributed Audio	▨	▨			▨	▨				▨			▨	
Distributed Video		▨	▨										▨	▨
Home Theater		▨				▨				▨	▨			
CCTV						▨				▨			▨	
Appliance Control	▨	▨		▨	▨	▨	▨	▨	▨	▨	▨	▨	▨	▨
Touch Screen	▨	▨		▨							▨	▨	▨	
PC Access/Control	▨	▨	▨	▨		▨	▨	▨	▨				▨	
Phone Access/Control	▨	▨	▨	▨	▨	▨	▨	▨				▨		▨
Remote Hand-Held Control	▨	▨			▨	▨		▨				▨	▨	▨
Voice Recognition		▨	▨				▨							
Expandable	▨	▨	▨	▨	▨	▨	▨	▨	▨	▨	▨	▨	▨	▨

system comes with four room modules expandable up to 255 modules.

Control modules consist of 16 optically coupled digital inputs, 16 relay outputs, and 8 analog inputs for monitoring such items as attic temperatures, outside temperatures, outside humidity (optional), basement flood sensors, water heaters, pool water temperature, etc., and communicate with the main control box through existing power or telephone lines. Control modules are used to control HVAC systems and devices such as water heaters, pool pumps, lawn sprinkler systems, electric gates, etc., and are usually mounted out of sight in the attic, garage, or closet. The basic system comes with one control module but is expandable up to 255 modules.

The cable TV modulator module is a device that takes the audio and video signals from Sophi's main unit and puts them on an unused cable channel. This allows any TV in the home to display Sophi's status. This module is available in a multi-channel version that will not only display system status but will display VCR output or CCTV camera output on an additional channel.

Sophi's security system uses standard wired or wireless sensors, such as door and window sensors, PIR sensors, fire and smoke detectors, and temperature sensors. It interfaces with most security systems. The system has 16 zones expandable up to 4,089 zones by adding more control modules. Security violations are displayed and announced on the TV or announced on the telephone or in-house speakers and are identified with preassigned names such as front door, Bobby's window, etc. Sophi has an optional wireless RF receiver for wireless sensor transmitters and personal emergency pendants. CCTV cameras can be added to monitor nurseries, front and back doors, and surrounding premises.

Sophi provides multi-zone heating and air conditioning for up to four zones, which is expandable. The system uses low voltage (24 VAC) motorized dampers in the HVAC duct to distribute air to the proper zones and is controlled by relays on the control module. Zone temperature is sensed by the room module in that zone. This module sends the temperature data over the existing AC power line to the main control box, which makes all the control decisions.

Sophi uses X-10 technology to control up to 256 lamps and electrical appliances. Incandescent lamps can be turned on, off, dimmed, or set to turn on/off up to four times a day on a daily basis or weekend schedule. All events are set with the handheld remote through the TV and can be controlled by any telephone in or outside the house.

TOTALHOME

Honeywell's TotalHome home management system is a relatively new and long awaited entry into the home automation field. With TotalHome Honeywell has created a whole-house home management system that integrates security, lighting, HVAC control, and appliance control into one easy-to-use system (called HBus). The system is controlled from strategically located display panels (keypads) and from any touchtone phone anywhere in the world.

With help from Honeywell the homeowner designs "modes" such as GOOD MORNING, AT WORK, AT HOME, SLEEP, and ON VACATION, to suit the way the family lives. Up to 16 lifestyle "modes" can be customized to meet your needs, and each mode includes specific instructions to tell your security system, thermostat, lights, and appliances exactly what to do.

In the "At Work" mode, TotalHome could automatically activate the security system, set back the thermostat, and turn off any small appliances accidentally left on plus monitor your house for emergencies such as fire, break-in, gas leak, etc. (TotalHome is monitored 24 hours a day by a UL-approved Honeywell Customer Service Center.)

Initial programming and any future program changes must be made by Honeywell. For convenience, changes can be made over the phone. Simply call in the changes you want to make, and customer service personnel will download the changes directly to TotalHome. There is a service charge every time you change programming. But for people who have trouble programming a VCR, this service may be well worth the extra cost.

The security end of TotalHome is a full-featured Honeywell Home Security System including perimeter protection (magnetic sensors, glass break, etc.), interior protection (PIR motion detectors), fire detection (smoke and heat sensors), duress alarm, and access control. The security system also features: entry/exit delay, partial arming, point identification (which allows the monitoring station to identify the exact point of entry in an emergency), separate interior zones, and battery backup.

HVAC control is accomplished by using Honeywell's Chronotherm III setback thermostat. With TotalHome, the Chronotherm adjusts the temperature up or down according to your modes for whole house comfort and maximum energy savings. While each mode may include thermostat settings, you can still adjust the Chronotherm manually anytime you like. The Chronotherm is accurate to within one degree of setting, with no temperature swings. You can expect energy savings of up to 30% with the Chronotherm III.

TotalHome utilizes X-10 power line technology for lighting and appliance control. TotalHome can control your lights to provide security lighting, scheduled lighting, and scene lighting. Appliance control includes turning on/off small appliances, pools and spas, yard sprinkler system, etc. Basically, TotalHome can control anything that can be controlled by X-10 modules and controllers.

TotalHome also offers several optional add-ons such as video entry systems, intercom/sound systems, central vacuum, water filtration, air cleaner, and humidifier. Honeywell can also custom design their LiteCom lighting control system for your home (see Chapter 3 for more on LiteCom).

10.
PC-Based Home Automation

For the homeowner who already owns a personal computer, there is no easier, more economical way to acquire home automation than through that PC. All it takes is a special software program ($100-$300) and various X-10-compatible plug-in modules and interfaces. There are two types of PC-based systems: "off-line" interface controllers and "full time" PC-based systems. Off-line controllers use your PC to program schedules (then the PC can be disconnected or used for other purposes). Full-time PCs are "dedicated" to running the automation programming and are not used for normal computing. With a computer-based system, home automation doesn't become obsolete. Upgrades can be added to allow the homeowner to maintain the latest features and services.

OFF-LINE PC SYSTEMS

CP290 Home Automation Interface
The CP290 Home Automation Interface from X-10 was one of the original "off-line" controllers available to X-10 users. After many years in the home automation market, the controller and computer software are still popular. One reason for this popularity is that the CP290 works on any computer with an RS-232 port. CP290 software is designed for IBM-compatibles, Macs, Apple IIe/IIc, and Commodore 64/128 computers. The software for IBMs and compatibles is menu-driven and lets users enter from the keyboard the names and locations of devices controlled. Software for the Mac lets user design the screen to look like his home and place icons representing devices in the appropriate locations. After pro-

gramming, the interface may be disconnected from the computer.

The CP290 can address all 256 X-10 codes. The actual number of modules that can be controlled is software dependent (256 for IBM and Macintosh, 72 for Apple IIe/IIc, 95 for Commodore 64/128). The CP290 can store 128 Timed Events. A Timed Event can be up to 16 devices on the same House Code programmed to go on or off at a particular time in a particular day or days. The CP290 has its own real-time clock and has battery backup to protect the time and program for up to 100 hours. The main advantage to the CP290 is price, about $60. The main disadvantage is that the CP290 only provides one-way control, in that it can only send commands to modules to activate them, unlike the Enerlogic ES-1400e which can not only transmit but also receive signals.

Enerlogic ES-1400e
Another off-line controller pioneer is the ES-1400e from Enerlogic. The ES-1400e is a programmable controller that sends commands, either immediately or on a timed basis, to receiver modules through the AC wiring of a home. Up to a total of 256 modules can be controlled and monitored by the ES-1400e. The system package includes software that allows the user to create programs for an IBM-compatible computer and download them to the ES-1400e control unit.

The ES-1400e home control unit not only transmits X-10 signals over the home's power lines, it also monitors the power lines, "listening" for any X-10 command sent

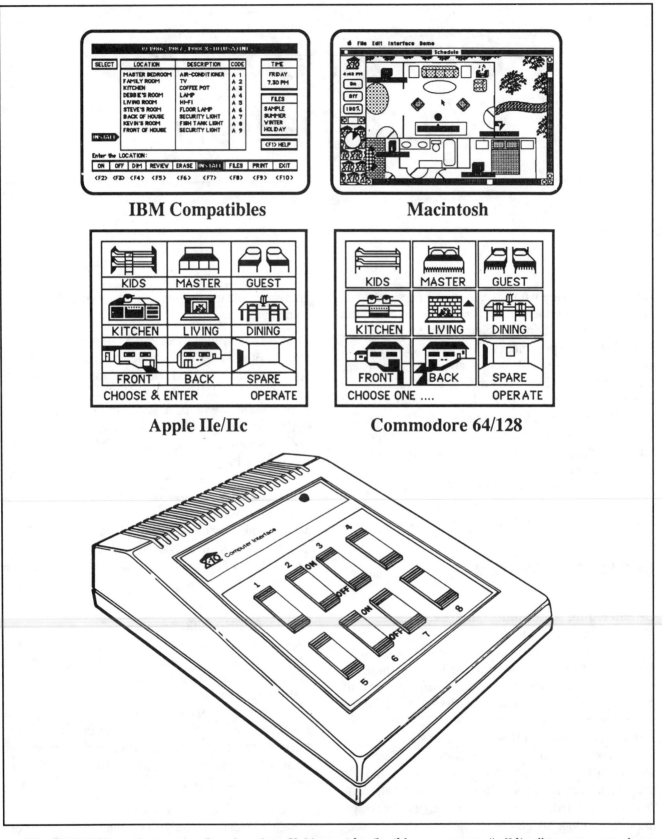

IBM Compatibles

Macintosh

Apple IIe/IIc

Commodore 64/128

The CP 290 Home Automation Interface from X-10 provides flexible, easy to use "off-line" system control.
Courtesy of X-10.

by such devices as mini-controllers, radio controllers, and burglar alarm interfaces. This capability of the ES-1400e allows for much more sophisticated control schemes for your X-10 system, including "mode" or "scenario" control. "Mode" or "scenario" control refers to the ability to set the house to an "at home" or "vacation" mode, for example, and let the control system initiate a series of behaviors such as security lighting, turning appliances off, etc. A random time feature (SECURITY) allows events to be performed at random times (12- or 24-hour mode), resolved to the nearest second.

Optional expansion modules available for the ES-1400e include: modem control, infrared control of external appliances, direct control analog and digital I/O modules, and echelon interface. In the near future Enerlogic expects to introduce a powerful telephone control unit that will interface with the ES-1400e and include such features as local or remote control by telephone, voice menus, remote programming, outbound dialing, and alarm notification. The new telephone control unit will even include a temperature sensor, a clock, and internal timer capabilities that will let it operate independently of the ES-1400e.

HomeBase

HomeBase, available from Home Control Concepts, has an easy-to-use Windows-like user interface. The system monitors your power line and allows advanced IF-THEN-ELSE, AND/OR control for a complete two-way X-10 system. The unit has battery backup and a real-time clock/calendar, which keeps track of sunrise/sunset. You can also remotely control your home from any computer anywhere in the world. This system requires a PC with a 2400 baud modem.

Event Control System

The Event Control System (ECS) from Omnipotence is a DOS-based program that can monitor and control lights and appliances, entertainment components, temperature, wired or wireless security sensors, and keypads. It also interfaces with infrared remote controls and telephones and understands speech. A button sequence from a keypad or handheld remote can be assigned to any task, so that when those buttons are pressed, the computer knows to send function instructions to the appropriate devices. Anything you want to have controlled/monitored must be defined as an "item" that has several

"states." For example, a defined item might be "day," "time," "temperature," or "security status," and their possible "states" may be Sunday, Monday, Tuesday ..., 1:00 p.m., 1:01 p.m., 1:02 p.m. ..., 60°, 65°, 70° ..., Armed/Disarmed. Once terms have been set, the user must define the events and corresponding actions that dictate how devices will be controlled.

Circuit Cellar HCS II

The Circuit Cellar HCS II is an expandable network-based control system incorporating direct digital inputs and outputs, direct analog inputs and outputs, X-10 transmission and reception, infrared remote control transmission and reception, remote displays, and more. HCS II consists of a supervisory controller connected to 31 specialized function models (called links) that perform remote data acquisition, closed-loop control, and display. An HCS II system need only include those links that suit the tasks to be performed. These comm-links are "smart" subsystems. Each link has a unique command set and, for multiple units of the same type, a unique address. The HCS II is most appropriate for computer buffs with programming experience.

Ménage UCIX

The Ménage UCIX is an affordable (about $600) programmable controller, which can send and receive X-10 and Leviton's DEC power line carrier signals (up to 256 addresses). You communicate with UCIX via a 32-key UHF remote control. The UHF remote allows you to control your lights, TV, VCR, CD player, and anything else with infrared or power line carrier control.

UCIX's infrared emitters transmit signals to your TV, VCR, CD, and other devices that use infrared for remote control. UCIX has 32K ROM and 32K of battery-backed RAM, which holds 900 programs or 200 IR codes or a proportional mix. An optional fiber optic kit allows direct routing of IR to receiving devices via optical fiber.

UCIX learns the infrared codes it needs from your existing remote controls. Once learned, you don't need the old remotes. A single UCIX remote can perform all the functions that now require several remotes. You can add special functions that are not on any of your existing remotes.

TimeCommander Home Control Systems

The TimeCommander Home Control System, from JDS

Technologies, plugs into any AC outlet and the serial port of any IBM-compatible computer. It transmits X-10 codes through the existing AC wiring to control up to 256 electrical devices, such as lights, appliances, security, heating/air conditioning, etc. In addition to sending X-10 commands, the TimeCommander monitors and identifies X-10 activity on the power line. Intelligent IF-THEN-AND-OR-ELSE routines and multiple commands (macros) can be defined and triggered by any combination of sources including timed schedule, phone (with a TeleCommand), intrusion (motion detectors, door/window sensors, etc.), and any other X-10-compatible controller.

Sophisticated time and event-based schedules are easily created with pop-down menus and an intuitive "point-and-click" data entry process. Once a schedule is programmed, the TimeCommander can be disconnected from the computer or used together for monitoring and manually controlling devices with the on-screen Mega Controller. An on-screen Status Display indicates on/off status of all 256 X-10 devices and the Activity Log stores and displays time and date of all X-10 activity — an invaluable tool for troubleshooting and monitoring system status.

The TimeCommander can be programmed to trigger a specified command when a defined sequence of X-10 codes is received. This feature can be used to allow sensitive equipment such as computers or door and gate openers to be controlled only when the proper sequence is received. The TimeCommander can also be programmed to receive X-10 sequences on an unused House code and transmit corresponding commands on all others, allowing any controller easy access to all 256 codes. For example, by setting all controllers to House code P and all controlled devices to House codes A through O, a standard 16-button maxi-controller can easily access any House and Unit code.

The TimeCommander can control your audio/video equipment and security system with the addition of the optional IR-Xpander and I/O-Xpander. The IR-Xpander connects to the TimeCommander to allow control of audio and video equipment by timed schedule or from any X-10-compatible controller. Preset macros can be programmed, allowing a single command to turn on the appropriate equipment, select the source (AM, FM, tape, CD, etc.), set the volume level, and adjust the lighting. By adding a TeleCommand System 100, you can control your audio and video equipment from any phone anywhere.

The I/O-Xpander provides multiple isolated inputs and outputs for direct control to and from external non-X-10 devices such as motion detectors. For security applications, intrusion detectors can be connected and programmed to trigger any output device such as siren, auto-dialer, etc., according to the TimeCommander schedule. The Activity Log can be used to store and display exact time and date of any intrusion or security violation.

With the addition of a TeleCommand, control is extended to every phone in your home, office, or car and around the world. Trigger preset macros or select scheduled routines using simple touchtone commands or specified ring sequences. The system can also be monitored and updated from any computer in the world by connecting a modem to the TimeCommander.

TeleCommand System 100

JDS Technologies TeleCommand System 100 Telephone-Controlled Automation System allows telephone control of any electrical device, such as indoor/outdoor lighting, appliances, security, computers, heating/air conditioning, door/gate openers, water heaters, audio/video equipment, sprinklers, office equipment, motors, pumps, etc., throughout your home by dialing simple, two-digit touchtone commands.

The TeleCommand System 100 comes preprogrammed, ready to use, and can be re-programmed by phone (on or off premise) to change access codes, restrictions, or operating parameters. The TeleComand is compatible with remote modules sold by X-10, Radio Shack, Sears, Stanley, Leviton, and Heath-Zenith, to name a few. To set up the TeleCommand, simply plug it into any AC outlet and telephone jack — no special wiring is needed.

TeleCommand features 100 Command Codes: 90 On, Off, Dim, Bright (House Codes A-J, Unit Codes 1-9); 10 All Lights On, All Units Off (House Codes A-J). The system uses non-volatile memory and is unaffected by power failures. An optional 12VDC battery can be connected to power the TeleCommand to maintain phone control of your security system if AC power fails.

The TeleCommand lets you access your computer at any time from any location without leaving it powered up, on line, and vulnerable to hackers. Simply call the TeleCommand and dial your Remote Access Code and the ON Command Code for the computer/modem you wish to power up. Once booted, you can enter your computer

The TeleCommand System 100 Telephone Controlled Automation System allows complete control of your X-10 system from any phone inside or outside the home. Courtesy of JDS Technologies.

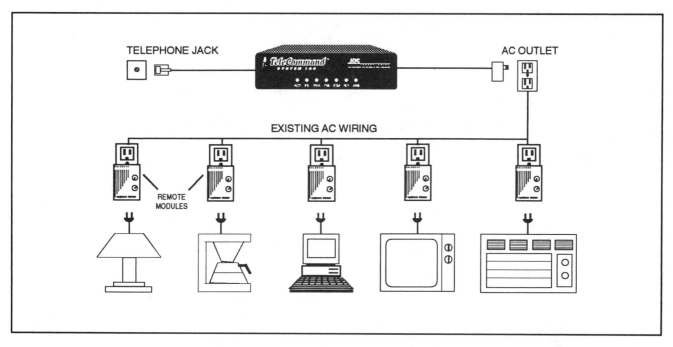

Courtesy of JDS Technologies.

password to access data files as usual. Up to 90 computers can be accessed over one shared telephone line.

Use your phone's memory to activate a series of commands at the touch of a button. By storing command codes in place of phone numbers, one button can shut off all the lights, turn down the heat, and arm your security system from your bed at night. The TeleCommand also has an Intercom feature that allows room-to-room communication using existing phones and a Hold feature that allows calls to be placed "on hold" and transferred to any extension phone.

For the ultimate in wireless X-10 remote control, just add the optional PocketCommander pocket-size cordless phone to your TeleCommand System 100. Pocket-Commander's ten-number memory can store Tele-Command codes in place of phone numbers for controlling multiple devices at the touch of a button. With the optional VoiceCommander voice-dialing telephone, you can place calls and, with the TeleCommand, control your entire house using simple spoken commands. It can be programmed to your voice in minutes using prompted instructions on its LCD display. The VoiceCommander stores 20 spoken commands, each of which can trigger a single X-10 device or a complex series of events. You can also use its auto-dialer/directory to store 50 additional phone numbers and touch-operated commands.

FULL-TIME PC SYSTEMS

Until recently, the only systems that made practical use of PCs for home automation were those that use the PC as a user interface to program a controller that operates independently from the PC. These systems include the X-10 CP290 and Enerlogic ES-1400e. One disadvantage of the off-line controllers programmed via PC is the need to power up the computer and load the appropriate software to make any changes. With full-time PC-based automation, the PC operates the system with no need for a third-party controller.

Dynasty
One such full-time PC-based home automation system is the Dynasty from Home Automation Laboratories. The Dynasty system links various components from different companies (e.g., computer interfaces, telephone interfaces, security systems, infrared remotes, temperature sensors, etc.) into one PC-based program, which runs full time on an IBM-compatible PC. The

DynaServer's hardware and software are customized to automate home control functions like heating and air conditioning, lights, audio/video, home theater, and security and telephone systems. The DynaServer Master System retails for about $2,000.

Dynasty control programs consist of "events" and "items." Events can be long or short groups of instructions that can contain IF-THEN-ELSE logic; commands to control lights, appliances, or audio/video equipment; calls to other events; and even commands for synthesized speech. Items are the basic unit in creating Dynasty programs and can take many forms. The basic categories of items are Component Items, which include peripheral devices like the infrared interface, speech interface, and security keypad; Device Items, such as light and appliance modules; Value Items, such as time, month, on/off; and Action Items, which initiate an action.

One of the advantages of Dynasty's event-oriented programming is that the user can set up control schemes as small chunks of code that are easy to understand and troubleshoot. Individual events within Dynasty can include up to 64 lines of code; activities that are more complex can be set up using multiple events or events that function as subroutines. What really sets Dynasty apart from conventional home control systems is its ability to use PC expansion devices and make them part of the system.

SOLVING INTERFACING PROBLEMS

The price for PC-based home automation is right; however, most systems still lag behind in one important area: interfacing. On a stand-alone controller, the homeowner can set up and send commands with the press of a button or two. On a PC controller, the process is usually more complex. Many of the programs are text-based and require some programming knowledge. To rectify this problem, computer programmers have been working on a graphic user interface (GUI), or "object-oriented programming" as an interface with PC controllers. Two companies that have recently partnered their graphically oriented system with home automation are Remote Measurement Systems and Ansan Industries, both for the Apple Macintosh.

I/O Port System Bridge and Master Control
Ansan's I/O Port System Bridge and Master Control software package provides two-way communications

between the Mac and modules and sensors via direct wiring, radio frequency, and power line control. The I/O Bridge Port monitors and controls 64 digital inputs and 8 analog input signals, 16 digital outputs, and 32 X-10 signals. By adding more Bridges, the system can be expanded to 512 digital inputs, 64 analog inputs, 128 digital outputs, and 256 X-10 modules.

The I/O Port System is a true multi-tasking system. It continues to monitor and control the home even while the user is word processing or using the computer for anything besides home automation. Ansan is also working on infrared communications that would allow the I/O Port Bridge to link with appliances and export the computer screen to TVs in the home.

The I/O Bridge Port System works in parallel with other home control systems (HVAC, security, etc.) by simply enhancing the current system's capabilities. The software is designed to allow the user to set up many specific "conditions" that must be met before the system takes action. For example, a condition could be set up to require not just one but two sensors be tripped before sounding an alarm. Every event is reported and saved on a disk file. That way, the homeowner can review exactly what occurred in the home.

EnviroMac

With Remote Measurement System's EnviroMac, users can program basic "control rules" by simply pointing to an entry box and typing in the appropriate commands (e.g., 7 a.m., module #5 ON). EnviroMac addresses up to 32 X-10 modules to control different appliances, lights, and temperature. EnviroMac's ADControl software links to the power line and devices from an ADC-1 external RS-232 serial port, which connects to the back of the Mac. The ADControl software works with all Macintosh computers.

The ADC-1 is equipped with 16 analog inputs (at 12-bit resolution), 4 digital inputs, 6 or 12 controlled outputs, and an X-10 power line module controller. As with Ansan's system, digital inputs can handle security signals from sensors and turn on lights and activate a siren if any sensor is triggered. The EnviroMac can also monitor sump pumps and maintain specific temperatures in the home according to time of day and occupancy. In addition to controlling the home, the EnviroMac can provide important detailed measurements of the home's performance. EnviroMac monitors energy usage throughout the day and by reviewing the data, the homeowner can easily see when the most energy is being used.

Remote Measurement System offers a complete line of sensors for the ADC-1 including: temperature, rainfall, wind speed, wind direction, soil moisture/conductivity, electrical energy consumption, relative humidity, and light levels. Virtually any sensor that changes its electrical properties in response to its environment can be connected to the ADC-1.

Automatic House Companion

The DeskMate Automatic House Companion software by Radio Shack lets homeowners use a Tandy or IBM-compatible computer to design an automation program to control as many as 256 modules in up to 128 separate timer events. The Automatic House Companion utilizes a graphic user interface featuring pull-down menus, pop-up dialog boxes, and the point and click convenience of a mouse for simple programming of the Plug 'n Power Interface. Once the interface is programmed, it may be detached from the computer to operate independently and free up the computer for other uses.

The software's floor plan allows the user to design an on-screen floor plan of his home and position icons representing electrical devices in various rooms. The Plug 'n Power remote module connected to the actual device carries the corresponding code setting. Routine Maker lets the user set up modes or scenarios. Schedule Maker schedules days, times, and actions for individual devices or routines created with Floor Plan and Routine Maker. A special Schedule Maker feature is a Security Mode, which randomly varies actual on/off times of the security system by as much as 30 minutes.

Voice Master and Sound Master

Voice Master and Sound Master allow you to add the convenience of voice control to your PC-based automation system. The Sound Master and Voice Master, both from Covox, Inc., let you teach your computer voice commands and assign them to a set of keystrokes. You can automate any sequence of keys in any software program with easy to use voice commands, bypassing complex menus or function-key sequences. They support playback of synthesized speech from the Speech Thing's software driver (see below). Your PC can use the Sound Master or Voice Master to record voice prompts or play back telephone messages or pre-recorded voice prompts. Both Sound Master and Voice

Master can also generate computer-synthesized speech from within the PC or from ordinary ASCII text using the optional Speech Driver Software package.

Voice Master and Sound Master are speaker-dependent, word-isolated voice recognition systems. Speaker-dependent means that you train the computer *only* to your voice. They can also be "trained" to understand non-voiced sounds, such as the ring of the telephone, doorbells, etc. Word-isolated means that you must pause slightly between each voice command so that the computer can "capture" the word, and not noise or unwanted sounds before or after the word.

Speech Thing

Covox's Speech Thing is a full featured 8-bit digital-to-analog converter with audio amplifier and software capable of adding clear and clean digitized sound and speech to any MS-DOS computer. Speech Thing attaches in-line with the parallel printer port, without interfering with the printer. A small audio wire carries the voice to the amplified speaker provided, or any other audio amplifier, intercom, or speaker system. Speech Thing is designed to play digitized or synthesized sound found in a wide variety of consumer, educational, and business software titles. You can also create talking software for customized applications such as home automation.

When connected to your IBM-compatible PC, the Speech Thing allows your PC to speak status messages, announce conditions in the home, remind you of appointments, play back recorded telephone messages, or play back recorded speech or sound files (requires Voice or Sound Master). For a truly interactive system, add either Voice Master or Sound Master voice recognition hardware/software to your PC-based home automation system. Voice commands can be substituted for pushing buttons to enable sophisticated home control, all for less than $300.

PROGRAMMABLE LOGIC CONTROLLERS

Homeowners have yet another choice for PC-based automation in addition to the systems already described — Programmable Logic Controllers. Programmable Logic Controllers (PLCs) are powerful industrial computers that have found their way into home automation as prices have fallen (most under $500). PLCs require professional installation and should not be considered by the typical do-it-yourselfer. PLCs are available through your building contractor or automation dealer/installer from companies such as Allen Bradley and Ormon Applications.

PLCs are composed of three functional parts: central processing unit (CPU), input terminals, and output terminals. The input/output terminals are wiring connections on which the user attaches light sensors, security sensors, electric valves, etc. Each input/output terminal has a corresponding address in the program and an external light indicating whether it is energized. The total number of input/output terminals is defined as the I/O count.

The memory section of the CPU contains the user's program. PLC memories are of two types: volatile and non-volatile. Volatile memory means a backup battery is used to maintain memory in case the PLC loses power. Non-volatile memory is electrically "etched" on an electronic chip and requires no battery backup. Most memory modules used with PLCs have this type of memory. The program is entered into memory with a programming device such as a handheld programmer or personal computer. It is created by entering the simple graphic commands of Ladder Logic, a language that duplicates the scanning format used by the CPU. But forget everything you have heard about computer pre-programming. PLCs were designed to be quick and simple to program.

11.
Smart House

Launched by the National Association of Home Builders in 1984, SMART HOUSE L.P. sought to create a safer wiring system for homes and a new way to differentiate between housing products. This soon expanded to include a safer, more convenient home gas delivery system. In 1987, the first SMART HOUSE prototype house was built near Baltimore, MD, and the process of turning an ideal system into a practical system began.

WHAT IS SMART HOUSE?

SMART HOUSE is an innovative energy and communications distribution system that puts in place the basic infrastructure that enables automated home management. It is an integrated system consisting of the wiring, outlets, and controls needed to provide remote and programmable control of house systems and appliances. The basic concept of SMART HOUSE is a family of three multi-purpose cables. These three cables carry power hybrid branch cable, telephone communications, audio/video, and low-voltage applications control signals throughout the home. The entire house can be wired using just these three types of SMART HOUSE cables, plus heavier conventional wiring to fixed-in-place appliances such as the furnace and range.

SMART HOUSE is a home management system that combines today's latest technology with an integrated home network of energy, communication, audio/video, and telephone cables. You can use your control panel, computer, handheld remote, or a simple wall switch to manage your home. You can even operate your house from a touchtone telephone. With SMART HOUSE you have the ability to program heating/cooling, entertainment, security, safety, lighting, gas and electric appliances to:

- turn on or off at programmed times
- operate together via pre-set house modes such as vacation, daytime, or romantic settings
- respond to activated sensors throughout the house

CONTROLS

In a SMART HOUSE, switches and controls are user programmable for maximum flexibility. The system can also be controlled from inside or outside the house by touchtone telephone. Other user interfaces may include wall-mounted control panels and touchscreen TVs. Besides these user controls, the SMART HOUSE can also use other types of inputs. Ambient light sensors can turn lights on automatically at dark; occupancy sensors can turn them off if no one is in the room.

The control system also allows interaction between SMART HOUSE-registered appliances, sensors, and other devices. For example, when the washing machine has completed its cycle, it can display a message on the TV telling you so. When the phone rings, the vacuum cleaner may turn off so the ring can be heard. Appliances can communicate maintenance or service messages ("check filter" or "compressor failure") to a touchscreen control panel. If occupancy or smoke detectors detect a potential intruder or a fire, they can be programmed to automatically call emergency monitoring services while alerting the homeowner by turning on lights and sounding an alarm over the stereo speakers.

FEATURES

Many SMART HOUSE features are available today; others are under development and will be available in the near future. Security/safety features will include:

- video monitoring
- automatic dial-out to police or monitoring station
- TV display of security/safety messages
- lighted exit paths
- zoned security

Air comfort features will allow for better temperature control throughout the house via zone controls. Setback and remote control will enhance home comfort. Energy management will be enhanced by on/off controls (remote, direct, or programmed), setback control, load management, and remote meter reading.

Entertainment

Entertainment features in a SMART HOUSE will include whole-house video distribution and monitoring and audio distribution and programmable control. Lighting will include multi-way dimming and switching, remote control, mood setting, preset lighting levels, light groupings, and programmable lighting by time of day, house mode, or action-response. Gas energy features will be greatly enhanced through the flexible gas piping and gas convenience outlets. A whole new generation of gas appliances is being developed, including SMART heating equipment, water heaters, gas grills, and gas fireplaces. SMART appliances will have the ability to communicate with each other or the system.

Each individual family will determine what products they want to attach in order to take advantage of the SMART HOUSE benefits most suited to them. Because SMART HOUSE is installed at the time of construction, the price of the system is included in the mortgage and thus more affordable. What sets SMART HOUSE apart from other approaches to home management is its unique wiring and integrated system of central control.

SMART HOUSE WIRE MANAGEMENT

Because of the extra conductors in hybrid cable, a new method has been developed to terminate it quickly, safely, and reliably every time. SMART HOUSE cable taps eliminate the need to separate hybrid cable into its individual conductors, strip back insulation, and connect wire nuts or screw terminals. Instead, only the outer sheath is removed, exposing the insulated conductors inside. The folded construction is flattened out and

placed between the two halves of a cable tap. When it is clamped on the hybrid cable with a special tool, prongs pierce the insulation to make contact with the conductors inside. The cable tap is then installed in a convenience center, where it serves as a backplate for plugging in the receptacles themselves.

The advantages of the cable tap approach are safety, speed of installation, and prevention of accidental miswiring. Proper polarity is guaranteed — no reversing the hot and neutral conductors, or mixing up power wires with control — and grounding connections are automatic. Because connections take place inside the cable tap, there is no exposed wiring in the convenience center box. The cable tap itself is touch-safe even after branch cable has been terminated, making it safe and easy to install receptacles.

SMART HOUSE communications cable is not terminated using cable taps. Instead, the coaxial cables are connected to distribution interface units and convenience centers using conventional push-down connectors. This low-voltage ribbon cable is terminated at SMART HOUSE outlets using insulation-displacement connectors similar to small branch cable taps.

The hybrid branch cable contains three #14 or #12 power wires (hot, neutral, and ground) plus six #24 low voltage control wires. Hybrid branch cable is UL-listed Type NM-B and installed through ordinary 1-inch diameter holes drilled in wood studs. Hybrid branch cable runs from the service center (see below) to combination wall outlets called convenience centers. Because SMART HOUSE hybrid cable is manufactured in #12 and #14 AWG sizes, appliances on dedicated circuits are connected using conventional Romex, BX, or conductors in conduit, along with a piece of applications cable to provide a communications link to the system controller.

Communications cable contains eight telephone wires and two coaxial cables. Communications cable runs from the service center to four-way splitters for TV and telephone wiring called distribution interface units. From these DIUs, communications cable runs to selected convenience centers throughout the house.

Applications cable is a low-voltage ribbon cable consisting of six #24 control wires plus two #18 wires for 12 VDC power. This low-voltage ribbon cable is installed as a dedicated bus that receives 12 VDC power from the continuous power supply and control signals from the system controller. This dedicated applications bus is

SMART HOUSE wiring being installed by trained SMART HOUSE electricians. Courtesy of SMART HOUSE L.P.

The new SMART HOUSE wiring system replaces conventional wiring with three efficient cables that carry all power, telephone, video, communications, and control signal throughout the house. Courtesy of SMART HOUSE L.P.

Modular SMART-REDI outlets in each room give homeowners multi-service access to 120 VAC power, telephone service, cable TV hookup, and whole-house audio/video distribution, all neatly combined at one location. Courtesy of SMART HOUSE L.P.

used for products that need high reliability, such as security products and smoke detectors.

SMART HOUSE OUTLETS

The SMART HOUSE uses three types of electrical outlets, called convenience centers, switch/sensor outlets, and applications outlets. The convenience center is a combination wall outlet that contains a duplex receptacle plus telephone and coaxial outlets. Two different types of receptacles will be available: SMART-REDI and SMART.

SMART-REDI receptacles are conventional NEMA 5-15 and NEMA 5-20 receptacles that plug into SMART HOUSE cable taps. Integrated SMART receptacles available in 1992 contain both the three familiar power prongs and six additional pins that provide low-voltage control signals to a new generation of "smart" appliances using special attachment plugs. Today's existing appliances will also be able to plug into these integrated receptacles but will receive 120 VAC power only. SMART receptacles include a relay controlled by an electronic chip that communicates with the system controller. This allows remote on/off control of the outlet. Both SMART-REDI and SMART duplex receptacles will come in GFCI and non-GFCI versions.

The applications outlet is similar to the switch/sensor outlet but is installed on the applications bus. This is a dedicated circuit of low-voltage applications cable that receives 12 VDC power from the continuous power supply and control signals from the system controller. The applications outlet is intended for products that should continue to function during a power outage, such as security sensors and smoke detectors.

The modular design of all three SMART HOUSE outlets makes it easy to change switches and sensors, or to upgrade from a standard SMART-REDI receptacle to an integrated SMART one. Each convenience center, switch/sensor outlet, and applications outlet contains a backplate called a cable tap, which connects to all conductors of the hybrid cable and has plug-in sockets for receptacles, switches, and sensors. These components are modular and can be plugged and unplugged from the backplate easily, without ever touching the actual wiring.

GAS MANAGEMENT

Gas will be supplied to SMART HOUSE appliances through a system of semi-rigid piping. Safe, convenient, easy-connect gas outlets can be located almost anywhere. They will accommodate appliances such as ranges, ovens, dryers, barbecue grills, and water heaters. Gas furnaces and air conditioners can be directly connected to the semi-rigid piping.

With innovative flexible gas piping and a distribution manifold, your gas system can be customized economically. You can have the warm ambience of a gas fireplace in your bedroom. Or extend your seasons of outdoor fun with a radiant gas heater and a spa on your deck. With a gas convenience outlet, you can plug in any gas appliance easily. Your gas grill can be used then put away until needed again. As a safety feature, no gas is routed to the outlet until the appliance is plugged in.

CONTROL CENTER

The control center, from Plexus Corporation, is a simple but powerful device used by the homeowner to monitor and control all SMART HOUSE communications, entertainment systems, appliances, and outlets within the home. An easy-to-read liquid crystal display presents information in a menu format that guides the user through each step of the setup and control process.

The heart of the Plexus Control Center is custom-designed microprocessor circuitry that translates the simple pushbutton commands of the homeowner into a set of concise instructions that are sent to the appropriate devices within the home. A series of ergonomically designed menus guides the homeowner through the process, enabling even untrained or infrequent users to take full advantage of the SMART HOUSE capabilities. Commands or status checks are initiated by selecting the desired option on the display menu and pressing the adjacent button. Each time a button is pushed, a more specific set of choices is presented to the user until the end result is achieved.

Each room in the home can be individually configured using the Plexus Control Center. Lights and appliances can be turned on or off automatically for energy management and security. Up to eight modes can be preset to accommodate the living patterns of an individual family. Personal Identification Numbers (PINs) can be assigned to individuals to prevent unauthorized access to the system or accidental input by children.

For the homeowner's convenience, the Plexus Control Center can be placed at multiple locations in the home,

SMART HOUSE gas outlets contain a single, easy-connect device to plug gas appliances into wall-mounted sockets as easily as electrical outlets. Courtesy of SMART HOUSE L.P.

such as the master bedroom and kitchen/entryway. The Plexus Control Center is a cost-effective, reliable device designed to be the primary control unit within the home. Built-in diagnostics help to isolate failures that may occur throughout the system.

Sears is developing a complete installation and service program for SMART HOUSE components. The plan includes a 24-hour response center that can remotely diagnose problems and dispatch a local service provider if needed. Although local contractors will perform the installation and service work, Sears will coordinate the work and provide secure warranty backing.

SERVICE CENTER

The service center is the combined service entrance for SMART HOUSE. Utility power, telephone, and TV feed into the service center and are distributed from it throughout the house. The service center components are installed together on a plywood backboard in a dedicated wall space. Installation of the components and wiring interconnections between them is made using templates supplied by SMART HOUSE. A typical service center consists of the following components: load center, system controller enclosure, coaxial headend, telephone gateway, continuous power supply (12 VDC). The following component is optional: remote control device.

The SMART HOUSE load center is similar to today's standard equipment, except that it will provide surge and ground-fault protection for all branch circuits. Homes are required to have 5 mA ground-fault protection for receptacles located in bathrooms, kitchen counters, basement, and outdoors. SMART HOUSE provides this same level of protection plus 30 mA UL-listed ground-fault circuit breakers on all 120 volt branch circuits to provide additional safety.

Continuous Power Supply (CPS), a battery-backed 12 VDC UPS component, supplies power to the system controller. It also supplies power to dedicated circuits of applications cable (called applications busses) installed to handle products such as security systems or IR controls, which communicate over the housewide network but don't need AC power to operate.

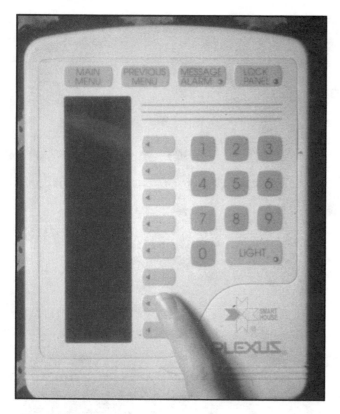

The SMART HOUSE Control Panel, one of the many SMART HOUSE Management Controls, is operated much like an easy-to-use automatic teller machine. Courtesy of SMART HOUSE L.P.

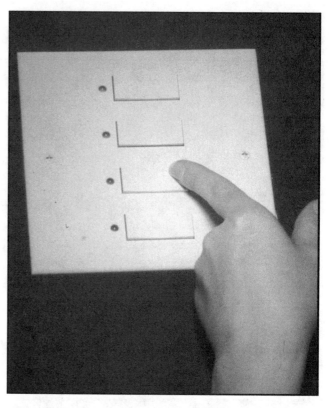

In a SMART HOUSE, wall switches can be programmed to control not only a light or set of lights, but also other features within the home, such as the television or shower. Courtesy of SMART HOUSE L.P.

The optional remote control device consists of remote control circuit breakers installed in the load center, with a separate control unit connected to the system controller. The RCD allows utility companies to turn major appliances on/off for energy management purposes (dryer, water heater, heat pump, etc.), by agreement with the homeowner.

The telephone gateway component is the communications nerve center for SMART HOUSE. It can handle up to four outside telephone lines and contains a built-in modem and answering machine. The telephone gateway is connected to the system controller, allowing the SMART HOUSE to be controlled by any touchtone phone.

SMART-REDI

You can prepare for SMART living by building a SMART-REDI house today. SMART-REDI homes func-

tion like traditional homes today while providing homeowners with exciting new features rarely found in new homes before now. SMART-REDI homes augment the entertainment, communications, security, and safety capabilities of a home. Because all of the wiring needed for energy and communication services is installed throughout the house at the time of construction, SMART-REDI homeowners can immediately take advantage of some of SMART HOUSE's benefits.

One benefit is whole-house cable TV and video distribution, which lets homeowners watch cable TV or a videotape playing on one VCR on any TV in the house. Another added advantage of SMART HOUSE's video distribution capabilities is the ability to plug video cameras inside or outside the home into the system. These cameras can then send a picture to any TV in the house, providing homeowners with video monitoring capabilities. Telephone service is also distributed throughout a SMART-REDI home, so telephone lines can be

The Baltimore Gas & Electric SMART-REDI House, located in Baltimore, MD, was the first SMART-REDI house built. Courtesy of SMART HOUSE L.P.

accessed from any room. SMART-REDI homes have the capacity to support up to four telephone lines, including a dedicated line for a fax machine or computer modem. These features make SMART-REDI and fully functional SMART HOUSEs perfect candidates for home offices.

Telephone service is provided through a component called the telephone gateway. The AT&T SMART-REDI telephone gateway is equipped with a whole-house intercom that lets homeowners use their touchtone phones to communicate within the house. When the house is upgraded, the SMART-REDI gateway will be replaced with a SMART telephone gateway that offers additional functions, including an option for an outside call-alert signal when the whole-house intercom is in use.

Another convenience in a SMART-REDI home is multiway dimming, which gives the homeowner simple control of a hardwired light or group of lights inside or outside the house. In a SMART-REDI home, lights can be dimmed without special dimmer switches.

SMART-REDI homes incorporate a heavy-duty surge suppressor to safeguard electrical and electronic equipment from lightning or other power surges; ground fault protection is also included to protect electrical wiring and products. Continuous power supply is also provided to supply battery backup to 12 VDC products such as security, safety, and fire protection.

In addition to the benefits found in SMART-REDI homes, the most important feature is the ability to be easily converted to fully functional SMART HOUSEs. With the basic components in place, only SMART-REDI homes are equipped to accept the activating electronic components whenever the homeowner chooses — without additional wiring.

UPGRADING TO FULL-SMART

The first step to upgrading a SMART-REDI home involves adding the System Controller electronics/software module. While the System Controller Enclosure is installed during the SMART-REDI phase, the System Controller module is not added until the system upgrade is performed. This module supplies the system's central control capabilities; a control panel is necessary to enable the homeowner to take advantage of all of the system's capabilities. SMART-REDI blocks in the Convenience Centers will be replaced with SMART blocks that contain microchips. When the System Controller module and the SMART duplex receptacle blocks are available, an installer or a service provider is needed to assist the homeowner in programming the house to best suit the family's needs.

No two SMART HOUSEs will be exactly alike. The beauty of SMART HOUSE is that each system can be designed to meet its family's individual lifestyle needs. SMART HOUSE is a modular system, designed to be able to accept current *and* future home automation products, which means it can continue to keep pace with changing needs. With the system in place, changes can be made and new products added at any time.

Key to Symbols

 Contact Switch, Balanced

 Contact Switch (Surface)

V Vibration/Shock Sensor

S Sound Detector/Discriminator

G Glass-Breakage Detector

I Passive Infrared Detector

F Contact Switch (Flush)

 Dual-Technology Device

I M Dual-Technology Sensor (PIR/microwave)

 Passive Infrared Detector-360° pattern (ceiling mounted)

Control Unit

Zn   Zoned Control Unit

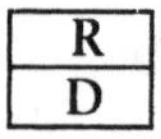

R / D   Remote Control - Digital Keypad

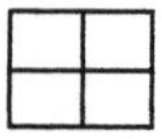

Long-Range Radio Transmitter

Line-Cut Monitor

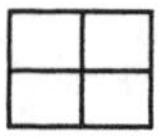

Signal Processor

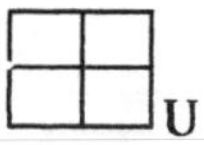

Signal Processor - Ultrasonic

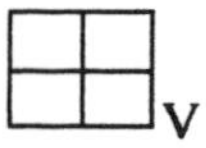

Signal Processor - Vibration/Shock

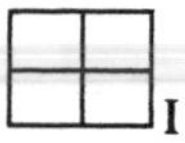

Signal Processor - Passive Infared

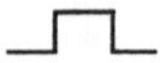

Foil Tape

Alarm Screen

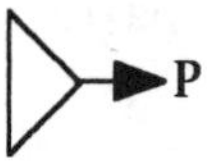

Photoelectric Transmitter

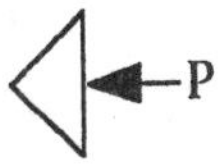

Photoelectric Receiver

Photoelectric Beam Path

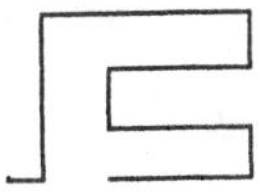

Floor Mat

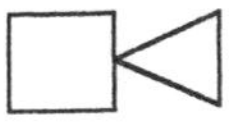

Horn/Siren Speaker

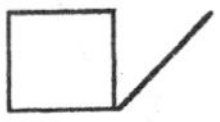

Buzzer

CCTV camera

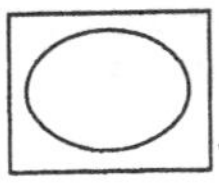

CCTV Monitor

IC   Intercom system

PLC   Powerline carrier transmitter/receiver (built-in or wall-mounted)

PLC   Powerline carrier transmitter/receiver (plug-in)

LAN   Wiring network panel

P B	Powerline carrier signal transmitter (built-in or wall-mounted)
∧ ∨	Stereo-speaker volume control
	Stereo-speaker outlet jack
⊗	Speaker with rough-in frame
	Heat detector
	Smoke detector
	Telephone outlet
A	Audio source outlet
T	HVAC thermostat
	CEBus TV outlet (dual cables)
T	Temperature Control Sensor
P	Floating Pool Alarm

Glossary

AC (alternating current) — The current available from the power outlets in American homes; it alternates direction sixty times a second.

ACTIVE SOLAR ENERGY SYSTEM — A system designed to convert solar radiation into usable energy for space, water heating, or other uses. It requires a mechanical device, usually a pump or fan, to collect the sun's energy.

ALARM CONDITION — A threatening condition, such as an intrusion, a fire, or a holdup sensed by a detector.

ALARM DISCRIMINATOR — A device used to minimize or eliminate the possibility of false alarms caused by extraneous sounds or vibrations. It can be adjusted to provide alarm discrimination under any job conditions.

ALARM SIGNAL — An audible and/or visual signal indicating an emergency that requires immediate action, such as intrusion, fire, smoke, unsafe equipment conditions, equipment failure, line tamper or failure. In general, all signals are treated as alarm signals, although alarm signals are sometimes differentiated from circuit faults or trouble signals.

ALARM SYSTEM — An assembly of equipment and devices designed and arranged to signal the presence of an alarm condition requiring urgent attention such as unauthorized entry, fire, temperature rise, etc.

AMPERE — A unit of electrical current equal to one volt across one ohm of resistance. Often abbreviated amp; its symbol is A.

AREA DETECTION — A technique for detecting an intruder's presence anywhere within a specifically defined, protected area, as opposed to detection at a specific point such as a door.

AUDIBLE ALARM — The term applies to any noise-making device, such as a siren, used to indicate an alarm.

AUDIO LISTEN-IN — Monitoring the sounds at a protected facility to determine when an intrusion occurs and/or to determine the nature of the intrusion after it has been detected by other means.

AUDIT — (1) Analysis of a specific building's consumption and potential to conserve utility-supplied energy; (2) an energy inspection typically associated with utility RCS (Residential Conservation Service) audits, which were mandated by Congress for larger utilities to provide until July 31, 1990.

AUTOMATION — (1) The technique of making an apparatus, a process, or a system operate automatically. (2) The state of being operated automatically. (3) Automatically controlled operation of an apparatus, a process, or a system by mechanical or electronic devices that take the place of human organs of observation, effort, and decision.

BATTERY BACKUP — Reserve power source in case of primary (AC) power failure.

BINARY — A numbering system using 2 as its base. The binary system uses two symbols — 0 and 1. Most alarm system devices are based on binary codes.

BRITISH THERMAL UNIT (Btu) — A unit used to measure quantity of heat, defined as the quantity of energy necessary to raise the temperature of 1 pound of water 1 degree Fahrenheit.

BUILDING ENVELOPE — The assembly of exterior partitions of a building that enclose conditioned spaces, through which thermal energy may be transferred to or from the exterior, unconditioned spaces, or the ground.

BURGLARY — An illegal entry into premises with the intent to commit a crime. (Legal definition varies by state.)

BUS — A connector module or interface for power distribution to and among appliances, or a rigid conductor in an electrical circuit, used to connect three or more circuits.

CALCULATION SYSTEMS — Systems usually based on one of the many building simulation models and an estimate of the amount of energy saved over some base case, which might be current building code. The savings are translated into several forms: Btu/ft 2, points, which are equivalent to a certain amount of usage/savings, or other designations such as "stars."

CAPACITANCE SENSOR — A protective device that detects a change in electrical capacitance of a metal object relative to ground. Touching a protected object, such as a safe, triggers an alarm.

CENTRAL MONITORING STATION — A system in which the alarm signal is relayed to a remote panel located at the facilities of a privately owned protection service company.

CERTIFICATION PROGRAM — A program typically operated by utilities, home builders' organizations, or not-for-profit organizations representing interested parties. Energy-efficiency standards are developed using local area demographics, construction practices, and area climatic conditions. It usually includes thermal envelope efficiency and space conditioning efficiency criteria. Certification programs generally rely on a specified inspection/verification process to ensure rating consistency. Houses either pass or fail the inspection for energy efficiency.

CHANNEL SEPARATIONS — Expressed in dB, a measurement of the amount of leakage between an electronic component's left and right channels; higher figures are better.

CIRCUIT — (1) A complete path in which electrons can flow. (2) One complete run of a set of electric conductors from a power source to various electrical devices (appliances, lights, etc.) and back to the same power source.

CLOSED CIRCUIT — A protective circuit consisting of all normally closed (NC) devices in series. A break in the circuit or activation of one or more sensors triggers an alarm.

COMFORT CONDITIONING — The process of treating air to simultaneously control its temperature, humidity, cleanliness, and distribution to meet the comfort requirements of the occupants of the conditioned space.

COMFORT ZONE — The range of temperatures over which the majority of persons feel comfortable (neither too hot or too cold).

CONDITIONED SPACE — That portion of the building that is heated and/or cooled.

CONTACTS — Electrically conductive points, or sets of points, that open and/or close circuits.

CONTROL PANEL — A device that arms, disarms, and supervises an alarm system at the user's premises.

CURRENT — The flow of electrons through a conductor.

DAYLIGHTING — The use of sunlight to supplement or replace electric lighting.

DAYLIGHTING CONTROL — A control system that varies the light output of an electric lighting system in response to variations in available light.

DECIBEL — A unit of measurement for sound intensity. Abbreviated dB.

DEDICATED LINE — A telephone line connecting two points, such as a protected premises and a central station, for alarm signaling. Also called leased line, direct wire, direct connect, and B.A. circuit.

DEMAND-SIDE MANAGEMENT (DSM) — Utility program designed to control energy consumption on the customer's side of the meter. Such programs include conservation/energy efficiency, load management, fuel substitution, and load building.

DETECTION PATTERN — Area of coverage for space protection devices.

DETECTION RANGE — The maximum effective distance that a sensor can detect an intruder. Used to describe space protection devices.

DETECTOR — Any device for detecting intrusion, equipment failure or malfunction, unsafe equipment operation, presence of smoke or fire, or any other condition requiring immediate action. Detectors include a means for translating the detected abnormal condition into some form of alarm signal — either a local or remote alarm, the latter over a reporting line, with or without electrical supervision.

DIGITAL COMMUNICATOR — A device that electronically dials one or more prerecorded telephone numbers using digital codes and reports alarm or supervisory information to a receiver.

DIGITAL KEYPAD — Used for arming and disarming an alarm system with numerical codes.

DIRECT SOLAR GAIN — Solar energy collected from the sun (as heat) in a building through windows, walls, skylights, etc.

DOLBY PRO LOGIC — An enhanced version of the basic Dolby Surround decoding system that employs special "logic" circuitry to improve sound localization, especially of on-screen dialogue. In addition to the two primary speakers, Pro Logic systems require the use of a front center-channel speaker and two rear-channel speakers for ambiance reproduction.

DOLBY SURROUND — A system developed for movie theaters, now available in some signal processors, preamplifiers, integrated amplifiers, and receivers, that adds one or two rear ambience channels to the ordinary stereo channels.

DOPPLER EFFECT (Shift) — The apparent change in frequency of sound or radio waves when reflected by or originating from a moving object. The operating principle of ultrasonic and microwave motion detectors.

DOUBLE GLAZING — Two thicknesses of glass, separated by an air space and framed in an opening, designed to reduce heat transfer or sound transmission.

DRY CONTACT — Metallic points making (shorting) or breaking (opening) a circuit.

DUCT — A passageway made of sheet metal or other suitable material used for conveying air or other gases at low pressures.

EFFICIENCY — The ratio of the useful energy delivered by a dynamic system (such as machine, engine, or motor) to the energy supplied to it over the same period or cycle of operation.

EFFICIENCY LIGHTING — The ratio of light from a lamp to the electrical power consumed, including ballast losses, expressed as lumens per watt.

ELECTROMAGNETIC INTERFERENCE — Interference caused by disturbances in the atmosphere (lightning, sunspots) or in the immediate vicinity (power lines, electrical motors). Abbreviated EMI.

EMISSIVITY — The property of emitting radiation; possessed by all materials to a varying extent.

EMITTANCE — The emissivity of a material, expressed as a fraction. Emittance values range from 0.05 for brightly polished metals to 0.96 for flat black paint.

END-OF-LINE RESISTOR — A resistor that introduces a specific impedance to a circuit. Deviations beyond certain limits trigger an alarm. Used to supervise protective circuits.

ENERGY COST SAVINGS — The difference between a home whose energy costs are being measured and a comparable home with no energy-saving construction or improvement features. For an existing energy-efficient home, it is the difference in operating costs between the home as it exists and the home after it has received energy-saving improvements.

ENERGY-EFFICIENCY RATING — A certification of a home's energy efficiency or a relative indication of its energy efficiency on a graduated scale.

ENERGY-EFFICIENT MEASURES — Items that reduce a home's consumption of utility-supplied energy, including measures such as insulation and low-emissivity windows and renewable energy technologies such as passive solar design and solar hot water systems.

ENERGY-EFFICIENT MORTGAGE PROGRAM — The energy improvement programs of the VA, FHA, Fannie Mae, Freddie Mac, and the Farmers Home Administration. These are national programs available to all qualified home buyers and homeowners at the time of purchase or refinance.

ENERGY-EFFICIENT MORTGAGES (EEMs) — When a homeowner or home buyer applies for a home loan, at the time of purchase or refinance, he or she can roll the cost of needed energy improvements into the mortgage, amortizing the cost of the improvements over the life of the mortgage.

ENERGY MANAGEMENT SYSTEM — A control system (often computerized) designed to regulate the energy consumption of a building by controlling operation of energy consuming systems such as the heating, ventilating and air conditioning, lighting, and water heating systems.

ENERGY RATING — A designation of the relative efficiency of a property.

ENERGY-SAVING CONSTRUCTION OR IMPROVEMENT FEATURES — Features that contribute to the lowering of energy use in a residence. They include, but are not limited to, the following: insulation (wall, ceiling, floor, slab, crawl, basement, window, door); air infiltration reduction (gaskets, caulking, weatherstripping, controlled mechanical ventilation); heating and cooling equipment (setback thermostats and high-efficiency furnace, air conditioning, water heater, and fireplace); duct loss reduction; glazing (amount of glazing, R-value, solar fraction, solar orientation); and passive and active solar features.

ENERGY-SAVING MEASURE — Any device, equipment, material, process, construction method, system, structure, or combination thereof that will result in a reduction of energy usage, when compared with conventional energy-related practice in the area of the project.

ENTRANCE DELAY — The time between activating a sensor and the transmission of an alarm signal by the control panel. This delay allows you to turn off your alarm after returning home without sending an alarm signal to the central station.

EXIT DELAY — This permits a person to turn on the alarm system and to leave through a protected entrance without causing an alarm.

EXTERNAL LOAD CONTROLS — Fixed or movable shading elements (awnings, wing walls, overhangs, eaves, shade screens) that control solar heat gain to exterior envelope components.

FOOTCANDLE — A unit of illumination on a surface that is 1 foot from a uniform point source of light of 1 candle and is equal to 1 lumen per square foot.

FUEL NEUTRAL — Rating system that factors in heating and cooling equipment efficiency without favoring one energy type or technology.

GENERAL LIGHTING — Lighting designed to provide a substantially uniform level of illumination throughout an area, exclusive of any provision for special visual tasks or decorative effect.

GLAZING — A covering of transparent or translucent material (typically glass or plastic) used for admitting light. Glazing retards heat losses from re-radiation and convection.

GRADE AA CENTRAL STATION; GRADE A CENTRAL STATION; GRADE B CENTRAL STATION — Underwriters' Laboratories (UL) designations for different classes of central stations, based on degree of protection afforded and specific requirements for equipment, personnel, procedures, records, and maintenance. Requirements are outlined in the UL publication, *Standards for Safety, Central Station Burglar Alarm Systems, UL611.*

GROUND LOOP — When two or more grounded points in an electrical system develop a conductive path between them, rendering all or part of the circuit ineffective.

HEAT GAIN — An increase in the amount of heat contained in a space, resulting from direct solar radiation, heat flow through walls, windows, roof, and other building surfaces, and the heat given off by people, lights, equipment, and other sources.

HEAT LOSS — A decrease in the amount of heat contained in a space, resulting from heat flow through walls, windows, roof, and other building surfaces, and from exfiltration of warm air.

HEATING LOAD — The rate at which heat must be added to a space to maintain the desired temperature within the space.

HEATING, VENTILATING, AND AIR CONDITIONING SYSTEM (HVAC) — A system that provides heating, ventilating, and/or cooling within or associated with a building.

HERS CHARACTERISTICS — (1) Rates, on a scale, the relative energy efficiency of any house — new and existing, efficient and inefficient; (2) provides a rating based on efficiency of the thermal envelope, space heating and cooling efficiency, and water heating efficiency; (3) estimates annual costs; (4) recommends improvement measures; (5) is fuel neutral; (6) requires on-site inspections and quality control; (7) typically, is state sponsored (or approved) and third-party delivered; (8) has goal of providing voluntary, market-driven incentives to encourage increased efficiency; (9) provides documentation that a house meets or exceeds a minimum standard for efficiency designated at a point on the scale.

HOME ENERGY RATING SYSTEM (HERS) — HERS measure and rate, on a scale, the relative energy efficiency of any house, regardless of age, efficiency, or fuel use. (See HERS CHARACTERISTICS.)

HOMERUN — A wiring method that connects each outlet or sensor directly to the electrical or control panel instead of several outlets/sensors on a continuous loop.

HOT WIRE — Ungrounded conductor carrying electrical current. Usually identified by black or red insulation, but may be any color other than white, gray, or green.

INCANDESCENT LAMP — An electric lamp consisting essentially of a glass or quartz bulb evacuated or filled with an inert gas in which a filament, commonly of tungsten, gives off light when it is heated to incandescence by an electric current.

INFILTRATION — The uncontrolled inward leakage of air through cracks and gaps in the building envelope, especially around windows and doors.

INFRARED — The part of the invisible spectrum that is contiguous to the red end of the visible spectrum and that comprises electromagnetic radiations of wavelengths from 0.8 to 1000 microns.

INTERNAL SHADING DEVICE — Any object on the interior side of the window that reduces the intensity of solar radiation reaching the living or working areas. Internal devices are much less effective at preventing heat gain than exterior shading devices.

KILOWATT (kW) — 1000 watts.

KILOWATT-HOUR (kWh) — 1000 watt-hour.

LIGHTING POWER DENSITY — Total lighting power consumption per unit area, typically measured in watts per square foot.

LINE SEIZURE — Characteristics provided by the integral circuitry of tape dialers and digital communicators, which "seize" in-use phone lines to ensure transmission of emergency signals.

LINE SUPERVISION — Electronic protection of an alarm line accomplished by sending a continuous or coded signal through a circuit. A change in the circuit characteristics, such as a change in impedance due to the circuit having been tampered with, will be detected by the monitor. The monitor initiates an alarm if the change exceeds a predetermined amount.

LOAD — The amount of power required by a circuit or device in operation.

LOAD MANAGEMENT PROGRAMS — Programs that have the effect of reducing electric peak demands, or shifting electric demand from the hours of peak demand to non-peak periods.

LOW-E — A special coating that reduces the emissivity of a window assembly, thereby reducing the heat transfer through the assembly.

LUMEN — A measure of the amount of light available from a source equivalent to the light emitted by one candle.

LUMEN/WATT — A measure of the efficacy of a light fixture; the number of lumens output per watt of power consumed.

LUMINAIRE — A complete lighting system consisting of a lamp or lamps together with the part designed to distribute light, to position and protect the lamps, and to connect the lamps to the power supply.

MAGNETIC CONTACT — A sensor used to protect movable objects — usually doors and windows. It consists of two separate parts, a magnetically activated switch and a magnet. Moving the magnet causes the switch mechanism to open and/or close because the magnetic field is removed.

MEDICAL ALERT — A signal initiated by a person in need of medical attention, transmitted to a remote receiving station where information is kept relative to the individual's medical problem.

MOTION DETECTION — Detection of an intruder by making use of the change in location or orientation in a protection area as the intruder moves about.

NATIONAL/LOCAL THRESHOLD — That point on the uniform scale at which energy-efficient mortgage benefits kick in.

NEUTRAL WIRE — Grounded conductor that completes a circuit by providing a return path to the source. Always identified by white or gray insulation.

NICAD (nickel cadmium) — A high performance, long-lasting rechargeable battery that may be used as an emergency power supply for an alarm system.

NODE O — A centering point of component parts.

NORMALLY CLOSED — A circuit or switch in which the contacts are closed during normal operation. Breaking or opening the circuit triggers an alarm.

NORMALLY OPEN — A circuit or switch in which the contacts are open during normal operation. Shorting or closing the circuit triggers an alarm.

OCCUPANCY SENSOR — A control device that senses the presence of a person in a given space, commonly used to control lighting systems.

OHM'S LAW — Voltage = current x resistance.

OPERATOR (of a window sash) — The mechanism, including a crank handle and gear box, attached to an operating arm or arms for the purpose of opening and closing a window. Usually found on casement and awning type windows.

PARALLEL CIRCUIT — Circuit interconnection in which all components share a common positive and common negative connection.

PASSIVE SOLAR GAIN — Solar energy that enters the building, providing heating and/or daylight to the building.

PASSIVE SOLAR TECHNOLOGIES — Technologies that combine architecture to benefit from solar radiation incidence on buildings for heating, cooling, and lighting, with good conservation techniques for the building envelope and energy-efficient equipment and controls. Passive solar technologies are typically sunspaces, direct gain systems, and thermal storage.

PEAK LOAD — The highest electrical demand within a particular period of time.

PHOTOCELL — A device that produces an electric reaction to visible radiant energy (light).

PHOTOELECTRIC SENSOR — A device that detects a visible or invisible beam of light and responds to its complete or near complete interruption.

PROGRAMMABLE CONTROLLER — A device that controls the operation of electrical equipment (air conditioning units, lights) according to preset time and schedule.

PROTECTED AREA — A term used to indicate the specific area being protected by a security system, the area under surveillance.

RACEWAY — A protective shield installed over surface wiring for safety and physical protection of the wires.

RADIO FREQUENCY — The frequency of certain electromagnetic waves. Abbreviated RF.

RADIO FREQUENCY INTERFERENCE — Electromagnetic interference in the radio frequency range. Abbreviated RFI.

RATING TOOL — A certified procedure for calculating total annual energy consumption and costs of a home, and for assigning a rating that establishes how the efficiency of a given home compares to the efficiency of all other homes.

REMOTE ALARM — An alarm signal that is transmitted to a remote central monitoring station.

RENEWABLE ENERGY TECHNOLOGIES — The use of, as resources, the energy inherent in sunlight and the direct and indirect results of its impact on our planet (photons, wind, falling water, temperature differentials, and plant matter), gravitational forces (the tides), and the Earth's heat. These technologies at the sites of homes tend to be limited to: passive solar space heating, cooling, and lighting; solar water heating; active solar space heating; photovoltaic generation of electricity; biofuel appliances; and wind generation of electricity.

RESET — To restore an alarm to its original (normal) condition after an alarm signal.

RESISTIVE — A property of a conductor by virtue of which the passage of current is opposed, causing electric energy to be transformed into heat.

RETROFIT — A modification to an existing building.

RJ31X JACK — A special telephone line jack that must be installed to connect digital communicators to the telephone line.

R-VALUE — A unit of thermal resistance used for comparing insulating values of different material. The higher the R-value of a material, the greater its insulating properties and the slower the heat flows through it. Also called R-factor.

SENSOR — A device designed to produce a signal or other indication in response to an event or a stimulus within its detection area.

SHADE SCREEN — A screen affixed to the exterior of a window or other glazed opening, designed to reduce the solar radiation reaching the glazing.

SHADING — (1) The protection from heat gains due to

direct solar radiation; (2) shading is provided by (a) permanently attached exterior devices, glazing materials, adherent materials applied to the glazing, or an adjacent building for non-residential buildings, hotels, motels, and high-rise apartments, and by (b) devices affixed to the structure for residential buildings.

SHADING COEFFICIENT — The ratio of solar heat gain through a specific glazing system to the total solar heat gain through a single layer of clear, double-strength glass.

SHUNT — To remove some portion of an alarm system from operation, allowing entry into a protected area without initiating an alarm signal.

SILENT ALARM — A remote alarm without any local indication that an alarm has been transmitted.

SLAVE — A mechanism under control of and repeating the actions of a similar mechanism.

SOLAR HEAT GAIN — Heat added to a space due to transmitted and absorbed solar energy.

SPIKE — A momentary increase in electrical current that can damage electrical equipment.

SUBMETERING — Breaking down the utility metering of a building to determine the proportionate energy use of specific building systems and appliances.

TASK LIGHTING — Lighting designed specifically to illuminate one or more task locations, and generally confined to those locations.

THERMAL BREAK (thermal barrier) — An element of low heat conductivity placed in such a way as to reduce or prevent the flow of heat.

THERMAL ENVELOPE — The building's shell — walls, foundation, floors, ceilings, windows, doors, and roof.

THERMOSTAT — An automatic control device designed to be responsive to temperature and typically used to maintain set temperatures by cycling the HVAC system.

THERMOSTAT, SETBACK — A device containing a clock mechanism, which can automatically change the inside temperature maintained by the HVAC system according to a preset schedule. The heating or cooling requirements can be reduced when a building is unoccupied or when occupants are asleep.

TRANSIENT — A brief power surge in an electrical line.

TRANSMITTER — A device that produces a radio frequency or other electrical signal for conveyance to a compatible receiver.

TRANSPONDER — A device that gathers and converts sensor data for transmission to a signal processor.

UL LISTED — Signifies that production samples of the product have been found to comply with established Underwriters Laboratories requirements. The manufacturer is authorized to use the Laboratories' listing marks on the listed products that comply with the requirements.

ULTRASONIC SENSOR — A sensor that detects motion by transmitting very high frequency sound and triggers an alarm when movement within the protected area creates a Doppler effect.

UTILITY AUDIT — A formal review of a home's energy use conducted by a utility company representative, with recommendations for energy-efficiency measures such as weatherstripping, caulking, and insulation.

U-VALUE (coefficient of heat transmission) — The rate of heat loss, in Btu per hour, through a square foot of a surface (wall, roof, door, or other building surface) when the difference between the air temperature on either side is 1 degree Fahrenheit. The U-value is reciprocal of the R-value.

VOLT — Unit of measure denoting electrical pressure. Abbreviated V.

VOLTAGE — Pressure at which a circuit operates, expressed in volts.

WALK-TEST — Testing a space protection sensor to ascertain its coverage pattern by walking through the protected area.

WATT — A unit of measure of electric power at a point in time, as capacity or demand.

WATT-HOUR — One watt of power expended for 1 hour.

WEATHERIZATION — Retrofitting a house's envelope with basic energy-efficiency measures, such as weatherstripping, caulking, and insulation.

WEATHERSTRIPPING — Specially designed strips, seals, and gaskets installed around doors and windows to limit air leakage.

ZONAL CONTROL (HVAC) — A method of designing and controlling the heating, ventilating, and air conditioning (HVAC) system of a residence so that living areas can be maintained at a different temperature than sleeping areas, using independent setback thermostats.

ZONES — Smaller subdivisions into which larger areas are divided to permit selective access to some zones, while maintaining other zones secure and to permit pinpointing the specific locations from which an alarm signal has been transmitted.

Appendices

1. Books, Videos, Magazines

BOOKS

All Thumbs Guide to Home Wiring
Electronics Book Club
Blue Ridge Summit, PA 17294-0810
or
CIE Bookstore
1776 East 17th St.
Cleveland OH 44114-3679
(800) 321-2155

An Installers Guide to CEBus Home Automation
Parks Associates, $149
5310 Harvest Hill Rd., Ste. 235, LB 162
Dallas TX 75230-5805
(214) 490-1113
(214) 490-1133 FAX

Approaching Home Automation: A Guide to Using X-10 Technology
Craig Elliot and Bill Berner, $19.99 plus $2.00 shipping and handling
Approaching, Inc.
1615 W. Cullom
Chicago IL 60613
(800) 484-9697 ext. 4547

Building Interior, Plants and Automation
Stuart D. Snyder
Prentice Hall
15 Columbus Cir.
New York NY 10023

The Complete Guide to Barrier-Free Housing
Gary D. Branson, $14.95
F&W Publications
1507 Dana Ave.
Cincinnati OH 45207
(800) 289-0963

The Complete Guide to Home Security
David Alan Wacker, $14.95
F&W Publications
1507 Dana Ave.
Cincinnati OH 45207
(800) 289-0963

SMART HOUSE: The coming revolution in housing
Ralph Smith, GP Publishing
SMART HOUSE Wiring, A comprehensive guide to installing the SMART HOUSE system
H. Brooke Stauffer and Ray C. Mullin, $20.95
National Association of Home Builders Research Center
(301) 249-4000

Understanding & Installing Home Systems — How To Automate Your Home
David Gaddis, $29.95
Home Systems
6 NE 63rd St., Ste. 300
Oklahoma City OK 73105
(405) 840-4751

VIDEOS

Home of the Future
$9.99 plus $2.50 S&H
Hometime
150 N. 6th St.
Philadelphia PA 19106
(800) 736-3033

Building Your First SMART HOUSE
SMART HOUSE L.P.
400 Prince George's Blvd.
Upper Marlboro MD 20772

MAGAZINES

Audio/Video Interiors
21700 Oxnard St., Ste. 1600
Woodland Hills CA 91367
(818) 593-3900

Circuit Cellar Inc.
4 Park St., Ste. 12
Vernon CT 06066
(203) 875-2751

Electronic House
P.O. Box 339
Stillwater OK 74076-0339
(405) 624-8015

Stereo Review
1633 Broadway
New York NY 10019

2. Catalogs, Technical Information, Trade Associations

CATALOGS

All Electronics Corp.
P.O. Box 567
Van Nuys CA 91408-0567
(800) 826-5432
Alarms, sensors, and electronic components

American Science & Surplus
601 Linden Pl.
Evanston IL 60202
(312) 475-8440
Electrical surplus

Complete Home Automation
1221 Thunder Trail, Box 2175
Goldenrod FL 32733-2175
(800) 766-4226 (orders)
(407) 830-5535

Digi-Key
701 Brooks Ave. S
Thief River Falls MN 56701-0677
(800) 344-4539
Mail order electrical supplier

ESS Distributors
10965 Santa Barbara Pl.
Alta Loma CA 91701
(800) 755-6796
Audio systems

Fair Radio Sales Co., Inc.
P.O. Box 1105
Lima OH 45802
(419) 227-6573
Military and industrial surplus electronic parts

Heath Company
(Home Automation by Heath)
Benton Harbor MI 49022
(800) 444-3284

Herko Electronics, Inc.
2300 Ridge Rd. W
Rochester NY 14626
(800) 388-1554 (orders & info)
(716) 227-1960 (tech line)
(716) 227-1490 FAX

Hi-Tech Industries, Inc.
226C E. Collins Dr.
Fort Wayne IN 46825
(800) 733-7444
(219) 484-0928

Home Automation Laboratories
(HAL)
5500 Highlands Pkwy., Ste. 450
Smyrna GA 30082-5141
(800) YEL-4-HAL (catalog requests)
(800) HOME-LAB (orders only)

Home Automation Systems
21 Seascape Dr.
Newport Beach CA 92663
(800) SMART-HM (orders & catalog orders)

Home Control Concepts
9353-C Activity Rd.
San Diego CA 92126
(800) CONTROL (orders only)
(619) 693-8887

Home Systems
6 NE 63rd St., Ste. 300
Oklahoma City OK 73105
(405) 840-4751
(405) 842-3419 FAX

Jameco Electronics
1355 Shoreway Rd.
Belmont CA 94002
(800) 831-4242
Mail order electronics and computers

Mountain West Alarm Supply
9420 E. Double Tree Ranch Rd.
Scottsdale AZ 85258
(800) 528-6169
Wholesale alarm products

Mouser Electronics
National Circulation Center
2401 Hwy. 287 N
Mansfield TX 76063-4827
(800) 34-MOUSER
Electronic parts catalog

Real Goods, Inc.
966 Mazzoni St.
Ukiah CA 95482
(800) 762-7325
Alternative energy catalog

Su-Mar Enterprises
1292 Montclair Dr.
Pasadena MD 21122
(800) 477-4181 (orders)
(410) 437-4181

Tech Toys International
P.O. Box 27983
Rancho Bernardo CA 27983
(619) 693-8892
Personal protection devices/X-10-compatible devices

Tenex Computer Express
56800 Magnetic Dr.
Mishawaka IN 46545
(800) PROMPT-1
(800) 776-6781

TECHNICAL INFORMATION

David Butler
RMS Syndication
P.O. Box 3839
Charlotte NC 28273-0001
Reprints of "At Home With Technology" weekly newspaper column, including exhaustive resource list.

Electric Power Research Institute (EPRI)
3412 Hillview Ave.
Palo Alto CA 94304
(415) 855-2411

For copies of EPRI reports or brochures contact:
EPRI Distribution Center
207 Coggins Dr.
P.O. Box 23205
Pleasant Hill CA 94523
(510) 934-4212
(510) 944-0510 FAX

Lab Notes
Home Automation Laboratories (HAL)
5500 Highlands Pkwy., Ste. 450
Smyrna GA 30082-5141
(800) YEL-4-HAL (catalog requests)
(800) HOME-LAB (orders only)

Silicon Valley Video Group
Attn: Steve Mueller
335 Bodega Way
San Jose CA 95119-1603
Prodigy ID: SJCR28A
X-10 technical information, 88 pages, $8.00.

TRADE ASSOCIATIONS

Custom Electronic Designer & Installers Association (CEDIA)
10400 Robert Rd.
Palos Hills IL 60465
(800) CEDIA30

Electronic Industries Association
1722 Eye Street NW, Ste. 200
Washington DC 20006
(202) 457-8700

Home Automation Association (HAA)
1223 Potomac NW
Washington DC 20007-3212
(202) 333-8579
(202) 337-3809 FAX

3. Home Automation Dealer/Installer Directory

The following pages contain an alphabetical listing of all known home automation dealers and installers by state. Considering the rapid growth that the home automation industry is currently experiencing, it is possible that not all dealers or installers in your area are listed in this directory. Although every attempt has been made to verify the accuracy of company information, some businesses may have moved, changed phone numbers, or gone out of business since this list was compiled. NOTE: Home automation companies not listed can contact the author through the publisher to be included in future printings.

Alabama

G & G Telecommunications, Inc.
4820 University Dr., Ste. 9
Huntsville AL 35806
(205) 830-4464

Southern Construction Products
517-B 35th St. North
Birmingham AL 35222
(800) 821-9296
(205) 250-9070

SVC Security Video
Concepts, Inc.
P.O. Box 530794
Birmingham AL 35253
(205) 940-7699

Arizona

ASSI Security of Arizona
2401 West Behrend, Ste. 87-89
Phoenix AZ 85027
(602) 581-0101

Kilowatt Electric
9214 North 5th Ave.
Phoenix AZ 85021
(602) 246-9329
(602) 944-2497 FAX

Last Chance Audio
P.O. Box 36532
Tucson AZ 85740
(602) 744-4282
(602) 744-4282 FAX

Lighting-Land
3550 East Indian School Rd.
Phoenix AZ 85018
(602) 956-8696
(602) 956-9874 FAX

Safeguard Security Systems
4801 East Indian School Rd.
Phoenix AZ 85018-5498
(602) 957-2851

Vjarnet Construction, Inc.
P.O. Box 31384
Phoenix AZ 85046
(602) 996-2827

Arkansas

Arkansas Home Automation, Inc.
1020 North Spruce
Little Rock AR 72205
(501) 664-7530

California

A. Arlie's Security System
P.O. Box 1015
Chino CA 91710
(714) 597-7777

All-Safe Alarms, Inc.
1000 South Main St., Ste. 652
Salinas CA 93901
(408) 484-9658

Antonucci & Associates, Inc.
25 Navy St. #7
Venice CA 90291
(310) 452-9011
(310) 399-6824 FAX

Athanor Engineering
5550 Franklin Blvd., Ste. 101
Sacramento CA 95820
(916) 456-4355
(916) 456-1697 FAX

Automated Environments
1531 Burgandy Rd.
Encinitas CA 92024
(619) 943-9385

Audio Visions Inc.
15375 Barranca Pkwy. B-107
Irvine CA 92718
(714) 753-0503
(714) 753-0501 FAX

Audio Video Engineering
6243 Calle Bodega
Camarillo CA 93012
(805) 338-7848

Automated Home Systems
P.O. Box 51224
Pacific Grove CA 93950
(408) 373-1615

Automation Systems Engineering
4102 Orange Ave., Ste. 107-30
Long Beach CA 90807
(310) 988-5050

Bonsey Electric
300 Union Ave. #33
Campbell CA 95008
(408) 377-9900

Building Automation
8401 Hialeah Court
Fair Oaks CA 95628
(916) 969-4949

Custom Home Electronics
6986 El Camino Real #B102
Carlsbad CA 92009
(619) 438-8242

Custom Works Engineering
1285 Las Tunas Dr.
San Gabriel CA 91776
(818) 359-2972

DMS Systems
5108 Spencer St.
Torrance CA 90503-2232
(310) 542-7712

David Young Associates
3 Encina
Irvine CA 92720
(714) 544-5773

Domestic Management Security
Systems
5108 Spencer St.
Torrance CA 90503
(310) 542-7712

Electrasonics West
9551 Fullbright Ave.
Chatsworth CA 91311
(818) 993-0600

Electronics & Design Assoc., Inc.
1801 South Bentley Ave., Ste. 306
Los Angeles CA 90025-4315
(310) 444-9575

Electrotech
17481 Valeworth Circle
Huntington Beach CA 92649
(714) 377-0849
(714) 377-0849 FAX

Engineered Environments
4059 Clipper Ct.
Fremont CA 94538
(510) 657-9240

Exclusive SmartHome Systems
10965 Santa Barbara Pl.
Alta Loma CA 91701
(800) 755-6796

Fields Telecommunications
32545-A Golden Lantern #470
Dana Point CA 92677
(714) 495-7109

Freenergy Company
25030 West Ave., Stanford #130
Valencia CA 91355
(805) 279-0373

Future Home Electric
6509 Kester Ave. #8
Van Nuys CA 91411
(800) 833-1400

Genesis Engineering, Inc.
25422 Trabuco Rd. #105-204
Lake Forest CA 92630
(714) 454-2492

Gold Country Security
P.O. Box 598
Pollock Pines CA 95726
(916) 644-5217

Golden Pacific Systems
1490 Camden Ave.
Campbell CA 95008
(408) 371-9177

Hidden Connections
3937 Magee Ave.
Oakland CA 94619
(510) 530-7622

High Output Electric
28643 North Avocado Pl.
Saugus CA 91350
(805) 296-1322

Home Automation Systems
21 Seascape Dr.
Newport Beach CA 92663
(714) 642-6610

Home Chat
2711 Grade Pl.
Spring Valley CA 91977
(619) 462-1860

Holosound
1548 Adams Ave. #202
Costa Mesa CA 92626
(714) 751-4656

Home Control Concepts
9353-C Activity Rd.
San Diego CA 92126
(619) 693-8887

Home Electronics Consultants
4332 Costello Ave.
Sherman Oaks CA 91423
(818) 981-8108

Home Tech Systems
P.O. Box 0349
Citrus Heights CA 95611
(916) 961-2126

Home Theater Designs
368 King Dr.
S. San Francisco CA 94080
(415) 952-1400

Inside Systems, Inc.
25252 McIntyre St.
Laguna Hills CA 92653
(714) 770-6050

Integrated Systems Designs
4095 Bridge St.
Fair Oaks CA 95628
(916) 863-6830

Intelligent House Systems
1501 Dana Pl.
Fullerton CA 92631
(714) 871-9143

Invostar, Inc.
17401 Jepsen C.
Huntington Beach CA 92647
(714) 848-2285

JDS Technology
16750 West Bernardo Dr.
San Diego CA 92127
(619) 487-8787

Lis Enterprise
23006 Hartand St.
West Hills CA 91307
(818) 713-2538

Living Systems
P.O. Box 514
Redondo Beach CA 90277
(310) 372-3243

Mad Martian
10551 Wellworth Ave.
Los Angeles CA 90024
(310) 479-3411

Michael J. O'Neill Corporation
136 South Linden Dr., Ste. 2
Beverly Hills CA 90212
(310) 276-4877

Moore Electric, Inc.
9540 Center Ave., Ste. 120
Rancho Cucamonga CA 91730
(714) 941-9483

Niche Electric
1140 Woodlake Dr.
Cardiff-By-The-Sea CA 92007
(619) 942-9483

Norris & Wong Associates
3739 Balboa St., Ste. 147
San Francisco CA 94121
(415) 221-7043

Norse Industries, Inc.
4020 Palos Verdes Dr. N., Ste. 108
Rolling Hills Estates CA 90274
(310) 544-4252

Paul Norris & Associates
559 40th Ave.
San Francisco CA 94121
(415) 221-7043

Primex Security & Home Automation
8750 Oland Ave.
Sun Valley CA 91352
(818) 768-8978
(213) 666-7757 FAX

Pyramid Light & Power
122 Pied Piper Lane
Santa Cruz CA 95060
(408) 458-0362

R & D Unlimited
3909 Starland Dr.
LaCanada CA 91011
(818) 952-1539

Rikar Antenna Engineering
P.O. Box 27054
Escondido CA 92027
(619) 745-0641

Robert's Home Audio & Video
1611 S. LaCienega Blvd.
Los Angeles CA 90035
(310) 276-3955

Safe & Sound
2400 Main St.
Santa Monica CA 90405
(310) 392-3031

Schweiter Enterprises
P.O. Box 947
San Ramon CA 94583
(510) 820-1851

Serena Industries, Inc.
1180-A Aster Ave.
Sunnyvale CA 94086
(408) 296-7444

Simply Automated Homes
437 Elwood Ave.
Oakland CA 94610
(510) 782-5535

SmartHouse Engineering &
Automation
5694 Mission Center Rd., Ste. 270
San Diego CA 92108
(619) 541-0210

Smith/Crockett Construction
Services
11426 Sutton Way, Ste. 116
Grass Valley CA 95945
(916) 273-4202
(916) 273-2141 FAX

Sound Clinic
Adirondack Row
San Diego CA 92139-2637
(619) 475-4546

Star Intelligence Resources
7514 Girard Ave., Ste. 1421
La Jolla CA 92037
(619) 483-7677

System Security
13337 East South St. #345
Cerritos CA 90701
(800) 392-9000

TeleGuard Security Systems, Inc.
16735 Saticoy St., Ste. 101
Van Nuys CA 91406
(818) 904-0269

The Home Automater
1921 Grenadier Dr.
San Pedro CA 90732
(310) 337-1077

3-Way Electric
49800 Hwy. 74, Unit E
Hemet CA 92544
(714) 927-8336

Trans Telecom Company
12079 Jefferson Blvd.
Culver City CA 90230
(310) 578-0022

Ultimate Enterprises
5643 Paradise Dr., Ste. 156
Corte Madera CA 94925
(415) 927-9551

Warren Security Systems, Inc.
P.O. Box 148
Sausalito CA 94966
(415) 456-4761

Wilson Audio Video Enterprises
20044 Ventura Blvd.
Woodland Hills CA 91364
(818) 883-2811

Colorado

Black Forest Home Security
6820 Brentwood Dr.
Colorado Springs CO 80908
(719) 495-2715

Electronic Systems Consultants
1020 East Hyman
Aspen CO 81611
(303) 925-1497

Martin's Handyman Service
P.O. Box 5760
Woodland Park CO 80866
(719) 687-6656

Mission Electric
10865 West 39th Pl.
Wheat Ridge CO 80033

Residential Systems, Inc.
400 Corporate Cir., Unit O
Golden CO 80401
(303) 277-9983

Sentient Homes, Inc.
3746 West 102nd Ave.
Westminster CO 80030-2438
(303) 469-9322

Vail Electronics Ltd.
P.O. Box 463
Edwards CO 81632
(303) 926-3065

Connecticut

AA Roberts Systems & Solutions
3 Beebe Lane
Storrs CT 06268
(203) 429-7862

Custom Audio-Video Systems
6 Elm Ct.
East Haven CT 06512
(203) 468-1599

Future Home Concepts
19 Clearview Ave.
Danbury CT 06811
(203) 778-4342

Future Home Systems
P.O. Box 260280
Hartford CT 06106
(203) 278-0564

Horizon Systems
125 George St.
East Haven CT 06512
(203) 469-8470

Intelligent Systems, Inc.
175 New Britain Ave.
Plainfield CT 06062
(203) 793-9951

Phoenix Security
444 Westport Ave.
Norwalk CT 06851
(203) 846-4611

Wesco Associates
197 Fern St.
West Hartford CT 06119
(203) 231-8228

W.J. Novak Electric
90 Post Rd.
Darien CT 06820
(203) 655-7508

Zelek Electric Company
11 Oak St.
Lyme CT 06371
(203) 434-9726

Florida

Atlantis Productions
4502 US Hwy. 1
Edgewater FL 32142
(904) 345-0103

Automated Electronics
3232 SW 35th Blvd., Ste. 420
Gainesville, FL 32608
(904) 336-9880

Coastline Communication Corp.
19501 N.E. 10th Ave., Ste. 306
N. Miami Beach FL 33179
(305) 653-7532

Complete Home Automation
1221 Thunder Trail, Box 2175
Goldenrod FL 32733-2175
(800) 766-4226
(407) 830-1124 FAX

Cybertech Home Systems
P.O. Box 560303
Montverde FL 34756
(407) 469-3142

Environmental Technology Control
598 Anchorage Dr.
North Palm Beach FL 33408
(407) 863-8900

Environmental Voice Systems, Inc.
9725 Fox Chapel Rd.
Tampa FL 33647
(813) 973-4020

Home Protection, Inc. (HPI)
2165 Sunnydale Blvd., Ste. H
Clearwater FL 34625
(800) 229-6693

Intellitech Sales Company
5220 Lake Catalina Dr.
Boca Raton FL 33496
(407) 998-9484

International Security Corporation
20725-33 NE 16th Ave.
Miami FL 33179
(800) 441-5645

IQ Communications Corporation
10735 SW 216th St., B-128
Miami FL 33170
(305) 233-1944

Media Control Technologies, Inc.
5420 N.W. 33rd Ave., Ste. 106
Fort Lauderdale FL 33309
(305) 486-3342
(305) 486-3365 FAX

Media Design, Inc.
5066 South Federal Hwy.
Stuart FL 34997
(407) 221-0224

Pro-Tech International Security
1689 N. Hiatus Rd., Ste. 133
Pembroke Pines FL 33026
(305) 433-4333

Radio Alarm
P.O. Box 10304
Riviera Beach FL 33419
(407) 852-5114

Rozar Electric
P.O. Box 2336
Havana FL 32333
(904) 539-6934

S.A.S. Home Systems, Ltd.
1220 North 19th Ave.
Lake Worth FL 33460
(407) 533-0772

Savi Technologies
1093 S. Semoran Blvd.
Winter Park FL 32792
(407) 678-0010

S.E.C. Systems Corp.
1140 Holland Dr., Ste. 3
Boca Raton FL 33487
(407) 241-7227

Georgia
Castle Computers, Inc.
2244 Josephine Ct.
Marietta GA 30062
(404) 565-1242

Electronic Home Consultants, Inc.
1401 Johnson Ferry Rd., Ste. 3281
Marietta GA 30062
(404) 977-2122

EnerSci, Inc.
3100 Briarcliff Rd. NE, Ste. 532
Atlanta GA 30329
(404) 409-8844
(404) 634-3067 FAX

Home Automation Laboratories
5500 Highlands Pkwy., Ste. 450
Smyrna GA 30082
(404) 319-6000

Home Electronics
740 Brookfield Pkwy.
Roswell GA 30075
(404) 642-8645

Home Theater Systems
140 Hilderbrand
Atlanta GA 30328
(404) 255-2673

Hawaii
AV-Com Inc.
1109 Maunakea St., Ste. F4
Honolulu HI 96817
(808) 526-9449
(808) 523-9532 FAX

Design Systems, Ltd.
1166 Waimanu St.
Honolulu HI 96814
(808) 545-1055

Insight Audio-Video
1750 Kalakava Ave., Ste. 3522
Honolulu HI 96820
(808) 942-3796

Mallard Electronic Systems
P.O. Box 4998
Hilo HI 96720
(808) 966-6722

Pacific Home Automation
1168 Kaluanui Rd.
Honolulu HI 96825
(808) 396-6292

Illinois
Automated Home Equipment
3600 E. State St., Ste. 210
Rockford IL 61108
(815) 394-0808

Debartolo Mission & School
7555 South Hermitage
Chicago IL 60620
(312) 846-4855
(312) 427-8698 FAX

City Wide Electric Company
44 East 108th St.
Chicago IL 60628
(312) 821-5217
(312) 928-7585 FAX

Copper Security, Inc.
5548 S. Pulaski Rd.
Chicago IL 60629
(312) 585-8585

Enterprise Security
2623 N. Kimball Ave.
Chicago IL 60647-6666

Heil Sound, Ltd.
#2 Heil Dr.
Marissa IL 62257
(618) 295-3000
(618) 295-3030 FAX

High Quality Electric
3892 Greenridge Dr.
Decatur IL 62526
(217) 877-0814

ISR, Inc.
1701 W. Quincy Ave.
Naperville IL 60540
(708) 416-6600
(708) 416-6601 FAX

Jack Koenig & Associates
1140 Half Day Rd.
Deerfield IL 60015
(708) 948-7136

NewTech Electric Company, Inc.
711 Raub St.
Joliet IL 60435
(815) 722-6489
(815) 727-9513 FAX

ONE
P.O. Box 539
Lake Bluff IL 60044
(708) 234-8840

Performance Innovations Corp.
77 W. Huron, Ste. 214
Chicago IL 60610
(312) 943-8665
(312) 642-9298 FAX

Star Home Automation
8841 West O'Brien Dr.
Orland Hills IL 60477
(708) 403-4842

Sundown One
1800 S. MacArthur Blvd.
Springfield IL 62704
(217) 523-0128

Tech Systems, Inc.
3150 Skokie Valley Rd.
Highland Park IL 60035
(708) 433-8582
(708) 433-8530 FAX

Wildfire Enterprises
Box 136 West Plaza
Wadsworth IL 60083
(708) 336-4282

Indiana
Computerland Warsaw
P.O. Box 720
Warsaw IN 46581-0720
(219) 269-4765

Covert Alarm Company
5149 North Keystone Ave.
Indianapolis IN 46205
(317) 257-3800
(317) 254-8335 FAX

Get Smart
1106 Edwardsburg Ave.
Elkhart IN 46514
(219) 264-2083

Habitat Systems. Inc.
1122 Rollingwood Lane
Fort Wayne IN 46845

Hi-Tech Industries
226 C East Collins Dr.
Fort Wayne IN 46825

Home Automation Unlimited
P.O. Box 9069
Fort Wayne IN 46899
(219) 428-0148
(219) 747-6614 FAX

Interactive Systems
4107 Golden Eagle Dr.
Indianapolis IN 46234
(317) 290-1000

PC Service & Sales
759 Lincolnway East
South Bend IN 46601
(219) 233-3161

Satellite Audio & Video
E. 2420 Morgan Ave.
Evansville IN 47711
(812) 479-3474

Tom Doherty's Custom Audio &
Video
200 W. Carmel Dr.
Carmel IN 46032
(317) 848-7503

21st Century Automation
3123 S. Michigan St.
South Bend IN 46614
(219) 291-8399
(219) 291-8411 FAX

User Friendly Operations
1830 Wayne Trace
Fort Wayne IN 46803
(219) 420-1830

Iowa
Automated Home & Business
1351 Watrous
Des Moines IA 50315
(515) 280-5233
(515) 285-1837 FAX

National Energy Consultants
871 Shaver Rd. NE
Cedar Rapids IA 52042
(319) 364-8805

Kansas
Future Home Audio/Video
2309 West 127th
Leawood KS 66209
(816) 941-2222

Genesys Automation, Inc.
11905 Westgate
Overland Park KS 66213
(913) 897-6581

Nautilus Software
103 West St., P.O. Box 645
Iola KS 66749
(316) 365-5749

Secure House L.C.
425 Ohio St.
Lawrence KS 66044
(913) 749-4687

Kentucky
Audio/Video Interior Design
P.O. Box 24543
Lexington KY 40524
(606) 275-1125

Gallimore Electric
Rt. 8, Box 1075
Murray KY 42701
(502) 759-1835

Hutchinson's Security
2156 Winchester Ave.
Ashland KY 41101
(606) 325-3794

Super Home Systems
2175 Watterson Trail
Louisville KY 40299
(502) 267-7045

Louisiana
Cableguard Systems, Inc.
7214 Washington Ave.
New Orleans LA 70125
(504) 486-7202

Landmar Security
343 Riverside Mall, Ste. 201
Baton Rouge LA 70801
(504) 336-4331

Southern Technologies of America
400 Bel Ann Dr.
Lafayette LA 70503
(318) 988-4912

Maine

Custom Electronics
46 West Shore Dr.
Freeport ME 04032
(207) 865-6396

Maryland

American Automation &
Communication, Inc.
P.O. Box 434
Riva MD 21140
(410) 573-0801

AMP Guard Electrical Systems
4331 Church Rd.
Hampstead MD 21074
(410) 239-7741

Custom Command Systems
115 Paint Branch Dr., Ste. 3181
College Park MD 20742
(301) 314-7767

Frick Electric Company
12507 Sunset Ave. Unit 2
Ocean City MD 21842

Friendly Home Automation
3701 Menlo Dr.
Baltimore MD 21215
(410) 367-9116

HED, Inc.
8552 Dakota Dr.
Gaithersburg MD 20877
(301) 948-0151

Home Automation Solutions
7 Thorburn Rd., Ste. 700
Gaithersburg MD 20878
(301) 762-8745

Home Entertainment Design, Inc.
9511 Foxlair Pl.
Gaithersburg MD 20882
(301) 948-0151

Hometron USA, Inc.
12625 Glen Rd.
Potomac MD 20854
(301) 258-9056

Intellitech Systems, Inc.
20 Gwynns Mill Court
Owings Mills MD 21117
(301) 363-8600

Professional Products, Inc.
4964 Fairmont Ave.
Bethesda MD 20814-5090
(301) 657-2141
(301) 657-2024 FAX

Su-Mar Enterprises
1292 Montclair. Dr.
Pasadena MD 21122
(800) 477-4181
(410) 437-3757 FAX

Techno-Home Electronics
P.O. Box 336
Kingsville MD 21087
(301) 561-1368

Massachusetts

Bay Electric
550 W. Yarmouth Rd.
West Yarmouth MA 02673
(508) 398-9265
(508) 398-9265 FAX

Distrinet Systems
119 Jones Rd.
Hopedale MA 01747
(508) 634-1442

Environmental Automation
762 Plain St.
Marshfield MA 02050
(617) 834-0230

Home Automation Systems
3 Little Bear Hill Rd.
Westford MA 01886-3938
(508) 692-3217

Home Automators
2 Newcastle Rd.
Boston MA 02135
(617) 254-0824

Intelligent Home & Office
P.O. Box 526
Holden MA 01520
(508) 829-9507

Lupping Electric
13 Fir St.
Wareham MA 02571
(508) 295-1647

MTS Services
236 Ayer Rd.
Harvard MA 01451
(508) 772-7211

St. Jac Enterprises
32 Spring Ave.
Sharon MA 02067
(617) 784-6687

Smart Buildings, Inc.
P.O. Box 987
Andover MA 01810
(508) 688-5818

TEMPO Music Service
P.O. Box 793
West Falmouth MA 02574
(508) 457-0132

Michigan

A.C.E. Systems, Inc.
132 Griags
Rochester MI 48307
(313) 652-6134

American Coach
130 West Chicago
Allen MI 49227
(517) 869-2253

Automated Environmental Controls
P.O. Box 1331
Ypsilanti MI 48197
(313) 482-5610

Best Electric
7513 Sunview Dr. SE
Grand Rapids MI 49548
(616) 698-8180

Comprehensive Protection Service
P.O. Box 15505
Ann Arbor MI 48106
(313) 572-8202

Innovative Electronics
42301 Birch Tree Lane
Mt. Clemens MI 48044
(313) 263-7582

Lighting Computers &
Automation Co.
2540 Oakdale Dr.
Ann Arbor MI 48108
(313) 971-1252

Masterview
2236 Jefferson Rd.
Otsego MI 49078
(616) 694-6322

Muligard/Audio Alert Security
Systems
23825 Military
P.O. Box 906
Dearborn Heights MI 48127
(800) 758-0330
(313) 562-1894 FAX

Sight & Sound, Inc.
1164 Sue St.
Saginaw MI 48609
(517) 781-4014

TALI-The Home Automation
Link, Inc.
2976 Ivanrest, Ste. 250
Grandville MI 49418
(616) 530-8711

Telephone Alarm Systems
310 N. Grand Ave., Ste. 109
Lansing MI 48933
(517) 482-1441

Minnesota
7825 Wayzata Blvd.
St. Louis Park MN 55426
(612) 542-1911

Applied Engineering Concepts
2745 Winnetka Ave., Ste. 191
Minneapolis MN 55427
(612) 542-7853

Current Electronics
201 W. Burnsville Pkwy.
Burnsville MN 55337
(612) 924-2434

Intelligent Home Systems
5665 Lake Sara Heights Dr.
Rockford MN 55373
(612) 479-6602

Relax Sight & Sound
321 1st Ave. North
Minneapolis MN 55401
(612) 333-6363

Sound Wiring
11975 Portland Ave. South
Burnsville MN 55337
(612) 895-9977

Supercalibrations
2158 St. Clair Ave.
St. Paul MN 55105
(612) 881-1261

Mississippi
Custom Home & Business
Automation Service
607 Spencer Dr.
Brandon MS 39042
(601) 825-7045

Missouri
A.M. Automation
P.O. Box 454
Liberty MO 64068
(816) 781-9191

AutoVox Systems Integration
P.O. Box 14024
Kansas City MO 64152
(816) 746-0085

Home Automation Living
508 Norma
St. Charles MO 63301
(314) 947-9993 ext. 1493

Hometech Enterprises, Inc.
6485 Chippewa
St. Louis MO 63109
(314) 832-9364

Integrated Electronics
422 Shawn Dr.
Belton MO 64012

MCL Technologies Group
202 West Dunklin
Jefferson City MO 65110
(314) 636-7110

PRO-TEC Alarm Systems &
Service, Inc.
P.O. Box 1422
Lee's Summit MO 64063
(816) 524-1801

Temperature Control Systems
440 Old Dorsett Rd.
Maryland Heights MO 63043
(314) 739-7777

Westco Security Systems, Inc.
105A Four Seasons Center
Chesterfield MO 63017
(314) 878-3272

Montana
MC Computers & Electronics
101 E. Mullan Rd., P.O. Box 7
Superior MT 59872
(406) 822-4891

Nebraska
Smarthome Technologies
P.O. Box 27526
Omaha NE 68127
(402) 341-3908

Nevada
Armed Alarm Company
316 California Ave., Ste. 157
Reno NV 89509
(702) 747-8433

Smart Home Automation
4350 South Arville #16A
Las Vegas NV 89103
(702) 367-2337

New Hampshire

C & F Associates
Old Chesterfield Rd.
Spofford NH 03462-0400
(603) 363-4794

Constant Security
Route 104, RR 3, Box 72-16
Meredith NH 03253
(603) 279-5200

Home Control Consultants
254-B N. Broadway, Ste. 205
Salem NH 03079
(603) 894-5059

New Jersey

Advanced Home Control
26 Green Terrace Way
West Milford NJ 07480
(201) 697-6905

Advanced Control Systems
947 Rahway Ave.
Westfield NJ 07090
(908) 654-4758

Alert Protective Systems
44A East Main St.
Ramsey NJ 07446
(201) 818-2505
(201) 818-2518 FAX

Architectural Electronics, Inc.
1128 Deal Rd.
Wayside NJ 07712
(908) 493-8888

Automation Technologies, Inc.
P.O. Box 2501
Crinnamison NJ 08077-4901
(609) 786-3700

Avius
369 Passaic Ave.
Fairfield NJ 07006
(201) 882-4600

Cestone Electric Co., Inc.
23 Jackson St.
Little Falls NJ 07424-1697
(201) 256-8426

Com + Plus, Inc.
3 Revmont Park South, Ste. 15
Shrewsbury NJ 07702
(201) 542-9494

The Cypress Group, Inc.
95 Cypress St.
Park Ridge NJ 07656
(201) 930-1731

Electronic Systems & Services
11 Old Mountain Rd.
P.O. Box 594
Lebanon NJ 08833
(908) 236-7171
(908) 236-7428 FAX

Energy Innovations Systems
P.O. Box 84
Demarest NJ 07627
(201) 342-8415

Frankentek, Inc.
P.O. Box 603
Medford NJ 08055
(609) 654-6888

Future Automation Systems Today
705 Cotswold Rd., Ste. 100
Somerdale NJ 08083
(609) 783-7422

High Tech Protective Services
190 A Blvd., P.O. Box 547
Hasbrouck Heights NJ 07604
(201) 288-4458

Intelectric, Inc.
1302 Lafayette Ave.
Woodbury NJ 08096-1050
(609) 845-3436

Intercept Engineering
11 Sioux Ave.
Rockaway NJ 07866-1821
(201) 663-0474

Media By Design
2 Williams Rd.
Landing NJ 07850
(201) 837-1778

Northern Valley Electric Company
111 Westervelt Pl.
Cresskill NJ 07626
(201) 567-7683

SAVI-Specialized Audio Video
Installations
142 Morris Ave.
Mountain Lakes NJ 07046
(201) 335-2726

Sawyers Control Systems
RR 3, Box 291
Pittstown NJ 08867
(201) 730-7107

Smart Systems Electric Corp.
6 Appletree Ct.
Livingston NJ 07039
(201) 533-9367

Voice Command Systems, Inc.
P.O. Box 431
Medford NJ 08055
(609) 953-8324

Wilson Alarm Systems, Inc.
202 W. Main St.
Millville NJ 08332
(800) 869-8095

New Mexico

Western Systems Design
1570 Pacheco, Ste. C-6
Santa Fe NM 87501-3937
(505) 983-9300

New York

Ambience Unlimited
5 Caroline St.
Saratoga Springs NY 12866
(518) 583-0770

Audio Command Systems
46 Merrick Rd.
Rockville Center NY 11570
(516) 766-5055

The Automated Home, Inc.
107 Cresthill Rd.
Yonkers NY 10710
(914) 337-2677

Automation Technologies
20-24 Wall St.
Binghamton NY 13901
(607) 771-6142

Casco Security Systems
300 Metro Park
Rochester NY 14623
(716) 271-3230

Custom Home Concepts, Inc.
313 Sheafe Rd., Ste. 22
Wappingers Falls NY 12590
(914) 462-8350

Classic Contracting & Electric
9 Wendy Dr.
Poughkeepsie NY 12603
(914) 298-0039

Data World, Inc.
107 W. Main St.
Cobleskill NY 12043
(518) 234-8201

Designed Media Systems
360 Westchester Ave.
Port Chester NY 10573
(914) 937-9422

Herko Electronics, Inc.
2300 Ridge Rd. West
Rochester NY 14626
(800) 388-1554

Home Buddy Systems
1242 Whitehaven Rd.
Grand Island NY 14072
(716) 773-2645

IB Technical Services
247 Ardmore Ave.
Staten Island NY 10314
(718) 494-5761

Island Security & Communications
602 Whiskey Rd.
Ridge NY 11961
(516) 744-1414

NovaWorks, Inc.
328 East 94th St.
New York NY 10128
(212) 534-7790

P.D.M. Services, Inc.
P.O. Box 745
Amherst NY 14226
(716) 691-3310

PSA Alarms, Inc.
2781 Cypress Ave.
East Meadow NY 11554
(516) 826-4797

Richie & Company
P.O. Box 227
Read Park Rd.
Lake Luzerne NY 12846
(518) 696-3117

Sonitec Security Systems, Inc.
20 West Lincoln Ave.
Mt. Vernon NY 10550
(914) 667-3399

Stoll Associates
1499 Eggert Rd.
Amherst NY 14226
(716) 837-4799

Stoneridge Electric Company, Inc.
P.O. Box 3845
Kingston NY 12401
(914) 331-4227

TEC Electric Corp.
24 Ashburton Ave.
Yonkers NY 10701
(914) 968-9209

Transtek International
31 Greene St.
New York NY 10013
(212) 219-8294

UEC Protective Systems, Inc.
1021 Columbia St.
Utica NY 13502
(315) 732-7339

The Well Connected Home
1167 RR 52, Ste. 106
Fishkill NY 12524
(914) 227-6364

North Carolina

Automated Environments, Inc.
P.O. Box 4014
Charlotte NC 28226-0099
(704) 364-0595

Baker Automation & Security
114 Barcliff Rd., Rt. #4
Raleigh NC 27606
(919) 362-4209

Comtec, Inc.
247 Charlotte St.
P.O. Box 8430
Asheville NC 28814
(704) 252-7092

Home Automated Solutions
117 Vashon Court
Cary NC 27513
(919) 469-4663

Home IQ Shop
67 Terrace Dr.
Weaverville NC 28787
(704) 658-2974

I.S.E. Systems
P.O. Box 3481
Wilson NC 27893
(919) 235-3573

K & M Satellite TV
526 E. Williams St.
Apex NC 27502
(919) 387-7077

Photo Scan Security & Com.
2701 Rowland Rd.
Raleigh NC 27615
(919) 876-8000

Wachovia Electric
1001 S. Marshall St., Ste. 19
Winston-Salem NC 27101
(919) 725-5609

North Dakota

Electronic Systems For Living
P.O. Box 3040
Bismark ND 58502-3040
(701) 222-3902

Ohio

ASE Surveillance Systems, Inc.
7163 E. Main St.
Reynoldsburg OH 43086
(614) 861-2090

Electrical Contractor
8519 Springboro Pike
Miamisburg OH 45342
(513) 435-1122

Excellence, Inc.
635 Yaronia Dr. N.
Columbus OH 43214
(614) 268-4445

High-Tech Homes, Inc.
3689 Silvercrest Dr.
Stow OH 44224
(216) 688-8627

Innovative Exceptions
P.O. Box 468022
Cincinnati OH 45246
(513) 777-4559

Lammon Electronics
770 S. Shoop
Wauseon OH 43567
(419) 335-1972

Mark III Mechanical
3025 W. Galbraith Rd.
Cincinnati OH 45239
(513) 522-3050

MCS Distributors
4805 Towpath Lane
Sylvania OH 43560
(419) 885-3412

National Sentry Security Systems
4022 Stonehaven Rd.
S. Euclid OH 44121
(216) 291-0555

North Coast Home Automation
20680 Centeridge Rd.
Cleveland OH 44116
(216) 356-4663

Newcome Electric Systems
Corporation
720-L Lakeview Plaza
Worthington OH 43085
(614) 848-5688

Smart Systems Technology, Inc.
7921 Keller Rd.
Cincinnati OH 45243
(513) 984-4412

Tabcom, Inc.
1026 Creek Lane
Rocky River OH 44116-2179
(216) 331-7511

Oklahoma

InfoMania Company
1209 E. Maple
Ft. Gibson OK 74434
(918) 478-2162

Lifestyles of Oklahoma
1304 S. Houston Ave.
Tulsa OK 74127
(918) 585-1883

Oregon

Security Alarm Corp.
217 Main St. SE
Albany OR 97321
(503) 967-8034

Pennsylvania

Antietam Alarm & Control
Systems
10185 Birchwood Lane
Waynesboro PA 17268
(717) 762-0746

Audiocrafters
113 Maple St.
Conshohocken PA 19428
(215) 940-0299

Automated Command & Control
Systems
124 Chestnut Lane, Box 335
Bechtelsville PA 19505
(215) 367-4528

Automation Plus, Inc.
3103 Hulmeville Rd.
Bensalem PA 19020
(215) 244-9580

Current Concepts
225 Noth 14th St.
Allentown PA 18102-3605
(215) 433-2112

GPM Corp.
510 Elm Ave.
North Vales PA 19454
(215) 699-4905

Intelligent Connections, Inc.
19 S. Central Ave.
Rockledge PA 19111
(800) 344-5572

John W. Eppler Electrical
513 Grand Ave.
Havertown PA 19083
(215) 789-1382

Marktech, Inc.
2385 Oakview Dr.
Pittsburgh PA 15237
(412) 367-2327

Mastervoice of Pennsylvania/
New Jersey
541 College Ave.
Haverford PA 19041
(215) 386-2760

Modules USA
317 Bustleton Pike
Feasterville PA 19053
(215) 364-6464
(215) 357-2545 FAX

Pro-Tech Electronics Co.
15686 Marsh Rd.
Waynesboro PA 17268
(717) 762-1809

Sophisticated Sound Systems
P.O. Box P343
Penndel PA 19047
(215) 752-1143

Transtek International
7000 Terminal Square, Ste. 200
Upper Darby PA 19082
(215) 734-1192

South Carolina

Hybrid Technical Systems, Inc.
4765 Franchise St.
Charleston SC 29418
(803) 552-2000

Seartron Home & Building
Automation Systems
2201 Hwy. 413
Anderson SC 29621
(803) 296-3112

Tennessee

Electronic Properties
6764 Slash Pine
Memphis TN 38119
(901) 754-6467

Home Control Technologies
926 SE Oakland Ave., Ste. 200
Johnson City TN 37604
(615) 283-4663

Home Wiring Group (HWG)
1809 Cloverleaf Dr.
Nashville TN 37216
(615) 226-2266

Progressive Technologies, Inc.
7724 Hwy 70
Bartlett TN 38133
(901) 382-1416

Sentry, Inc.
P.O. Box 621
Brentwood TN 37024-0621
(615) 373-4869

Sound Concepts, Inc
1567 Overton Park Ave.
Memphis TN 38112
(901) 276-4722

Texas

Architechtural Audio/Video
3729-B West Alabama, Ste. 650
Houston TX 77027
(713) 522-7512

Artificial Intelligence Marketing
18206 Shadow Valley
Spring TX 77379
(713) 376-6954

Automated Concepts
5900 Memorial Dr., Ste. 206
Houston TX 77007-8008
(713) 861-6595

Automation Consulting & Sales
515 E. Houston St.
San Antonio TX 78205
(512) 225-4969

Comcraft Service Sales
P.O. Box 524
DeSoto TX 75115
(214) 230-9217

Detailed Attention, Inc.
23 Mayfair Grove Ct.
The Woodlands TX 77381
(713) 292-6007

Heaton Diversified Systems
556 Sawdust Rd.
The Woodlands TX 77380
(713) 363-0014
(713) 367-3471 FAX

Home Automation Consultants
5766 Balcones #203
Austin TX 78731
(512) 323-5507

Home Entertainment
3510 Galleria
Dallas TX 75240
(214) 934-8585

Home Magic
201 West Stassney, Ste. 127
Austin TX 78745
(512) 243-2730
(512) 443-5582 FAX

IntelliHome
8350 N. Central, Ste. M-2076
Dallas TX 75206
(214) 361-4044

Kortek Industries
2000 Bering, Ste. 400
Houston TX 77057
(713) 783-0024

Media Design
130 E. Holland
San Marcos TX 78666
(512) 754-0083

Mesa Home Automation
7307 Kapok Lane
Austin TX 78759-3735
(512) 258-2695
(512) 258-4464 FAX

Mouser Electronics
2401 Hwy. 287 N
Mansfield TX 76063
(800) 346-6873

Select Automation Systems
201 W. Stassney, Ste. 127
Austin TX 78745-3156
(512) 243-2730

Texas Intelligent Systems, Inc.
3915 Artdale at Westpark
Houston TX 77063
(713) 977-4330

There's More to Life
6917 Brookvale Rd.
Ft. Worth TX 76132
(817) 294-2053

Voice Odysseys, Inc.
11104 West Airport Blvd., Ste. 222
Stafford TX 77477
(713) 933-3903
(713) 879-7739 FAX

Voice Total Environmental
Control
HCR 1, Box 17
Medina TX 78055-9605
(512) 589-7103

Utah
AES Systems, Inc.
1560 Riverside Ave.
Provo UT 84604
(801) 373-0498

Aspen Alarm & Home Automation
697 W. 1000 South
Woods Cross UT 84087
(801) 295-6227

Erdmann Electric, Inc.
270 N. 300 West
Springville UT 84663
(801) 489-6683

United Security Systems, Inc.
7515 S. State St.
Salt Lake City UT 84047
(801) 566-3666

Vermont
First Line Security
P.O. Box 6422
Rutland VT 05702
(802) 773-3402

Howard's Alarm Service
RD #2, Box 113
Isle La Motte VT 05463
(802) 928-3390

Interior's Unlimited
P.O. Box 779
Ludlow VT 05149
(802) 228-5255

Virginia
Custom Technology, Inc.
11403 Fieldstone Lane
Reston VA 22091
(703) 860-8959

Electrical Specialties
P.O. Box 296
Earlysville VA 22936
(804) 978-7969

Executronics Inc.
10 South King St.
P.O. Box 70
Leesburg VA 22075
(703) 777-0000

Frick Electronic Company
77 South Witchduck Rd.
Virginia Beach VA 23462
(804) 473-9955

Get Smart Home Automation
219 N. Dogwood Dr.
Harrisonburg VA 22801
(703) 434-6993

Monitor Systems, Inc.
P.O. Box 922, Village Center
Great Falls VA 22066
(703) 759-7990

Paragon Plus
1120 Kings Way Dr.
Virginia Beach VA 23455
(804) 464-5340

Proto-Tek, Inc.
9915 Oleander Ave.
Vienna VA 22181
(703) 938-6642

Robinson's Security System
1607 Pinchot St.
Richmond VA 23235
(804) 745-3743

Washington
Alarms, Inc.
P.O. Box 283
Mercer Island WA 98040
(206) 236-0700

Group One N.W., Inc.
12121 NE Northrup Way
Bellevue WA 98005
(206) 454-9900
(206) 454-5902 FAX

Heston Technical Services
1840 130th Ave. NE, Ste. 14
Bellevue WA 98005
(206) 881-6940

Jet City AVS
29761 53rd Ave. S
Auburn WA 98001
(206) 839-4372

Off The Shelf
14181 313th NE
Arlington WA 98223
(206) 435-4111

Taurus Automation
7423 Tacoma Ave. South
Tacoma WA 98408
(206) 472-5137

West Virginia
Alarmtronics Security
P.O. Box 262
Hurricane WV 25526
(304) 757-9461

Alert Security Service
P.O. Box 8100
Huntington WV 25705
(304) 529-7552

Wisconsin
Electrolarm Security Systems
1220 W. Court St.
Janesville WI 53545
(800) 322-9834

Professional Energy Systems
14640 W. Greenfield Ave.
Brookfield WI 53005
(414) 796-8281

Starcom Security Services
364 Backwater Trail
Nekoosa WI 54457
(715) 325-3125

Puerto Rico
Magic House of the Caribbean
St. 22-I-2 Royal Town
Bayamon PR 00619
(809) 730-2868

Smart Homes
Hwy. 110, KM 1.2
P.O. Box 4669
Aguadilla PR 00605
(809) 882-5964

Virgin Islands
VI Automation
168 Crown Bay, Ste. 310
St. Thomas VI 00802
(809) 779-2908
(809) 776-0020 FAX

Canada
A.C.E. Systems
#125-4664 Lougheed Hwy.
Burnaby BC V5C 5T5
(604) 291-9555
(604) 294-1758 FAX

ACS Security & Home
Automation
27 Sunbird Blvd.
Keswick ONT L4P 3R9
(416) 476-6502

Advanced Home Automation
186 Raglan Rd. W
Oshawa ONT L1H 7K4
(416) 655-5355
(416) 655-5356 FAX

Automated Mansions BBS
636 E. 29th Ave.
Vancouver BC V5V 2R9
(604) 875-6465
(604) 872-8830 FAX

Baran-Harper Group
77 Drakefield Rd.
Markham ONT L3P 1G9
(416) 294-6473
(416) 471-6776

Cottage & Castle Services
Bruce McLean
P.O. Box 215
Barrie ONT L4M 4T2
(705) 721-1037

Data-Home Systems, Ltd.
P.O. Box 286, 14 Porter Ave.
Hantsport NS B0P 1P0
(902) 684-9440
(902) 798-4469 FAX

Domotron
165 Frobisher #511
Pte. Claire QUE H9R 4R8
(514) 694-8248

Electrically First, Inc.
5000 Dufferin St., Unit C1&2
Downsview ONT M3H 5T5
(416) 665-7299

Innovation Electronic Systems
43 Pilkington Crescent
Thornhill ONT L4T 7J5
(416) 738-6747

Innovative Built-In Systems
83 Deacons Lane
Ajax ONT L1S 2T4
(416) 683-2253

Jantek
27 Restone Path
Etobicoke ONT M9C 1Y7
(416) 620-5255
(416) 620-7726 FAX

Media Sound & Visual
69 Wellington St.
London ONT N6B 2K4
(519) 679-7370

Ongoing Results, Ltd.
#8-117 Ringwood Dr.
Stouffville ONT L4A 8C1
(416) 642-3500
(416) 642-3545 FAX

PC Home Automation
1800 Bank St.
Ottawa ONT K1V 0W3
(613) 526-0751

Professional Computing Services
850 Legion Rd., Unit 18
Burlingham ONT L75 1T5
(416) 333-3193
(416) 333-4543 FAX

Quantum Electronic Systems
1700 Vanity Estates Dr. NW
Calgary ALBA T3B 2W9
(403) 247-9176
(403) 286-1407 FAX

Salco Technology, Inc.
260 Adelaide St. E, #135
Toronto ONT M5A 1N0
(416) 840-4771

Simply Automated Control
Systems, Inc.
2024 Douglas St.
Victoria BC V8T 4L1
(604) 380-7720

Smart Electric Ltd.
#210, 42160 12th St. NE
Calgary ALBA T2E 6K9

Sound Environments
455 Sentinel Rd., Ste. 513
Downsview ONT M3J 1V5
(416) 661-7514

Williams Enterprises & Industries
22 Sherry Lane
Nepean ONT K2G 3L6
(613) 226-8975

Wireless Technology
3333 Cavendish Blvd., Ste. 455
Montreal QUE H4B 2M5
(514) 486-1828
(514) 481-8020 FAX

International
Grupo Simplex
Edif Simplex Calle 52 E.
Apdo 2016 Panama
Panama G A, Rp of Panama
Tele: 507 63 5275

Laserbeam Developments Ltd.
3 Liverpool St.
Hamilton New Zealand
Tele: 64-71-391-646
64-71-381-638 FAX

Ottar aps
Provstevaenget 10
4330 Hvalsoe, Denmark
Tele: +45 42 40 70 77
+45 42 40 70 53 FAX

4. Buying Guide

Closed Circuit Television (CCTV)

ATV Research, Inc.
1301 Broadway, Box 620
Dakota City NE 68731
(402) 987-3771

CCTV Corp.
315 Hudson St.
New York NY 10013
(212) 989-4433

Knox Security Engineering Corp.
1930 W. Main St.
Stamford CT 06902
(203) 622-7300

M & S Systems
2861 Congressman Lane
Dallas TX 75220
(214) 358-3196

Video Surveillance Corp.
1050 E. 14th St.
Brooklyn NY 11230
(718) 258-1310

Computer Cards and Peripherals

Allen Bradley
Milwaukee WI 53204
(414) 382-2000

Ansan Industries Ltd.
4704 American Rd.
Rockford IL 61103
(815) 874-6881

Audio Design Associates (ADA)
602-610 Mamaroneck Ave.
White Plains NY 10605
(914) 946-9595

C & K Systems, Inc.
107 Woodmere Rd.
Folsom CA 95630
(916) 351-1131

Command Control, Inc. (CCI)
8800 Roswell Rd., Ste. 130
Atlanta GA 30350
(404) 992-8430

Omnipotence, Inc.
2236 Cambridge Dr.
Sarasota FL 34232
(813) 371-5085

Ormon Applications
Schaumburg IL 60173
(708) 843-7900

Remote Measurement Systems, Inc.
2633 Eastlake Ave. East, Ste. 200
Seattle WA 98102
(206) 328-2255

Consultants

Bondi Productions
583 W. Thames St.
Norwich CT 06360
(203) 887-4827

Command Control, Inc. (CCI)
8800 Roswell Rd., Ste. 130
Atlanta GA 30350
(404) 992-8430

Diablo Research Corp.
130 Kifer Court
Sunnyvale CA 94086
(408) 730-9555

EGIS Inc.
1701 K St. NW, Ste. 750
Washington DC 20006
(202) 828-8350

Hi-Tech Industries, Inc.
226C E. Collins Dr.
Ft. Wayne IN 46825
(800) 733-7444

Home Control Concepts
9353-C Activity Rd.
San Diego CA 92126
(619) 693-8887

Hometek Advanced Living Environments
P.O. Box 261189
San Diego CA 92196-1189
(619) 538-9030

Intelihome
8350 N. Central, Ste. M-2076
Dallas TX 75206
(214) 361-4044

International Services Corp.
6 NE 63rd St., Ste. 300
Oklahoma City OK 73105
(405) 840-4653

Parks Associates
5310 Harvest Hill Rd., Ste. 235, LB 162
Dallas TX 75230-5805
(214) 490-1113

Robert N. Pyle & Associates, Inc.
1223 Potomac St. NW
Washington DC 20007-3213
(202) 333-8190

Rose Associates
Four Main St.
Los Altos CA 94022
(415) 941-1215

Developmental Hardware

Circuit Cellar, Inc.
4 Park St.
Vernon CT 06066
(203) 875-2751

Command Control, Inc. (CCI)
8800 Roswell Rd., Ste. 130
Atlanta GA 30350
(404) 992-8430

Cyberlynx Computer Products
2885 E. Aurora Ave., Ste. 13
Boulder CO 80303
(303) 444-7733

Diablo Research Corp.
130 Kifer Court
Sunnyvale CA 94086
(408) 730-9555

Energy Management Systems/HVAC Systems

Arzel Technology, Inc.
26210 Emery Rd.
Cleveland OH 44128
(216) 831-6068

Bryant, Day & Night and Payne (BDP)
7310 W. Morris St., P.O. Box 70
Indianapolis IN 46206
(315) 432-6177

Zone Perfect
Calidyne Corp.
5900 Olson Memorial Hwy.
Minneapolis MN 55422
(612) 544-6807

Carrier Corp.
Box 4808 Carrier Pkwy.
Syracuse NY 13221
Call local dealer

Clark & Co., Inc.
P.O. Box 10
Underhill VT 05489
(802) 899-2971

Cyberlynx Computer Products
2885 E. Aurora Ave., Ste. 13
Boulder CO 80303
(303) 444-7733

Designtech International, Inc.
7401 Fullerton Rd.
Springfield VA 22153
(703) 866-2000

Electric Power Research Institute (EPRI)
3412 Hillview Ave.
Palo Alto CA 94303
(415) 855-2000

Emerson Electric
9797 Reavis Rd.
St. Louis MO 63123
(314) 577-1550

Enerzone Systems Corp.
2660 Freewood
Dallas TX 75220
(214) 902-9191

GE Meter & Control
130 Main St.
Somersworth NH 03878
(603) 749-8126

Heatcraft Refrigeration Products Div.
P.O. Box 1699
Atlanta GA 30371
(800) 848-2270

Heat-N-Glo Fireplace Products, Inc.
6665 W. Highway 13
Savage MN 55378
(612) 890-8367

Honeywell Home and Building Control
1985 Douglas Dr.
Golden Valley MN 55422
(800) 345-6700

Hunter Fan Company
2500 Frisco Ave.
Memphis TN 38114
(901) 743-1360

Integrated Communication Systems, Inc.
1000 Holcomb Woods Pkwy., Ste. 412
Roswell GA 30076
(404) 641-1551

Interactive Technologies, Inc.
2266 Second St. N
North St. Paul MN 55109
(800) 777-1415

Itron, Inc.
15516 East Euclid Ave.
Spokane WA 99215
(509) 924-9900

Johnson Controls, Inc.
507 E. Michigan St.
P.O. Box 423
Milwaukee WI 53201
(414) 274-4000

PDI Corp.
180 Admiral Cochrane Dr. #125
Annapolis MD 21401
(410) 224-2130

RCS
(Residential Control Systems)
3983 S. McCarran Blvd., Ste. 190
Reno NV 89502
(916) 929-2956

Rodco Products Co., Inc.
2565 16th Ave.
P.O. Box 944
Columbus NE 68601
(800) 323-2799

Ted Farrell Enterprises, Inc.
300 Enterprise St., Ste. O
Escondido CA 92029
(619) 738-8410

Valera Corp.
800 Proctor Ave.
Ogdensburg NY 13669
(800) 267-1909

Entertainment Systems

ADCOM
11 Elkins Rd.
East Brunswick NJ 08816
(908) 390-1130

Analog and Digital Systems, Inc. a/d/s/
One Progress Way
Wilmington MA 01887
(617) 729-1140

Atlantic Technology
343 Vanderbilt Ave.
Norwood MA 02062
(617) 762-6300

Audioaccess
26046 Eden Landing Rd., Ste. 5
Hayward CA 94545
(415) 293-0183

Audio Command Systems
46 Merrick Rd.
Rockville Center NY 11570
(516) 766-5185

Audio Design Associates (ADA)
602-610 Mamaroneck Ave.
White Plains NY 10605
(914) 946-9595

AudioEase
15350 E. Hinsdale Dr.
Englewood CO 80112-4245
(303) 766-9300

B.I.C. America
883 E. Hampshire Rd.
Stow OH 44224
(216) 928-2011

Bose
The Mountain
Framingham MA 01701
(508) 879-7330

Carver
P.O. Box 1237
Lynnwood WA 98046
(206) 775-1202

C-Cor Electronics, Inc.
60 Decibel Rd.
State College PA 16801-7580
(800) 233-2267

Custom Command Systems, Inc.
115 Paint Branch Dr., Ste. 3181
College Park MD 20742-3261
(301) 314-7767

Datawave
16611 Arminta St.
Van Nuys CA 91406-1611
(818) 908-WAVE (9283)

Denon
222 New Rd.
Parsippany NJ 07054
(201) 575-7810

Design Acoustics
1225 Commerce Dr.
Stow OH 44224
(216) 686-2600

Ezcony International Corp.
2335 NW 107th Ave., Box 111
Miami FL 33172
(305) 599-1352

Fisher
21350 Lassen St.
Chatsworth CA 91311
(213) 998-7322

Harmon Kardon
8380 Balboa Blvd.
Northridge CA 91325
(818) 893-9992

Hitachi
3890 Steve Reynolds Blvd.
Norcross GA 30093
(800) 241-6558

Home Automation Laboratories
(HAL)
5500 Highlands Pkwy., Ste. 450
Atlanta GA 30082
(800) HOME-LAB (orders only)
(404) 319-6000
(404) 438-2835 FAX

Home Systems
6 NE 63rd St., Ste. 300
Oklahoma City OK 73105
(405) 840-4751

Hometronics
4405 Massachusetts Ave.
Indianapolis IN 46218
(317) 545-6239

IHS Systems
13223 Black Mountain Rd. #1-103
San Diego CA 92129
(619) 484-2085

JVC
41 Slater Dr.
Elmwood Park NJ 07407
(201) 794-3100

Kenwood
Box 22745
Long Beach CA 90801-5745
(213) 639-9000

Luxman
19145 Gramercy Pl.
Torrance CA 90501
(310) 326-8000

Magnavox
1 Phillips Dr.
Knoxville TN 37914
(615) 521-4391

Marantz
1150 Feehanville Dr.
Mt. Prospect IL 60056
(708) 299-4000

McIntosh
2 Chambers St.
Binghamton NY 13903-2699
(607) 723-3512

Mitsubishi
5757 Plaza Dr.
Cypress CA 90630
(714) 220-2500

MKO Electronic Systems, Inc.
1832 Borman Court, Ste. 1
St. Louis MO 63146
(314) 453-0006

M & S Systems, Inc.
2861 Congressman Lane
Dallas TX 75220
(214) 358-3196

Multiplex Technology, Inc.
3200 East Birch St.
Brea CA 92621-6258
(800) 999-5225
(714) 996-4100

The New Millennium Company
7739 E. Broadway Blvd., Ste. 262
Tucson AZ 85710
(602) 577-3174

NHT
537 Stone Rd., Bldg. E
Benicia CA 94510
(707) 747-0151

Niles Audio Corp.
12331 S.W. 130th St.
Miami FL 33186
(305) 238-4373

Onkyo
200 Williams Dr.
Ramsey NJ 07446
(201) 825-7950

OWI Inc.
1160 Mahalo Pl.
Compton CA 90220
(310) 638-4732

Panasonic
1 Panasonic Way
Secaucus NJ 07094
(201) 348-7000

Pioneer Electronics
2265 E. 220th St.
Long Beach CA 90810
(800) 421-1404

ProScan/Thomson Consumer
Electronics
600 N. Sherman Dr.
Indianapolis IN 46201
(317) 267-5000

RHB Sound, Inc.
4042 Pacific Ave.
Riverdale UT 84405
(801) 399-4900

Russound/FMP
5 Forbes Rd.
Newmart NH 03857
(603) 659-5170

Sharp
Sharp Plaza
Mahwah NJ 07430
(201) 529-8200

Sonance
961 Calle Negocio
San Clemente CA 92672
(800) 582-7777

Sony Corporation of America
Sony Dr.
Park Ridge NJ 07656
(201) 930-6432

Soundstream Technologies
120 Blue Ravine Rd.
Folsom CA 95630
(916) 351-1288

Toshiba
82 Totowa Rd.
Wayne NJ 07430
(201) 628-8000

USTEC Products
470 South Pearl St.
Canandaigua NY 14424
(800) 836-2312

Video Link
12950 Bradley Ave.
Sylmar CA 91342
(818) 362-0353

Yamaha
Box 6660
Buena Park CA 90622
(800) 492-6242

Zenith
1000 Milwaukee Ave.
Glenview IL 60025
(706) 391-7000

Home Automation Training and Dealerships

Hi-Tech Industries
226-C E Collins Dr.
Fort Wayne IN 46825
(219) 484-0928

Home Control Concepts
9353-C Activity Rd.
San Diego CA 92126
(619) 693-8887

Intellitricity, Inc.
3307 Northland, Ste. 130
Austin TX 78731
(512) 323-5507

International Services Corp.
6 NE 63rd St., Ste. 300
Oklahoma City OK 73105
(405) 840-4653

Home Theater

AMX Corporation
11995 Forestgate Dr.
Dallas TX 75243
(800) 222-0193

Audiosource
1327 N. Carolan Ave.
Burlingame CA 94010
(415) 348-8114

Paramount Pictures Home Theater
Products
1950 E. Orangethorpe
Fullerton CA 92631
(800) 777-9948

Pioneer Electronics (USA)
2265 E. 220th St.
P.O. Box 1720
Long Beach CA 90801
(213) 746-6337

Pulsar Video Systems, Inc.
7660 Clairmont Mesa Blvd.
San Diego CA 92111
(800) 828-3811

Roomtune, Inc.
P.O. Box 57
Sugarcreek OH 44681
(216) 852-2222

Sharp Electronics Corp.
LCD Products Group
Sharp Plaza
Mahwah NJ 07430-2135
(201) 529-0321

Snell Multimedia/Lucasfilm
THX Audio
143 Essex St.
Haverhill MA 01832
(508) 373-6114

Soundstream Technologies
120 Blue Ravine Rd.
Folsom CA 95630
(916) 351-1288

Uni-Screen, Inc.
263 Kansas St.
Horicon WI 53027
(414) 485-3123

Intercoms
Aiphone Corp.
1700 130th Ave. NE
Bellevue WA 98005
(206) 455-0510

Broan MFG. Co., Inc.
926 West State St.
Hartford WI 53027
(414) 673-4340

DFE Inc.
1705 W. Main
Oklahoma City OK 73106
(800) 822-4868

Doorking
120 Glasgow Ave.
Inglewood CA 90301
(310) 645-0023

Fanon Courier
14811 Myford Rd.
Tustin CA 92680
(714) 669-9890

Intelecom
6488 Avondale Dr., Ste. 125
Oklahoma City OK 73116
(405) 842-0163
(405) 842-0162 FAX

M & S Systems
2861 Congressman Lane
Dallas TX 75220
(214) 358-3196

Nutone
Madison and Red Bank Roads
Cincinnati OH 45227-1599
(800) 543-8687

Telecall America
14620 NE 95th St.
Redmond WA 98052
(206) 881-2742
(206) 881-3085 FAX

Lighting Control
BRK Electronics
780 McClure Rd.
Aurora IL 60504
(800) 323-9005

Cable Electronic Products
Division of Leviton Mfg. Co., Inc.
P.O. Box 6767
Providence RI 02940
(401) 781-5400

Carpi Lighting
6430 E. Slauson Ave.
Los Angeles CA 90040
(213) 726-1800

C & K Systems, Inc.
107 Woodmere Rd.
Folsom CA 95630
(916) 351-1131

Conservation Technology, Ltd.
130 N. Waukegan Rd.
Deerfield IL 60015
(708) 945-0303

Designtech International, Inc.
7401 Fullerton Rd.
Springfield VA 22153
(703) 866-2000

Honeywell Home & Building
Control
1985 Douglas Dr.
Golden Valley MN 55422
(800) 345-6700

Leviton Mfg. Co., Inc.
59-25 Little Neck Pkwy.
Little Neck NY 11362
(800) 323-8920

Lightolier
100 Lighting Way
Secaucus NJ 07094
(201) 864-3000

LiteTouch Inc.
3550 South 700 West
Salt Lake City UT 84119
(801) 268-8668

Lutron Electronics Co. Inc.
7200 Suter Rd.
Coopersburg PA 18036-1299
(215) 282-3800

Novitas Inc.
Consumer Products Division
1657 Euclid St.
Santa Monica CA 90404
(310) 452-7890

Prescolite Controls
1206 Tappan Cl.
Carrollton TX 75006
(800) 346-6377
(214) 242-6581

Vantage Controls Inc.
4415 South 500 West
Salt Lake City UT 84123
(801) 266-2165

Miscellaneous
Best Power Technology Inc.
P.O. Box 280
Necedah WI 54646
(800) 356-5794
Uninterruptible power systems

DSK
325 North Oakhurst Dr., Ste. 404
Beverly Hills CA 90210
(213) 550-7600
Safer Home Test Kit

Glentronics
2053 John's Dr.
Glenview IL 60025
(708) 998-0466
Basement Watchdog

Green Technologies, Inc.
5490 Spine Rd.
Boulder CO 80301
(303) 581-9600
Greenplug

Heat-N-Glo Fireplace Products, Inc.
6665 W. Hwy 13
Savage MN 55378
(612) 890-8367
Remote control gas fireplace

Hemco
P.O. Box 878
Westminster CA 92684
WT-1 Wall Timer

The New Millennium Company
7739 E. Broadway Blvd., Ste. 262
Tucson AZ 85710
(602) 577-3174
Electronic Guard Dog

Ortner Technologies Corp.
RD #2, Box 233
Mount Joy PA 17552
(800) 7-ORTNER
AutoTell vehicle detector

Pineda Products, Inc.
425-A Pineda Court
Melbourne FL 32940
(407) 254-7785
At-Ease home radon monitor

Power Access Corp.
P.O. Box 235
Collinsville CT 06022
(800) 344-0088
Automatic door opener

Square D Company
3203 Nicholasville Rd.
Lexington KY 40503
(800) 747-0914
Remote controlled circuit breakers

Powerline Control

Circuit Cellar, Inc.
4 Park St.
Vernon CT 06066
(203) 875-2751

Enerlogic Systems, Inc.
2 Townsend W., Ste. 6
Nashua NH 03063
(603) 880-4066

Home Control Concepts
9353-C Activity Rd.
San Diego CA 92126
(619) 693-8887

IHS Systems
13223 Black Mountain Rd. # 1-103
San Diego CA 92129
(619) 484-2085

Jance Associates Inc.
P.O. Box 234
East Texas PA 18046
(215) 398-0434

JDS Technologies
16750 West Bernardo Dr.
San Diego CA 92127
(619) 487-8787

Leviton Mfg. Co., Inc.
59-25 Little Neck Pkwy.
Little Neck NY 11362
(800) 323-8920

Powerline Control Systems
9031 Rathburn Ave.
Northridge CA 91325
(818) 701-9831

Radio Shack
1500 One Tandy Center
Fort Worth TX 76102
(817) 390-30112

X-10 (USA) Inc.
91 Ruckman Rd.
Closter NJ 07624-0420
(201) 784-9700

Remote Controls

Cable Electronic Products
Division of Leviton Mfg. Co., Inc.
P.O. Box 6767
Providence RI 02940
(401) 781-5400

Designtech International, Inc.
7401 Fullerton Rd.
Springfield VA 22153
(703) 866-2000

Home Control Concepts
9353-C Activity Rd.
San Diego CA 92126
(619) 693-8887

IHS Systems
13223 Black Mountain Rd. #1-103
San Diego CA 91129
(619) 484-2085

Infrared Research Labs, Inc.
820 Davis St., Ste. 444
Evanston IL 60201
(800) 328-0475
(708) 328-8043

Memorex
P.O. Box 901021
Fort Worth TX 76101
(800) 223-9829
(817) 878-6700

Pioneer Electronics (USA)
2265 E. 220th St.
P.O. Box 1720
Long Beach CA 90801
(213) 746-6336

Radio Shack
1500 One Tandy Center
Fort Worth TX 76102
(817) 390-3011

Recognition Corporation
46-23 Crane St.
Long Island City NY 11101
(800) 223-6009
(718) 392-6442

Somfy Systems, Inc.
2 Sutton Pl.
Edison NJ 08817
(908) 287-3600

Universal Electronics, Inc.
6138 Riverview Rd.
Peninsula OH 44262
(216) 657-2616

X-10 (USA), Inc.
91 Ruckman Rd.
Closter NJ 07624-0420
(201) 784-9700

Residential Access Control Systems

Corby Industries, Inc.
1501 E. Pennsylvania St.
Allentown PA 18103-1588
(215) 433-1412

Destron IDI
2545 Central Ave.
Boulder CO 80301
(303) 444-5306

EMX Inc.
20600 Chagrin Blvd., Ste. 503
Shaker Heights OH 44122
(216) 662-9240

Handykey
1800 Abbott St.
Salinas CA 93901
(408) 754-4448

Indala Corp.
711 Charcot Ave.
San Jose CA 95131
(408) 754-7010

Secura Key
19749 Bahama St.
Northridge CA 91324
(818) 882-0020

Thorn Automated Systems
835 Sharon Dr.
Westlake OH 44145
(216) 871-9900

Robots

General Robotics Corp.
14618 W. 6th Ave., Ste. 150
Golden CO 80401-5256
(303) 277-1574

Rhino Robots Inc.
308 S. State St.
P.O. Box 4010
Champaign IL 61820
(800) 562-1888

Security Systems

Ademco
165 Eileen Way
Syosset NY 11791
(516) 921-6704

AMP, Inc.
P.O. Box 3608
Harrisburg PA 17105
(800) 522-6752

Apex Security Alarm Products
3301 Bramer Dr.
Raleigh NC 27604
(800) 272-7937

C&K Systems, Inc.
107 Woodmere Rd.
Folsom CA 95630
(916) 351-1131

Cable Electric Products
Division of Leviton Mfg. Co., Inc.
P.O. Box 6767
Providence RI 02940
(401) 781-5400

Dancraft Enterprises
5520 W. 118th Pl.
Inglewood CA 90304
(310) 643-8782

Designtech International, Inc.
7401 Fullerton Rd.
Springfield VA 22153
(703) 866-2001

Dicon Systems Inc.
631 Executive Dr.
Willowbrook IL 60521
(708) 850-7255

Farady, Inc.
805 S. Maumee St.
Tecumseh MI 49286
(517) 423-2111

First Alert Professional Security
Susyems
172 Michael Dr.
Syosset NY 11791
(516) 921-6066

Fyrnetics Inc.
1055 Stevenson Ct., Ste. 120W
Roselle IL 60172
(708) 893-4592

Handykey
1800 Abbot St.
Salinas CA 93901
(800) 626-4448

Home Automation Laboratories
(HAL)
5500 Highlands Pkwy., Ste. 450
Atlanta GA 30082
(404) 319-6000
(404) 438-2835 FAX
(800) HOME-LAB (orders only)

Interactive Technologies Inc.
2266 N. Second St.
North St. Paul MN 55109
(612) 777-2690

Leviton Mfg. Co., Inc.
59-25 Little Neck Pkwy.
Little Neck NY 11362
(800) 323-8920

Napco Security Systems
333 Bayview Ave.
Amityville NY 11701
(516) 842-9400

Radio Shack
1500 One Tandy Center
Fort Worth TX 76102
(817) 390-3011

Silent Knight Security System
7550 Meridian Cl.
Maple Grove MN 55369
(612) 493-6400

Transcience
633 Hope St.
Stamford CT 06907
(800) 243-3494

Voyager Security Systems
7550 Meridian Cl.
Maple Grove MN 55369
(612) 493-6460

Video Link
12950 Bradley Ave.
Sylmar CA 91342
(818) 362-0353

X-10 (USA) Inc.
91 Ruckman Rd.
Closter NJ 07624-0420
(201) 784-9700

Sensors — Alarm

Ademco
165 Eileen Way
Syosset NY 11791
(516) 921-6704

BRK Electronics
780 McClure Rd.
Aurora IL 60504
(708) 851-7330

C&K Systems, Inc.
107 Woodmere Rd.
Folsom CA 95630
(916) 351-1131

Cable Elctronic Products
Division of Leviton Mfg. Co., Inc.
P.O. Box 6767
Providence RI 02940
(401) 781-5400

D.A.S. Distribution
P.O. Box 404
West Suffield CT 06093
(203) 668-1664

Designtech International, Inc.
7401 Fullerton Rd.
Springfield VA 22153
(703) 866-2001

Detection Systems, Inc.
130 Perinton Parkway
Fairport NY 14450
(800) 289-0096

Dicon Systems Inc.
631 Executive Dr.
Willowbrook IL 60521
(708) 850-7255

ESS Distributors
10965 Santa Barbara Pl.
Alta Loma CA 91701
(800) 755-6796

First Alert Professional Security
Systems
172 Michael Dr.
Syosset NY 11791
(516) 921-6066

Home Safeguard Industries, Inc.
29706 Baden Pl.
Malibu CA 90265
(310) 457-5813

Intellisense
2171 Watterson Tr.
Louisville KY 40299
(502) 266-5019

Jameson Home Products
2820 Thatcher Rd.
Downers Grove IL 60515
(708) 963-2850

Leviton Mfg. Co., Inc.
59-25 little Neck Pkwy.
Little Neck NY 11362
(800) 323-8920

Litton-Poly-Scientific, Security
Systems
1213 N. Main St.
Blacksburg VA 24060
(703) 953-4751

Optex (USA) Inc.
365 Van Ness Way #510
Torrance CA 90501
(310) 212-7271

Racon, Inc.
12628 Interurban Ave. S
Seattle WA 98168-3383
(206) 241-1110

Radio Shack
1500 One Tandy Center
Fort Worth TX 76102
(817) 390-3011

Raytek
1201 Shaffer Rd.
P.O. Box 1820
Santa Cruz CA 95061-1820
(408) 458-1110

Visonic Ltd.
20 Northwood Dr.
Bloomfield CT 06002
(800) 223-0200
(203) 243-0833

Sensors — Environmental

GAS DETECTION

A.D.D.M. International Inc.
3091 Trinity St.
P.O. Box 572
Oceanside NY 11572
(516) 766-5997
(516) 678-0259 FAX

Pama Gas-Alarm
Dynamation Inc.
Ann Arbor MI
(313) 769-0573
(313) 678-0259 FAX

Macuraco Inc.
Englewood CO 80151
(303) 781-4062
(303) 761-6640 FAX

TEMPERATURE DETECTION

Blue Grass Electronics Inc.
602 W. Jefferson
La Grange, KY 40031
(502) 222-7174
(502) 222-5138 FAX

Marsh Products Inc.
Batavia IL 60510
(708) 879-8008
(708) 879-8072 FAX

WATER/LEAK DETECTION
C.A.M. Co., Inc.
Big Rock IL 60511
(708) 556-3110

Datasonic Inc.
Mineola NY 11501
(516) 248-7330

MULTIPLE-SENSOR SYSTEMS
Hydro-Temp Inc.
Baton Rouge, LA 70821
(504) 291-1200

Winland Electronics Inc.
418 South Second St.
P.O. Box 473
Mankato MN 56001
(800) 635-4269
(507) 387-2488 FAX

SMART HOUSE
SMART HOUSE L.P. is a consortium of manufacturers that work with SMART HOUSE to develop and manufacture components for the SMART HOUSE System.

SMART HOUSE L.P.
400 Prince George's Blvd.
Upper Marlboro MD 20772-8731
(800) 759-3344

Ademco
165 Eileen Way
Syosset NY 11791
(516) 921-6704

VISTA Security System
Alcatel Canada Wire Inc.
1515 N. Warson Rd.
St. Louis MO 63132
(314) 428-1550
SMART-REDI and SMART components

AMP Inc.
Product Information Center
Harrisburg PA 17105
(800) 522-6752
SMART-REDI and SMART components

Ansan Industries, Ltd.
4704 American Rd.
Rockford IL 61103
(815) 874-6881
I/O port system

AT&T Network Systems
200 Park Plaza, RM 2 FL 44
Naperville IL 60566
(708) 979-1977
Telephone gateway

Broadband Networks
2820 E. College Ave., Ste. B
State College PA 16801
(800) 473-7337
SMART-SOURCE coaxial headend

Carrier Corp.
P.O. Box 70
Indianapolis IN 48206
(317) 243-0851

HVAC
C-COR Electronics Inc.
60 Decibel Rd.
State College PA 16801-7580
(800) 233-2267
Coaxial headend

Custom Command Systems, Inc.
115 Paint Branch Dr., Ste. 3181
College Park MD 20742-3261
(301) 314-7767
Video touchscreen

Diablo Research Corp.
130 Kifer Court
Sunnyvale CA 94086
(408) 730-9555
Product development

Ducane Industries
800 Dutch Square Blvd., Ste. 200
Columbia SC 29210
(800) 798-1610
SMART barbeque gas grill

Eaton Corp.
Cutler-Hammer Products
4201 N. 27th St.
Milwaukee WI 53216
(800) 833-3927
Cutler-Hammer service entrance components

Halstead Industries
300 N. Greene St.
Greensboro NC 27401
(919) 272-1966
Copper gas piping products

Heat-N-Glo Fireplace Products, Inc.
6665 W. Highway 13
Savage MN 55378
(800) 669-HEAT
SMART gas fireplace

Inncom International, Inc.
P.O. Box 966
Old Lyme CT 06371-0966
(800) 543-1999
Telephone console and control panel

Lennox Industries, Inc.
P.O. Box 799900
Dallas TX 75379
(214) 497-5000
Multi-zone gas/electric HVAC system

M.B. Sturgis, Inc.
555 Fee Fee Rd.
Maryland Heights MO 63043
(314) 291-6665
Gas appliance connector

Micro Cogen, Inc.
1335 Midway Dr.
Alpine CA 92001
(619) 445-3536
Gas cogenerator

Molex, Inc.
2222 Wellington Ct.
Lisle IL 60532-1682
(708) 969-4550
SMART-REDI and SMART components

Multiplex Technology, Inc.
3200 E. Birch St.
Brea CA 92621-6258
(714) 996-4100
CCTV

New Stuff
255 N. Valley Dr.
Grants Pass OR 97526
(503) 479-3212
Cable fasteners

Onan Power Electronics
9713 Valley View Rd.
Minneapolis MN 55344
(612) 943-4600
Continuous power supply

Onan Power Corp.
1400 73rd Ave. NE
Minneapolis MN 55432
(612) 574-5000
Standby power generator

PDI Corp.
180 Admiral Cochrane Dr.
Annapolis MD 21401
(410) 224-2130
Energy management system

Parity, Inc.
10655 Weymouth St., Ste. 3
Bethesda MD 20814
(301) 897-0836
Node addressing tool

Pioneer Electronics (USA) Inc.
2265 E. 220th St.
Long Beach CA 90810
(213) 835-6177
SMART consumer electronics
products

Plexus Corp.
55 Jewelers Park Dr.
Neenah WI 54957
(800) 236-7597
Control panel

Powerline Control Systems
9031 Rathburn Ave.
Northridge CA 91325
(818) 701-9831
Exterior controllers

Production Diagnostics, Inc.
2121 N. Fielder Rd.
Arlington TX 76012
(817) 261-2264
Remote shower switch

RMC Research
1085 Morris Ave.
Union NJ 07083
(800) 236-7597
Product development

Siemens Energy & Automation
P.O. Box 89000
Atlanta GA 30356-9000
(404) 751-2000
Electrical system components

Simpson Electric Company
853 Dundee Ave.
Elgin IL 60120-3090
(708) 697-2260
Testing equipment

Smart Interface
746 Oro Viego Rd.
Las Cruces NM 88001
(505) 522-3070
Wireless remote

Sturgeon Bay Metal Products
1018 Green Bay Rd.
P.O. Box 28
Sturgeon Bay WI 54235
(414) 743-2221
Cable straps

Uspower Climate Control, Inc.
954 Marcon Blvd.
Allentown PA 18103
(800) 669-1138
Geothermal HVAC system

Voyager Security Systems
7550 Meridian Circle N
Maple Grove MN 55369
(800) 523-3773
Spread spectrum security system

Ward Manufacturing
115 Gulick St.
P.O. Box 9
Blossburg PA 16912
(717) 638-2131
Gas piping and gas manifolds

Water Heater Innovations, Inc.
3107 Sibley Memorial Hwy.
Eagan MN 55121
(612) 688-8827
Marathon water heaters

Waterfurnace International
9000 Conservation Way
Fort Wayne IN 46809
(219) 478-5667
Geothermal heat pump

The Watt Stopper, Inc.
296 Brokaw Rd.
Santa Clara CA 95050
(408) 988-5331
Occupancy/light level sensor

Westinghouse Security Systems
3040 Riverside Dr., Ste. 122
Columbus OH 43221
(800) 321-8899
Wireless security system

The Wiremold Company
60 Woodlawn St.
West Hartford CT 06110
(800) 621-0049
Service entrance cable manager

Solar
Siemens Solar Industries
4650 Adohr Lane
Camarillo CA 93011
(805) 482-6800

Solartronics
76 Benbro Dr.
Buffalo NY 14225-4806
(800) 635-0381

Sunnyside Solar, Inc.
RD 4, Box 808
Brattleboro VT 05301
(802) 257-1482

Sun Quest Inc.
1555 Rankin Ave.
Newton NC 28603
(800) 627-5080

Telephones and Accessories
CDT
80 Pickett District Rd.
New Milford CT 06776
(203) 355-3178

Doorking
120 Glasgow Ave.
Inglewood CA 90301
(310) 645-0023

Intelecom
6488 Avondale Dr., Ste. 125
Oklahoma City OK 73116
(405) 842-0163

JDS Technologies
16750 West Bernardo Dr.
San Diego CA 92127
(619) 487-8787

Knox Security Engineering Corp.
1930 W. Main St.
Stamford CT 06902
(203) 622-7300

Northwest Bell Phones
9394 W. Dodge Rd., Ste. 100
Omaha NE 68114
(402) 390-8600

Phonex Corp.
6952 High Tech Dr.
Midvale UT 84047
(801) 566-0100

Questech International, Inc.
4951-B E. Adamo Dr., Ste. 238
Tampa FL 33605
(813) 247-4900

Radio Shack
1500 One Tandy Center
Fort Worth TX 76102
(817) 390-3011

Southern Telecommunications
8281 E. Evans Rd. #102
Scottsdale AZ 85260
(602) 443-9228

Telecom Logic
15403 Proctor Ave.
Industry CA 91745
(818) 330-8866

The New Millennium Company
7739 E. Broadway Blvd., Ste. 262
Tucson AZ 85710
(602) 577-3174

Voice Control and Voice Messaging

Covox Inc.
675 Conger St.
Eugene OR 97402
(503) 342-1271

Home Automation Laboratories (HAL)
5500 Highlands Pkwy., Ste. 450
Atlanta GA 30082
(404) 319-6000
(404) 438-2835 FAX
(800) HOME-LAB (orders only)

Mastervoice, Inc.
10523 Humboldt St.
Los Alamitos CA 90720
(310) 594-6581

Water Management

American Products
10951 West Los Angeles Ave.
P.O. Box 8085
Moorpark CA 93020-8085
(805) 523-2400

Ansan Industries Ltd.
4704 American Rd.
Rockford IL 61109
(815) 874-6881

AquaProducts, Inc.
25 Rutgers Ave.
Cedar Grove NJ 07009
(201) 857-2700

Aqua/Trends
P.O. Box 810444 Woodlands Station
Boca Raton FL 33481
(407) 272-9838

Chardonnay
15812 Arminta St.
Van Nuys CA 91406
(818) 787-7779

Chronomite Laboratories, Inc.
21011 S. Figueroa St.
Carson CA 90745
(800) 447-4962

Home Systems
6 NE 63rd St., Ste. 300
Oklahoma City OK 73105
(405) 840-4751

Jacuzzi Whirlpool Bath
100 N. Widget Lane
P.O. Drawer J
Walnut Creek CA 94596
(510) 938-7070

KBI Industries, Inc.
P.O. Box 2096
Michigan City IN 46360
(219) 879-5000

Kohler Company
444 Highland Dr.
Kohler WI 53044
(414) 457-4441

Kreepy Krauly USA, Inc.
13801 NW 4th St.
Sunrise FL 33325
(800) 374-4300

Rain Bird National Sales
145 N. Grand Ave.
Glendora CA 91740
(818) 963-9311

Raindrip Inc.
21305 Itasca St.
Chatsworth CA 91311
(818) 718-8004

RainMatic Corp.
828 Crown Point Ave.
Omaha NE 68110
(402) 453-5300

Ultraflo Corp.
P.O. Box 2294
Sandusky OH 44870
(419) 626-8182

Weather-Matic
P.O. Box 180205
Dallas TX 75218-0205
(214) 278-6131

Whole House

AMX Corp.
11995 Forestgate Dr.
Dallas TX 75243
(800) 222-0193

Ansan Industries, Ltd.
4704 American Rd.
Rockford IL 61109
(815) 874-6881

Circuit Cellar, Inc.
4 Park St.
Vernon CT 06066
(203) 875-2751

CSI/Carrier
2645 Snyder Ct.
Walnut Creek CA 94598
(510) 932-1346

Custom Command Systems, Inc.
115 Paint Branch Dr., Ste. 3181
College Park MD 20742-3261
(301) 314-7767

Digital Technology Inc.
1000 Riverbend Blvd., Ste. R
St. Rose LA 70087
(504) 467-1466
(504) 467-2146 FAX

Enerlogic Systems Inc.
2 Townsend W., Ste. 6
Nashua NH 03063
(603) 880-4066

Farady Inc.
805 S. Maumee St.
Tecumseh MI 49286
(517) 423-2111

Group Three Technologies
2125-B Madera Rd.
Simi Valley CA 93065
(805) 582-4410

Home Automation, Inc.
2313 Metairie Rd.
P.O. Box 9310
Metairie LA 70055
(504) 833-7256

Home Automation Laboratories
(HAL)
5500 Highlands Pkwy., Ste. 450
Atlanta GA 30082
(800) HOME-LAB (orders only)
(404) 319-6000
(404) 438-2835 FAX

Home Systems
6 NE 63rd St., Ste. 300
Oklahoma City OK 73105
(405) 840-4751

Hometronics
4405 Massachusetts Ave.
Indianapolis IN 46218
(317) 545-6239

Honeywell Home & Building
Control
1985 Douglas Dr.
Golden Valley MN 55422
(800) 345-6700

IHS Systems
13223 Black Mountain Rd. #1-103
San Diego CA 92129
(619) 484-2085

Intelligent Systems, Inc.
175 New Britain Ave.
Plainview CT 06062
(203) 793-9951

Intellitricity, Inc.
3307 Northland, Ste. 130
Austin TX 78731
(512) 323-5507

JDS Technologies
16750 W. Bernardo Dr.
San Diego CA 92127
(619) 487-8787

Mastervoice, Inc.
10523 Humboldt St.
Los Alamitos CA 90720
(310) 594-6581

Omnipotence, Inc.
2236 Cambridge Dr.
Sarasota FL 34232
(813) 371-5085

Remote Measurement Systems, Inc.
2633 Eastlake Ave., Ste. 200
Seattle WA 98102
(206) 328-1787

Square D Company
3203 Nicholasville Rd.
Lexington KY 40503
(800) 747-0914

Telestate International
2010 Avenue G, Ste. 914
Plano TX 75074
(214) 422-9665
(214) 423-3840 FAX

Unity Systems Inc.
2606 Spring St.
Redwood City CA 94063
(415) 369-3233

Windows and Window Coverings

Andersen Windows, Inc.
100 Fourth Ave. N.
Bayport MN 55003-1096
(612) 439-5150

Bautex Motorized Drapes
10860 Alder Cl.
Dallas TX 75238
(214) 343-1610

Bramen Co. Inc.
P.O. Box 70
Salem MA 01970
(800) 234-7765

European Rolling Shutters
150 Martinvale Lane
San Jose CA 95119
(408) 629-3740

Levolor Corp.
595 Lawrence Expy.
Sunnyvale CA 94086
(408) 245-4000

Lutron Electronics Co., Inc.
7200 Suter Rd.
Coopersburg PA 18036-1299
(215) 282-3800

Makita USA, Inc.
14930 Northam St.
La Mirada CA 90638-5753
(714) 522-8088

Pease Exterior Rolling Shutters
7100 Dixie Hwy.
Fairfield OH 45104
(800) 543-1180

Roll-A-Way Insulating Security
Shutters
10601 Oak St. NE
St. Petersburg FL 33716
(800) 245-9505

SM Automatic
10301 Jefferson Blvd.
Culver City CA 90232
(310) 559-6405

Solartronics, Inc.
76 Benbro Dr.
Buffalo NY 14225-4806
(800) 635-0381

Somfy Systems, Inc.
2 Sutton Pl.
Edison NJ 08817
(800) 22-SOMFY
(901) 287-3600

Sunbilt Solar Products
109-101 180th St.
Jamaica NY 11433
(718) 297-6040

Sun Quest Inc.
1555 Rankin Ave.
Newton NC 28658
(800) 627-5080

Truth Division, SPX Corp.
700 W. Bridge St.
Owatonna MN 55060
(507) 451-5620

Velux-America Inc.
P.O. Box 5001
Greenwood SC 29648
(803) 223-3149

AWNINGS
Somfy Systems Inc.
2 Sutton Pl.
Edison NJ 08817
(800) 22-SOMFY
(901) 287-3600

Pease Industries Inc.
7100 Dixie Hwy.
Fairfield OH 45104
(800) 543-1180

Inter Trade Inc.
3175 Fujita St.
Torrance CA 90505
(213) 515-7177

AUSTRIAN PUFFS
SM Automatic
10301 Jefferson Blvd.
Culver City CA 90232
(800) 533-5520

Somfy Systems Inc.
2 Sutton Pl.
Edison NJ 08817
(800) 22-SOMFY
(901) 287-3600

BLINDS
SM Automatic
10301 Jefferson Blvd.
Culver City CA 90232
(800) 533-5520

Velux-America Inc.
P.O. Box 3208
Greenwood SC 29648
(803) 223-3149
For skylights only

CURTAINS/DRAPERIES
Lightwood Mfg. Inc.
16088 SE 106th Ave.
Clackamas OR 97015
(800) 356-2580

Solar Drape
250 Wales Ave.
Tonawanda NY 14150
(716) 692-9375

ROMAN SHADES
Castec Inc.
7531 Coldwater Canyon
N. Hollywood CA 91605
(800) 828-2500

SM Automatic
10301 Jefferson Blvd.
Culver City CA 90232
(800) 533-5520

Somfy Systems Inc.
2 Sutton Pl.
Edison NJ 08817
(800) 22-SOMFY
(901) 287-3600

SECURITY SCREENS
Imperial Screen Co., Inc.
Lawndale CA 90260
(213) 772-7465

Maxwell Alarm Screen Mfg.
2326 Sawtelle Blvd.
Los Angeles CA 90064
(800) 472-7336

Sentry Security Screens
1510 Gary St.
Bethlehem PA 18018
(215) 758-8818

SHADES
Castec Inc.
7531 Coldwater Canyon
N. Hollywood CA 91605
(800) 828-2500

Mecho Shade Systems Inc.
42-03 35th St.
Long Island City NY 11101
(718) 729-2020

Somfy Systems Inc.
2 Sutton Pl.
Edison NJ 08817
(800) 22-SOMFY
(901) 287-3600

SM Automatic
10301 Jefferson Blvd.
Culver City CA 90232
(800) 533-5520

Solar Drape Ltd.
250 Wales Ave.
Tonawanda NY 14150
(716) 692-9375

SHUTTERS
Inter Trade Inc.
3175 Fujita St.
Torrance CA 90260
(213) 515-7177

Pease Industries Inc.
7100 Dixie Highway
Fairfield OH 45014
(800) 543-1180

Roll-A-Way
10597 Oak St. NE
St. Petersburg, FL 33716
(800) 245-9505

Somfy Systems Inc.
2 Sutton Pl.
Edison NJ 08817
(800) 22-SOMFY
(901) 287-3600

Todd Company
1301 S. Bowen Rd., Ste. 260
Arlington TX 76013
(817) 461-TODD

SKYLIGHTS
ACP Corporation
50 Utter Ave.
P.O. Box 515
Hawthorne NJ 07507
(201) 423-2900

Andersen Corporation
100 4th Ave. N
Bayport MN 55003
(612) 439-5150

Bramen Co. Inc.
P.O. Box 70
Salem MA 01970
(800) 234-7765

Roto Frank of America
P.O. Box 599
Chester CT 06412
(203) 526-4996

Truth
SPX Corporation
700 West Bridge St.
Owatanna MN 55060
(507) 451-5620

Velux-America
P.O. Box 3208
Greenwood SC 29648
(803) 223-3149

Ventarama Skylight Corp.
140 Cantiaque Rock Rd.
Hicksville NY 11801
(516) 931-0202

Wasco Products, Inc.
P.O. Box 351
Sanford ME 04073
(207) 324-8060

VERTICAL BLINDS
SM Automatic
10301 Jefferson Blvd.
Culver City CA 90232
(800) 533-5520

WINDOW QUILTS
Sunbilt Solar Products
109-1 180th St.
Jamaica NY 11433
(718) 297-6040

Wiring and Network Systems
ESS Distributors
10965 Santa Barbara Pl.
Alta Loma CA 91701
(800) 755-6796

Hometronics, Inc.
4405 Massachusetts Ave.
Indianapolis IN 46218
(317) 545-6239

Multiplex Technology, Inc.
3200 E. Birch
Brea CA 92621
(714) 996-4100

ChannelPlus video distribution
system
Square D Company
3203 Nicholasville Rd.
Lexington KY 40503
(800) 767-0914
ELAN Home Electronics Network

Index

A complete catalog of Betterway Books is available FREE by writing to the address shown below, or by calling toll-free 1-800-289-0963. To order additional copies of this book, send in retail price of the book, plus $3.00 postage and handling for one book, and $1.00 for each additional book. Ohio residents add 5½% sales tax. Allow 30 days for delivery.

Betterway Books
1507 Dana Avenue
Cincinnati, Ohio 45207

Stock is limited on some titles; prices subject to change without notice.